Alan Curbishley
VALLEY OF DREAMS

Alan Curbishley

VALLEY OF DREAMS

HarperCollins*Publishers*

HarperCollins*Publishers*
1 London Bridge Street
London SE1 9GF

www.harpercollins.co.uk

First published by Harper*Sport* 2006
This edition published 2018

1

A CIP catalogue record for this book
is available from the British Library

ISBN 978-0-00-831879-6

For Carol, Claire and Michael, thanks for your love and support over the years. I couldn't have done it without you. 1–2–3, love you lots, and to Mum, Dad, Billy, not forgetting Alf, Della, Laura and Paul. Thanks for always being there.

Contents

Acknowledgements

It's difficult to know exactly where to start when it comes to saying thanks and mentioning the people who played a part in my time at The Valley, but in no particular order, let me thank: Arnie Warren for being instrumental in getting me to The Valley and keeping me there as a manager; Lennie Lawrence for signing me and then giving me the chance to coach; Roger Alwen and Mike Norris for the opportunity to break into management; Richard Murray for putting me in sole charge and for being such a supportive and understanding chairman; Martin Simons for his dedication to the cause and for always being able to put a smile on my face; Steve Gritt for being a great managerial partner in the early days; Les Reed for his coaching ability and friendship; Peter Varney for his friendship and for being a great chief executive; and Keith Peacock and Mervyn Day for making my off the field team so strong and enjoyable to work with. I also want to thank all of the Charlton directors who were involved with the club during my time, all of the players from the 'old brigade' during those difficult but enjoyable days when I first started in management, and all of the players who were part of Charlton teams during the 15 years I was a manager with the club.

I want to thank Jimmy Hendry, Paddy Powell, Alex Silverman, Jimmy Hamson, Jim Fibbins, Jeff Vetere, Mike Stevens, Derek Ufton, Richard Collins, Bob Whitehand, Dr John Fraser, Glynn Snodin, Bez Dine, Chris Parkes, John Yarnton and his late wife Barbara, Peter 'Scoop' Burrowes, Audrey Hannant, Tom Morris for his pictures, Colin Cameron for his help with all the facts and statistics at the end of this book, Mick Cole for being Mick Cole, Johnny and Sally 'Star Fish' Hayes, community scheme manager Jason Morgan, who was at the club throughout my time as manager and had as much success as me, Paul Geary and his ground staff, who always made sure that even when we didn't have the best facilities we had the best pitches, and Jim Smith, Joe Royle, Ron Saunders and Barry Lloyd who played a part in my career as a player and manager. I would also like to thank Michael Doggart, Tom Whiting and Neil Dowden at HarperCollins.

My special thanks to Kevin Brennan for all of his work in collaborating with me in the writing of this book and to Sir Alex Ferguson for his Foreword and for being a good friend and advisor over the years.

There were an awful lot of people who helped me and were a part of my story during my time at The Valley. Unfortunately there isn't the space to include all of them in these acknowledgements, but they know who they are and the part they played. Finally, to all the Charlton fans: we went through a lot together and the send-off you gave me will live with me forever.

Alan Curbishley

FOREWORD

One of my most vivid memories of Alan, Charlton and The Valley was the day I came down with Manchester United to play an FA Youth Cup match. We won the game 5–2, but it wasn't so much the result which left a lasting impression, it was the club and what they seemed to be about.

The date was 12 January 1995 and it was little more than two years after Charlton had finally got back to The Valley after more than seven years away, when they had to ground share with Crystal Palace and then West Ham United. The Valley that day was a very different place to the way it is now. The stadium was neat but with only a small capacity, the players got changed in one set of portakabins, and the board entertained their guests in another set of portakabins. But despite all of that the club put on a tremendous spread for us and had also invited a lot of their old heroes to the match, including members of the 1947 FA Cup winning team. When you walked into the place there was a real warmth and spirit to the club, and even back then I had the feeling that they were going to build on what they had. The club were back where they belonged at their own ground and I could sense how much it meant to the fans and the board of directors.

I also knew how much it meant to the two young managers who had been given the joint task of helping to build the club's fortunes. Both Steve Gritt and Alan Curbishley were cutting their managerial teeth in the game, and the two went on to do a fine job together, before Alan was given the opportunity of taking sole control in the summer of that same year.

From the very first time I met Alan I had the feeling that he was going to do something in the game, and as a young manager he always seemed to have the kind of drive and ambition that I felt would help him succeed. What he and Charlton managed to achieve during his years in charge was nothing short of amazing.

As a young manager Alan always seemed to have a calm authority about what he did and that is still true to this day. I've been known to get a wee bit excited on the touchline during the course of my career, but that isn't really the case with Alan. He has a great demeanour. He has a controlled, calm attitude and also has the experience to go with it. After 15 years as a manager he knows the game, and despite what he achieved with Charlton and the level of success he enjoyed in establishing them as a Premiership club, he has never changed as a person. We live in an era where too often there are managers who are concerned with their image and how they are perceived in the media and by the public. Alan always got on with his job in a straightforward and honest way, and he has proved over the years just what a capable and effective manager he is.

The success both he and Charlton enjoyed was no fluke. Alan and the club had to work hard at it, and as far as I'm concerned one of the major turning points for Charlton was the way they were able to bounce back after being relegated following one season in the Premier League in 1999. They kept their team together, the players wanted to work and play for the manager, and the board provided a platform for it all to happen.

I've always said that in order for you to succeed as a manager you need someone there who understands the complexities of the job and is willing to back you. Alan had that in Charlton chairman, Richard Murray. He and the board stuck with him through some of the tough times, while Alan stayed put and did not up sticks to another club, and at the same time produced teams which consistently did well on the pitch. There was the right kind of trust, understanding and loyalty on both sides and that helped the club to grow both on the pitch and off of it.

The atmosphere at The Valley has always been fantastic whenever we've played matches there and the Charlton fans certainly know how to get behind their team. I think I inadvertently helped to raise the decibel level one season in December 2000 when we were involved in a 3–3 draw. I must hold the record for the manager with the most 3–3 draws in the Premiership and that year it was Charlton's turn. We were 3–1 up in the game and I decided to take Roy Keane off towards the end of the match. Charlton promptly went on to score twice and the game ended as a draw. Maybe it's not one of the tactical substitutions I'm most proud of, but I think they still talk about the match as being one of the most entertaining at The Valley since the club returned to the ground!

Anyone in the game knows exactly how hard everyone at Charlton worked to make sure they became an established Premiership club, and nobody worked harder than Alan. He did not have the money and resources of other clubs, but consistently produced good teams who competed with, and beat, the big boys. Managing these days is not an easy business and it involves a lot more than looking after a football team. Alan learned his trade from those days back in the early 1990s as joint manager with Steve Gritt when the club didn't even have a ground of its own, to being a highly respected Premiership manager. It's a remarkable achievement and he deserves full credit for the part he played in the success story of Charlton Athletic Football Club.

When I go to The Valley these days and see how the stadium has developed, I can't help but be impressed by what has happened since that Youth Cup match, but the one thing that hasn't changed is the warmth and sincerity of the place. When we played there in a League game at the end of the 2004–05 season I had a wonderful afternoon. We won the game but it was what happened afterwards that made my day. I found out that Charlton had a few famous faces from their past at the ground and among them were John Hewie and Eddie Firmani. Hewie was a particular hero of mine and I remember seeing him score from the penalty spot for Scotland against Spain at Hampden in 1957. Alan kindly took me to see the pair of them and it was a genuine thrill for me to meet players who I had admired since I was a youngster.

They were two of a number of great players and characters who have been associated with Charlton over the years, people who left their mark and made a real contribution to the club. In recent years nobody has made more of a contribution to the Charlton cause than Alan Curbishley. His last game in charge of the club, of course, came against us at Old Trafford, in what I know was an emotional afternoon for him. The story of his time at Charlton Athletic serves as a great example of just how much he has achieved during his career as a manager so far.

Alex Ferguson

1 All Good Things . . .

I'd often wondered what it would be like when the end finally came and on a Friday afternoon in April 2006 I found out.

In many ways it was a surreal experience. After 15 years as manager of Charlton Athletic I found myself in The Valley boardroom sitting with the two men who I had worked so closely with as the club had risen from the depths of despair with no ground and no money, to an outfit that can now rightly claim to be an established part of the Premiership. It had been an amazing journey and one in which both Chairman Richard Murray and Chief Executive Peter Varney had both played massive roles.

Richard was the man who had been there right at the beginning when I had taken over the team jointly with Steve Gritt, and he was the man who had made the decision to give me sole charge of the side back in the summer of 1995. Peter had joined a couple of years later and the three of us worked closely together in the most exciting period I believe the club has ever experienced. It was a simple formula as far as Richard was concerned. He appointed us and let me get on with running the team, while Peter got on with running the club. The result had been two promotions and seven seasons in the Premiership, during which time the club and its Valley ground had gone from strength to strength.

Part of the reason for that was the stability that Richard believed was so important to the success of Charlton. Now, as the three of us sat awkwardly in the boardroom together, I was about to take the first step in breaking that long-established stability by leaving the club that had been such a big part of my life for so long. The awkwardness came from the fact that the three of us didn't really know how to react to the situation. We may have all worked together, but more than that, we were friends as well. We felt comfortable talking about club business and the plans we had, and we could joke with each other, but this was a totally different situation. In a funny sort of way I don't think any of us had really thought about what it would be like if the partnership was broken up, but that was exactly what was about to happen.

I could see it was a shock for Peter and he looked visibly shaken when Richard explained the situation to him and the fact that the reason we were all there was to sort out an amicable settlement to my contract which still had a little more than a year to run. Despite Richard asking me to extend the deal, I had decided as early as the previous summer not to do so. Instead, I just wanted to let it run out and then take a long look at things and think about my future.

When I made that decision I knew it wouldn't be one that Richard would be happy with. During all my time at the club he had made a point of ensuring that I had at least two or more years left on any contract I had. It was quite understandable that he should want things that way. Having your manager committed for three or four years obviously makes matters easier for lots of reasons, particularly when it comes to signing players and planning for the future.

In September 2005 Richard asked to see me because he wanted to discuss an extension to my contract. We had already spoken briefly a couple of months earlier, but only because he wanted to flag it up and not very much was said in terms of detail for any deal. By the time we spoke in September Charlton were second in the table having got off to a great start with some terrific attacking play that saw us pick up five wins out of the first six matches, four of them away from home. But despite the start and the fact that only Premiership champions Chelsea were keeping us off top spot, I told Richard that I didn't want to sign and instead we agreed to talk again at Christmas.

By that time the team's fortunes had changed dramatically after a dreadful run which had seen us lose seven out of eight matches in the League and slump to 12th place. It was an example of the sort of extremes in form that seemed to characterize much of our season, but despite the bad run Richard had never once been on the phone to have a go at me or criticize what was going on. Obviously he was as disappointed as the rest of us, but typically he chose not to get on my back and instead left me alone to manage the team, just as he always had done, and despite the run he was still keen for me to sign a new deal with the club. Just as before, I told him I didn't want to, for the simple reason that I had it in my mind to get the season out of the way and then think about my future in the summer. My priority was getting the team back on track and picking up points. My only thoughts at the time were to make sure we reached the magic 40-point mark which virtually guarantees a side safety and the reassurance of playing Premiership football for another season.

Once that had been achieved with a home win against Newcastle in March, Richard quite naturally wanted to plan for the future and talk to me about the way forward for the club just like we had done in previous seasons. We started to have discussions and talked about various players we might consider as transfer targets, but I had also made up my mind that I was not going to sign a new contract. It had nothing to do with the fact that my name had become linked as a possible successor to Sven-Goran Eriksson when it was announced he would be leaving his post as head coach of England after the World Cup, or with the fact that I had been linked with the Glasgow Rangers job just before Christmas. Having made the decision way back in September before any of that had happened, I felt comfortable with it. As far as I was concerned I was prepared to see out my contract at Charlton but I wouldn't commit myself to a new deal and a further extension, despite the substantial money involved.

As the season drew to a close Richard and I had a meeting over lunch in a restaurant at Ruxley Manor near the club's training ground in New Eltham. It was relaxed and informal as we discussed the club and what the plans would be for the next season, but when the subject of my contract came up I once again told him that I would not be signing a new deal. As we left the restaurant he turned to me and admitted, 'You've given me something to think about. If you're not going to sign I'm going to have to consider everything.'

Two days before my April meeting with him and Peter in the boardroom I had another lunch with Richard at the same restaurant for another round of talks. We discussed a wide range of things including the role that would be played by Andrew Mills, who at the time was a football agent. The club had recently engaged him speci-fically to help with the head hunting of potential transfer targets, and the possible sale of players. Lots of clubs are doing this sort of thing at the moment and we saw it as a way forward for Charlton as we tried to compete in a very competitive market.

But although we were talking about what was likely to be happening in the weeks and months ahead, as well as planning for the next season, I was also aware that if I was still at The Valley after the summer I would be going into the new campaign with just one year left on my contract. Richard had already mentioned the fact that a situation like that caused him problems. For a start, any new player coming into the club would be well aware that the manager trying to sign him on a four-year contract only had one year left on his own deal.

There was also the problem of how I might be perceived generally. In recent years people like Sir Bobby Robson, Gordon Strachan and Kevin Keegan had all left their jobs early, for different reasons, once it had become public knowledge that they were only going to be around for one more season. Also, the England thing had dragged on and on, and even though by this time I felt pretty sure I was out of the running, the FA still hadn't made an official announcement. It was just another problem Richard had because he hadn't heard from the FA and was becoming impatient with the whole process and the way it affected the club.

As we ate our lunch I told him that the England job wasn't really on my agenda. I was more concerned with the club and myself and that was why I had asked him for a meeting. During my time at Charlton everything we'd done and everything we'd attempted to do had been for the best of the club. I had called the meeting mainly to highlight the problems having just one year left to run on my contract would cause, and Richard understood my position.

I could quite easily have signed a new three-year deal, taken the money and got on with it. But I have never done anything just for the money and I didn't want to be in a position where I felt I'd signed a new contract and couldn't honour it. I think all my emotions came out and Richard knew exactly how I felt.

He knew that if I did fulfil the year I had left on my contract there was no way I would want things to go wrong, and he knew that if I stayed the work ethic that I had always had would still be there, but at the same time he didn't really see it as commitment. I was concerned about the club and I was prepared to do a year, but I knew how difficult that was going to be. By the time Richard had finished his dessert I think we both knew we were coming to the same conclusion.

To turn down the offer of a contract was a big financial decision, and I don't know how many people in my position would have done it, but I had made up my mind and I think Richard knew I was not going to change the way I thought. He stopped to have a last word just as we were walking to our cars.

'Perhaps,' he said, 'we should think about an early termination. You know the position I'm in, and this is a difficult situation.'

I understood what he was saying. 'I'll have a think about things,' I told him and we arranged to have another meeting eight days later.

I drove home thinking that perhaps that was it and my time at Charlton might be over, but pretty soon I began to think about the next day and the training we had planned in preparation for our home match with Blackburn at the weekend. Whatever was going on with me I knew that it had to be business as normal as far as the team were concerned and I was determined to do all I could to make sure we signed off with a win in what was going to be our last home League game of the season.

The next day my wife Carol had an appointment in London and I said I'd pick her up so that the two of us could drive home and have a chat in the car. I wanted to let her know what had been going on and talk about the meeting I'd had with Richard. On the way back home we hit some horrendous traffic and were hardly moving when I took a call from Andrew Mills. He was full of enthusiasm as we discussed various players and whether we might be interested in them as transfer targets. In the end poor Carol had to sit there for about 40 minutes listening to us talking, and when the call ended I couldn't help having an uneasy feeling. There was Andrew bursting at the seams with enthusiasm for the task he'd been given, and I was talking about plans for the following season, not really knowing what was going to happen. Even if we could manage to afford the fees and wages of certain players, I knew I would have to sit down with them and say I want you to sign for four years, and by the way I've only got one year left on my own contract. How would that look?

When we got to Docklands I suggested to Carol that we stop off for a meal at The Lotus Chinese restaurant. It's a place owned by a friend of ours, Steve Cheuk, and I knew we would be able to eat and talk without being disturbed. I told Carol all about what had gone on and although I think she was a bit shocked at first she understood how I felt and also how I had been feeling for some time. I knew I'd been snappy and short tempered with my own family in recent months and that wasn't a good sign. Being at a club for 15 years as their manager is a very long time and I knew nothing could go on for ever.

On the way home we listened to the last part of Middlesbrough's UEFA Cup semi-final with Steaua Bucharest, as they overcame the Romanian side to secure a place in the final. It was a great win for them and for their manager Steve McClaren.

'Wasn't it only a few months ago that one of their fans was throwing his season ticket at McClaren?' asked Carol.

'Yes,' I said. 'If I see out my contract I wonder how long it will be before a fan throws something at me!'

I fell asleep as soon as my head hit the pillow when we got home, which was a rare occurrence for me, because I often have trouble sleeping, but by 3.30 in the morning I was wide awake and couldn't get back to sleep again. I kept thinking about all the problems the club would have regarding recruitment for the following season and wondering how things could be planned long-term if I only had one year left on my contract. I had an early breakfast at 6am and was at the training ground by 8.20am. I wanted to speak to Richard and knew I couldn't wait until the following week for our planned meeting.

I phoned him and went through all the things we had talked about before and then reminded him that if we left our meeting for virtually another week, important time would be lost for him and for the club. Managers and players would soon be on holiday taking a break, and the close season has a habit of disappearing very quickly. If Richard was thinking of recruiting a new manager, then that process could take some weeks, so time wasn't on his side and it was agreed that we would meet that afternoon at The Valley.

Perhaps for a while he had thought the situation might go away and perhaps I was thinking that if I did my year I might change my mind and stay. But it just seemed wrong and I felt happier that the meeting had been arranged. By the time I'd put the phone down coach Mervyn Day and assistant manager Keith Peacock had arrived. I hadn't said anything to them about what had been going on and, just as we had done so many times before, the three of us set about the final training session before the next day's game with Blackburn. It must have seemed like any other Friday to everyone and at the end of training I did my usual weekly press conference.

Apart from the questions about England that had been a constant feature for months I was also asked by Sky TV's Andy Burton whether I was going to be at Charlton in the summer. 'Yes,' I said. 'I expect to be here because I'm prepared to honour the one year I have left on my contract.' It wasn't a lie because I was prepared to stay on for another year, and at that time nothing had officially been done to say that was not going to be the case, but at the same time I knew I was about to go into a meeting with Richard at The Valley that would probably end my association with the club. I'm on the committee of the League Managers' Association, but I hadn't taken any advice from them, even though I knew there had been some horror stories regarding managers and their contracts when it came to them leaving a club.

I walked into the meeting on my own but I felt comfortable. I had a 15-year relationship with Richard and nearly a 10-year relationship with Peter. After about 20 minutes of talking it was decided that I was going to leave. I felt it was the best thing for me and the best thing for the club, but we still had the tricky situation of me having one year left on my contract.

Richard asked Peter to leave so that the two of us could talk alone. We juggled a few things around but we reached a conclusion in about 10 minutes.

In many ways the negotiations were typical of the sort of relationship we'd always had. I'm sure that 99 per cent of the time the conversation would have been a lot more aggressive between other chairmen and managers, but that was just how we were. Richard then suggested we take some time out. He wanted to talk to Peter and I needed to ask my solicitor Mike Morrison to draw up the termination agreement that I had just been offered and fax it over for all of us to sign.

It was when I got back in the room that the awkward feeling I've already described began to set in. I suddenly started to realize what was happening. I hadn't just been at the club for 15 years as their manager I'd also been a player with them and had first signed way back in 1984. Apart from just under three years at Brighton between 1987 and 1990, I had been associated with Charlton for almost 22 years, which is a very long time.

Both Richard and Peter obviously realized this too and knew what a big part of my life Charlton had been. By the time I got back into the room they had formulated a plan. The next day's game against Blackburn was going to be used as a celebration of my time at the club. They felt that after all we'd achieved and done together they were going to do things in style.

The plan was to put an embargo on the news of my departure. They didn't want me to tell the players until 15 minutes before the 5.15 pm kick-off. They didn't want me to tell Mervyn or Keith until 90 minutes before the game, and they insisted they wouldn't be telling anyone else until the appropriate time. Richard had decided that he would go onto the pitch at 5 pm to tell the fans. Even the club directors weren't going to be told until just before the kick-off and they wanted them, along with the two teams, to form a guard of honour and give me the send-off they believed I deserved.

'We're not going to have a manager who has been here for 15 years just walk off into the sunset and not get the thank you and recognition he deserves,' insisted Richard. 'This is Charlton and we do things differently.'

As the three of us sat there in the awkward silence waiting for the fax from Mike Morrison to arrive, I knew exactly what they meant. Charlton are different for so many reasons and they will always be a unique club in my eyes. Managing them and being a part of the place for so long had been very special, but I also knew the old saying was right.

All good things must come to an end.

2 First Impressions

'Who badges, Who badges. Get your 10p Who badges here.' It was 9.30 in the morning and I was screaming at the top of my voice, trying to attract the attention of fans who had just started to pour through the gates of The Valley. I didn't realize it at the time, but I was standing in the corner of the famous old covered end, just about where the players' tunnel entrance is now. The Valley looked very different in those days and the first impression I had was just how vast it was. In particular, the massive East Terrace seemed to reach up to the sky, and later that day it looked even more impressive as it became absolutely packed with people.

I was a 16-year-old apprentice at the time. It was May 1974 and I was about to earn more money in a day than I did in a couple of months playing for West Ham's youth team. Long before I ever decided to put my first foot on the management ladder my eldest brother Billy was leading the way, only in his case it had nothing to do with eleven blokes kicking a football around for a living. Instead, it was all about looking after one of the world's biggest rock bands – The Who. As their manager, he organized a tour that year which included some big venues, one of which happened to be an open-air concert at The Valley.

I was still living at home with my mum and dad in Canning Town, and for two weeks before the gig our front room was turned into a temporary badge-making factory. The idea was for my younger brother Paul and me to make little badges with pictures of The Who on them, and just to keep it all in the family, the pair of us were supervised by another brother, Alfie, who was a few years older than me. We'd had a little machine installed at home and were churning out hundreds of badges which we planned to sell to fans on the day for 10p each. Paul and my best mate, Pat Willis, were going to sell them with me and we reckoned that if things went well for us we stood to make about £70 each, which was an absolute fortune considering I was earning £8 per week at West Ham.

The three of us arrived bright and early on the day after making our way from east to South East London. Although it was only about 8 am, there seemed to be hundreds of people all around the ground and it was already a bit chaotic. A lot of fans who had arrived during the night came well prepared and actually pitched their tents in Harvey Gardens outside some of the houses surrounding the ground, without the people who lived in the homes knowing too much about it.

We all had passes to go anywhere and after unloading our badges in a specially provided room at the ground, we set about trying to make some money. To be honest, it wasn't exactly a hard sell, because our customers were Who fanatics and they gobbled up anything to do with their heroes, including our little badges. We were doing a roaring trade, but then I recognized another little avenue which I thought could earn us even more money for our day's work.

Not surprisingly, the stewards who were in charge of the crowd that day wanted to make sure the whole thing went off without any trouble, and one of the things they decided to do was stop anyone entering the stadium with cans or bottles of booze. The fans were left with the stark choice of finishing their drinks there and then, emptying them into cartons, or throwing them into skips. I think some people went off and got cartons of soft drinks that they emptied to make way for the harder stuff, but a lot of other people were prepared to just throw their beers in a big skip, so they could get in and make sure they had a good place to watch the concert from.

It wasn't long before I saw that one of these skips was beginning to fill up with unopened cans of beer, and it was then I had my extra money-making idea. We started taking the cans and put them at the bottom of the bags we had with us for carrying the badges. Pretty soon we were walking through the crowds that were gathering on the pitch and on the terraces, not only selling our badges, but also offering the punters a little extra something to make sure they kept their voices well lubricated. I've no doubt that we probably sold the same beer back to people who had tossed it into the skip earlier that day.

The concert kicked off in the early afternoon and was scheduled to finish at about 11 pm. The Who were the main band and came on last, which was great for us, because by that time we had done all of our selling and could relax as we prepared to take in the whole thing from backstage. By this time The Valley was absolutely full, and the massive East Terrace towered over the stadium. The other thing that struck me was just how far it went back, and when it was packed full with people, it really was an amazing sight. It was later estimated that there had been something like 47,000 people crammed on and around the terrace at the time. The pitch was also jammed with fans, and wherever you looked there seemed to be a sea of faces. An aerial shot of the stadium was viewed later by the authorities at the Greater London Council and they estimated there were 88,000 at the concert. The only area that wasn't swarming with human bodies was the stage. It had been set up to jut out at about the halfway line, and just before the band were due to play promoter Harvey Goldsmith decided to have a quick word with the assembled masses.

It was the usual thing you might expect at a concert: 'Are you all looking forward to seeing The Who? Let's all have a good time. Can the people at the front try not to jump up too much. Will the people at the back make sure they don't push forward.' By this time I was standing in the wings and as Harvey carried on giving the crowd his dos and don'ts, I suddenly saw a can of beer come flying through the night air. I was too far back for it to be a threat, but poor old Harvey nearly caught the full force of it as the can came crashing down beside him.

I knew straight away that it had almost certainly found its way into the stadium thanks to our little scheme, and I was just thankful that it didn't do any damage. I'm sure the last thing Harvey and my brother would have wanted was for their concert to turn into some sort of riot, fuelled by a load of boozed-up fans, who had got their drink courtesy of Bill's younger brother.

Happily Harvey ran for cover and wasn't hurt, The Who came on and played brilliantly, I made a nice few bob, and I still maintain to this day that the flying can of beer was sold to the culprit by Pat Willis – and not by me!

People who have only seen The Valley in recent years will find it hard to believe what the stadium looked like back then. It certainly wasn't the sleek all-seater ground that most Premiership teams and their fans have become used to. In many ways it was a bit ramshackle and looked as though it could do with a bit of sprucing up, but the one thing it most certainly had was character. The concert that day was an unforgettable experience for anyone who was there, but it wasn't just The Who that left a lasting impression on me, it was The Valley as well. Little did I realize at the time just how much of the rest of my life would be linked to that vast bowl of a place tucked away in South London, just a stone's throw from the River Thames.

3 Location, Location

I have to admit that my move to Charlton as a player in 1984 had more to do with the housing game than the beautiful game.

I sometimes have to pinch myself when I start to think just how much football has changed in this country since I first entered the game as an apprentice with West Ham back in the 1970s.

It may only be a matter of thirty years or so, but in terms of the money and finances involved in football at the top level now, we are light years removed from what went on then. A Premiership player these days can, and should, be able to make himself financially secure over the length of a contract in the top flight of English football. Even an average player in the top flight these days can be earning around £500,000 per year. When you're earning literally thousands of pounds each week you'd have to be extremely dumb or extremely unlucky to blow it all and end up with nothing to show for your career.

By the mid-1980s I'd managed to establish myself as a midfield player in the old First Division. It was the top tier of English football and we were well paid for playing the game, but the money that was being handed out was nothing compared with what today's Premiership footballers get. I had progressed from playing youth football for West Ham at the time of that Who concert, to making a breakthrough into their first team after signing professional forms in 1975. My first professional contract with them was worth £50 per week and by the time I left Upton Park I was earning £200 per week. In 1979 I was transferred to Birmingham for £225,000, and more than doubled my money with the move. After spending four years with them I moved across the city to join European Cup holders Aston Villa in a £100,000 switch which gave me a guaranteed salary of £40,000 a year. I was earning decent money and playing football as a professional had given me a good standard of living, but I certainly wasn't rolling in it. In fact, a friend of mine who was a printer actually earned more than I did.

My wife Carol and I had moved home to the Midlands after leaving West Ham, but we obviously had friends and family back in London who we saw pretty regularly. My fellow Who badge seller, Pat Willis, decided to get married in the summer of 1984 and it was when I was down for the wedding that I started to take stock of a few things. While we'd been away from the south house prices had rocketed in London. I'd paid £42,000 for my house in Birmingham and more than four years later, at the time of Pat's wedding, it was probably worth no more than £52,000. After talking to some of our friends that day it was clear an equivalent place in the south would be worth something like £90,000. Carol and I soon realized that we were being left behind in the property stakes, and that if we didn't do something about it quickly, we'd never be able to move back, so I made the decision to try and sell our house and rent a property up there.

At the time this all coincided with the fact that Villa had changed managers. It was Tony Barton who had led Villa to their European Cup triumph and brought me to the club, but he ended up getting the sack and Graham Turner arrived from Shrewsbury with his own ideas about how he wanted things done. I got on with the pre-season training that year but never got a look-in when it came to the first team, and by the time October had come around Turner made it clear that if anyone came in for me I could go.

In those situations more than 20 years ago there was very little a player could do except get his head down, work as hard as he could and keep plugging away in the hope that circumstances changed. I don't think it's quite the same these days with some players: if they are left out of the side they don't seem prepared to get on with things in the same way I had to, and I think the reason for the change in attitude has been the amount of money they are now paid. In my case I actually managed to get back in the Villa first team, but at the same time, Arnie Warren, who was working as chief scout for Charlton manager Lennie Lawrence, got in touch and made it known that they would be interested in signing me.

It was decision time for me and, for the first and only time in my entire career in the game, I made a decision that was purely financial instead of being all about football. We had actually sold our house in the Midlands by the time Charlton made their official bid for me, and it was a chance for us to move and buy something in the south. I could have stayed at Villa and still bought a house in London, but somehow the idea of a move just fitted in nicely.

Charlton were hardly at the top of the English game. In fact, they'd nearly gone out of existence all together the previous season. They had literally been within minutes of disappearing as a club until a package put together by Sunley Holdings, which was headed by John Fryer, was accepted by the High Court and the Football League. At the time Lennie's team were struggling to keep their heads above water in the Second Division and it looked as though they had a relegation battle on their hands.

I'd known Arnie for quite a few years and he'd desperately tried to sign me for QPR as a school kid when he was working for them, but I was West Ham through and through, so I was always going to sign for the Hammers. Arnie had kept in contact and knew that I'd had a rough time of it under Turner at Villa, so Lennie decided to make his move. Charlton bid £38,000 for me. Not exactly a fortune, but it was probably still more than they could afford and I believe John Fryer and Sunley's were the people behind the finance for the deal because I think I was bought with one of their cheques.

I played for Villa on a Saturday in a home game against Liverpool and actually did pretty well, against a midfield that included Steve McMahon and Mark Walters, but the offer was on the table and I had to make my decision about a move to Charlton. In the end I decided to go for it, motivated by the house-price situation, and with the thought in the back of my mind that I would only be spending about six months at The Valley before someone else came in for me and I'd be off. At least it meant that I was in the south again and not losing out on the housing boom, and with Carol eight months pregnant with our first baby, it seemed like the right time to be heading back to London.

Jimmy Hill was on the Charlton board and was acting chairman when I made arrangements with Arnie to have a meeting before signing for the club. I was a bit surprised that he wanted to hold the talks at the Royal Lancaster Hotel in London's West End, rather than at The Valley. We were staying with Carol's parents, which was only a stone's throw from Upton Park, so a quick trip across the Thames would have been pretty easy but Arnie insisted on the Hotel. Everything went well, Jimmy and Lennie outlined their plans for Charlton and how they wanted the club to move forward, we had a nice meal in an Italian restaurant and I agreed to sign for them.

The next day we had to meet at The Valley for my medical and I quickly began to realize why they hadn't wanted to meet me there 24 hours earlier; as I drove into the ground the place looked like an absolute mess. Only a few days earlier I'd played at Villa Park in front of 40,000 fans and suddenly I was looking at the reality of signing for a club like Charlton. I sat under the main stand in Lennie's office and he sent out for a couple of roast-beef sandwiches from the Royal Oak pub, which was just around the corner from the ground – they turned out to be the best thing about the day.

I passed my medical and went for a stroll around the stadium. It didn't exactly help lift my spirits. It was a grey December day and The Valley was empty and uninviting. There was fencing up all around the place and the big East Terrace that had looked so impressive ten years earlier for that Who concert just looked tired and sad. It was the first time I'd been back to the ground for some time and it didn't seem too inspiring.

After my badge-selling exploits I'd actually got to play on The Valley pitch for West Ham, when we beat Charlton 3–1 in an FA Youth Cup match. I also went there on a Friday night in April 1976 to watch Johnny Giles play for West Bromwich Albion, and a couple of years later my brother Paul had a trial with Charlton after West Ham released him, so I watched him play in a 6–2 reserve game win against Brentford. In 1980 I played for Birmingham in a match at the stadium when we were going for promotion under Jim Smith. We won the game 1–0, but the main reason I remember it was for an incident involving our winger Alan Ainscow. He was getting a lot of stick from Jim, who was shouting non-stop at him from the touch-line. Just when Alan thought it couldn't get any worse he managed to misjudge a pass, letting the ball run right under his foot and down into the tunnel. Jim went ballistic as his face turned crimson and the veins on his neck began to bulge. He screamed at Ainscow as he went to retrieve the ball, but even he was lost for words when it was thrown back with Alan staying in the tunnel – he'd obviously had enough of Jimmy's verbal abuse!

If my walk around The Valley had made me wonder what I was getting myself into, the next day at training only helped to put more doubts into my mind. I got to the training ground bright and early in the sponsored car Villa allowed me to keep for a couple of months, eager to be positive about the whole move and put in a good session on my first day. Back then Charlton didn't have the sort of training facility they have now. In fact, it was shared with the public. By night the clubhouse and dressing rooms were used as some sort of social club, and by day we came in and used it for training.

There was a bar with its shutters down and a pool table in the main building, with a single-bar electric heater on the wall, and the whole place seemed pretty shabby. If that wasn't bad enough, worse was to follow when I walked into the dimly lit dressing room. I think it was the smell that got to me first and as I looked over into the corner I saw what my nose had already prepared me for. Someone had been sick, probably one of the punters from the night before who'd had too much to drink and then threw up as they made their way to the toilets. Welcome to Charlton Athletic.

Some of the players started turning up and began playing pool. I knew some of them like Derek Hales and Mike Flanagan, and a few asked me what I was doing there and why had I signed for Charlton. It was as if they were trying to work out why I had taken such a backward step in my career by coming to a club like Charlton. Another familiar face was Robert Lee. I'd helped coach him when he was a kid at West Ham and I was in the first team at Upton Park. We'd been encouraged to take the youngsters each week for evening coaching sessions and I took one group at Redbridge in Essex that included Robert and John Moncur who later played for Tottenham and the Hammers, while another West Ham team-mate, Pat Holland, coached another group of kids in Tilbury. I used to like coaching the kids but never really kept tabs on what happened to a lot of the youngsters, so it was funny joining a club and playing with Robert in the same side.

The Charlton assistant physio Bill Gallagher came in and threw a load of training gear onto a table. It was a case of first come, first served, but although I'd got there early I didn't benefit when it came to the training gear because it was all in a bit of a state. The kit consisted of old Charlton first-team shirts, either red or yellow, and a lot of it had seen better days. Despite all of this I actually enjoyed the training and was really enthusiastic. I noticed that Robert was the same, but to be honest I couldn't see too much enthusiasm in some of the others. I finished training and on the way home I began to wonder exactly what I'd done. Any enthusiasm I might have had in training was gone by the time I arrived home and my first words as I walked through the door summed up exactly how I felt.

'Carol,' I said. 'I think I've just made the biggest mistake of my life.'

It was just a gut reaction to the way I was feeling and I said pretty much the same thing to Mervyn Day, who was still at Villa.

'You can't believe the difference,' I told him. 'I don't know what I've done Merv. I just wish I could turn the clock back 48 hours.'

What I had done, although I had no way of knowing it at the time, was to start a relationship with Charlton that was to last for more than 22 years. At the time all I was thinking about was the fact that the next six months were going to be vitally important to me and the club. Charlton were in danger of being relegated, and if I was going to get another move by signing for a bigger and better club, I realized I had to really perform well and be noticed. I certainly would never have believed when I made my debut for the club in the 2–1 defeat by Crystal Palace at Selhurst Park on Boxing Day 1984 that my life over the years which followed would become so wrapped up in Charlton Athletic, and the club would come to mean so much to me.

I made my home debut three days later in a game against Grimsby. We had a team photograph taken before the match. I can remember wondering where the crowd was when we ran out for the kick-off. There were just 3,853 people there and the ones that stayed away missed out on a hat-trick from Robert Lee and a goal from me as we won 4–1.

Despite my misgivings about the situation I'd landed myself in, I got on with things and soon started to realize that, as a midfielder, I had half a chance with people like Robert, Derek Hales and Mike Flanagan in the team. They were good players and I felt there was something there that could be built on. Lennie had told me when I signed that he intended to bring players into the club, because he was going to have some money to spend from the new owners, but the real trick that season was to make sure we stayed in the Second Division. It suddenly dawned on me that I might slip from the First Division to the Third in the space of about six months. In the end we stayed up by the skin of our teeth.

Although I didn't get the move in the summer that I'd originally hoped for, Lennie was as good as his word when it came to his ambitions for the club and pretty soon I wasn't the only new face at The Valley. He'd brought in left-back Mark Reid and striker John Pearson towards the tail end of the season and then in the summer the club pushed the boat out by signing right-back John Humphrey, defenders Steve Thompson and John Pender, as well as midfielder George Shipley. From being relegation candidates at the end of 1985, there was suddenly a real feeling that we had a side capable of pushing for promotion.

We started the season well with only one defeat in our first six matches and although we beat Stoke 2–0 at home in our seventh game the match turned out to be possibly the saddest there's ever been at the stadium. It was the day, 21 September 1985, that the team played its last game at The Valley, with the club having previously announced its intention to ground share with Crystal Palace at Selhurst Park. The first the players knew about the whole thing was on the Thursday morning prior to our home game with Palace two weeks earlier. Lennie told us there would be an announcement saying we would be playing at Selhurst and that our last match at The Valley would be against Stoke. John Fryer and Sunley's had pumped around £2 million into the club when they had rescued it 18 months earlier but it didn't include ownership of the ground. One of the club's previous chairmen, Michael Gliksten, still owned The Valley and had agreed a seven-year lease with a new consortium. In the summer of 1985, and in the wake of the Bradford City fire disaster, the East Terrace was closed after action from the Greater London Council concerning its safety. At the same time Gliksten decided that he wanted to use two acres of The Valley site behind the West Stand and the speculation at the time was that he might want to develop the land. The board claimed that the combined effect of the closure of the East Terrace and the possible restrictions to the West Stand would make staging games at The Valley impossible, and so the club struck a deal to share with Palace following that game with Stoke.

It was obviously a terrible moment for the fans and by all accounts they made their feelings known, but I wasn't there to witness it because I'd been injured and was just working my way back to fitness. A couple of days before the Stoke game Lennie gave me the option of either being a substitute for the first team, or having a run-out in the reserves who were due to play a game at Highbury against Arsenal. I decided to get a full 90 minutes under my belt and turned out for the reserves, but we got hammered 12–0, and it could have been a lot worse.

There was no way a club like Charlton could put out two strong teams on a Saturday and we sometimes struggled to field just one. Arsenal had some of the best youngsters in the country playing for their reserves and the difference in class showed. We did some running at The Valley on the Monday morning following the match, and Lennie decided that those who played in the Highbury game should do even more than the rest because the result was so bad.

It wasn't the nicest thing to have to do after getting whacked two days earlier, but I just got on with it and had a bit of a moan later. A lot of players these days seem to like to have a grizzle before they're asked to do some hard training, as if it's going to change the manager's mind. It never works that way and so my view was that you might just as well get on with it.

When we were getting changed Lennie came over to have a word. He told me that I couldn't have got much out of the game because of the result and that the team must have played really badly. That wasn't really the case and I told him I'd seen some of the best young players I'd ever come across. You didn't have to be a football expert to see that they'd go on to be a real force in the game, because the Arsenal side had people like Tony Adams, Martin Hayes, Niall Quinn, Dave Rocastle and Michael Thomas in it. Not bad for a reserve team, and not surprising that a lot of that side went on to form the core of the Arsenal team that won the First Division Championship in 1989.

The news that the club was leaving The Valley obviously hit the fans badly. Not only were we moving away from our own ground, we were going to share with a team the supporters regarded as the enemy. In their eyes it couldn't have been worse, but in a funny way I don't think the move affected the team as much as many thought it would. You have to remember that over half the side were new recruits, we'd been at the club a matter of months rather than years, and I think that in a strange way that helped us, because it wasn't quite the wrench it could have been.

By the time we played our first game at Selhurst I was back in the side, and the thing I remember most about it was that virtually none of us knew how to get to our new 'home'. Luckily Mike Flanagan, who lived near me, gave me a route that I still use to this day if I ever have to go over there. Happily we all managed to arrive on time and beat Sunderland 2–1 in front of 5,552 people. It was the start of more than five and a half years at Selhurst Park. It was also another win that eventually led to us being promoted. That season we finished second to Norwich and a point in front of Wimbledon to make sure South London would have two sides playing in the First Division the following season.

Despite all the problems the club had encountered we actually made sure of promotion with an away win at Carlisle in the last but one game of the season. Lennie was chaired around the ground by some of our supporters who had made the long trek north to cheer us on. We celebrated with fish and chips on the team bus and a few cans of beer, which is so different to what would happen today. It's all about refuelling properly now and alcohol has been replaced by sports drinks. As I sat there on the journey back to London I had time to reflect on what had gone on during my short time with the club. From staying up by the skin of our teeth we'd gone on to surprise everyone and win promotion.

It was the first of so many unlikely things to happen to Charlton during my time with the club. Some of them I can't really imagine happening ever again, and winning promotion that year was one of them. We'd left The Valley and against all the odds managed to get ourselves into the top flight. I think as bad as the move was for many people it actually had a galvanizing effect on us all. We were more of a team than ever and we really did all play for each other.

As we went into the summer break I felt a lot better about things. I may have taken a career gamble when I decided to sign for Charlton, but it had paid off. I was going to be playing in the First Division once again and I couldn't wait to get started.

4 Sweet and Sour

It may be a bit of a cliché, but in football you really don't know what's around the corner. Getting promotion and looking forward to playing in the First Division again was a sweet feeling during the summer of 1986, but that feeling very quickly began to turn sour as the new season loomed and I found myself battling against the effects of an Achilles injury.

I'd played with it during the run-in to promotion and thought that I'd be able to get it fixed during the close-season, but the reality was that I just couldn't seem to shake it off. I wanted it sorted out but the method of diagnosis and treatment back then was so different to the way things happen these days. Even after having the injury opened up and finding out the problem, I still spent months trying to get myself fit enough to play.

The medical people couldn't really find anything wrong with me and eventually the surgeon decided to open up my heel and found I had a cyst that was causing the trouble, but that was only the start of my problems. They may have found the cause but the after-effects of surgery on my Achilles left me struggling to regain full fitness by the time pre-season training had finished. I really didn't know what to do and ended up going to see the military physiotherapists at Queen Mary's rehabilitation centre, where Falklands veterans like Simon Weston had treatment, but I still couldn't shake off the effects. Eventually I became the first patient admitted to the physiotherapy unit at Lilleshall, spending five weeks there and only returning each weekend for a couple of days' break, but it did work and I got very fit up there.

However, by the time I got back to full training with Charlton, Lennie had done what all managers have to do in the situation he was in: he had to strengthen the squad and two of the players he brought in were midfielders – Andy Peake and Colin Walsh. So although I was fit I still found it hard to get back in the side and the injury took a lot out of me both physically and mentally. Being injured and out of the team is never a pleasant experience for a player, and pretty soon you're spending more time on the treatment table than with your own teammates.

That first season in the top division saw Charlton struggle to stay up and in the end we finished fourth from bottom, but only survived after a thrilling play-off win against Leeds in a deciding encounter at St Andrews. I was so far off being in the first team that I didn't even go to Birmingham.

Looking back now I have to say it was a pretty miserable season for me and in the end I only made 12 appearances. After struggling with the injury for so long, I got myself sorted out, but never got near the first team until November, when I celebrated my 29th birthday by playing in the 4–1 defeat at Watford. I was never able to get a regular place in the team and, as things turned out, the play-off final wasn't the only big occasion I missed out on.

We also managed to reach the final of the Full Members Cup

that season, which was played at Wembley in March, but the only look-in I got that day was being photographed on the pitch with the rest of the squad long before the match kicked-off.

The competition had at least given me the chance to play in a couple of games and I think Lennie probably felt a bit bad about the fact that through no real fault of my own I'd found myself struggling to get a place in the side. He knew that I'd taken a big gamble to join the club when Charlton might well have been heading for the Third Division. It had seemed as though the whole thing was working out and then I got hit by the injury.

Lennie had to do something and there was no way he could just sit around and wait for the injury to clear up so that I could play again. Colin Walsh and Andy Peake had come in and done a really good job, which left me on the sidelines. The Full Members Cup at least meant that I could get a run out in the first team, even if it was playing wide right in our 2–1 semi-final win against Norwich at Selhurst.

In the week leading up to the final we had a home League game against Oxford, in which I played. It was a terrible affair and the whole team played badly in a goalless draw. The final was on Sunday and after training on Friday Lennie called a team meeting. It was pretty short and to the point, in which he basically said that he didn't really care about the Full Members Cup, it was the League which was the most important thing and he clearly hadn't been too impressed with the showing against Oxford. He then said he was going to name the side for Wembley and he didn't want any arguments or questions about his selection.

'I don't want anyone coming to see me after I give you the

team,' he said, and then proceeded to name the side, but I wasn't in it. Peter Shirtliff had been out of the team because of injury, but he at least got a place on the bench, which was more than I got.

Lennie turned quickly after reading out the names and started heading for his office upstairs at the training ground, but despite what he said about not wanting any questions or arguments, I wasn't about to take his decision to leave me out lying down. I raced after him and bolted into his office before slamming the door behind me. We had a real shouting match and even Arnie Warren took cover after poking his head around the corner and realizing it was better to stay out of the way.

I came out really upset and at one point refused to take all the training gear and suit that had been specially made for the Wembley final; I also vowed not to go to the team hotel at Lancaster Gate in London the night before the game, but was eventually talked into relenting by Shirty, who phoned up and persuaded me it was the right thing to do for the team.

We had our meal at the hotel on the Saturday night and I was still in a mood because of what had happened. Quite by chance Jim Smith, my old manager at Birmingham, who was in charge of QPR at the time, wandered into the hotel. He asked me whether I was in the team and was really surprised to hear that I wasn't. He could see I was upset about what had happened.

'Have a glass of red wine,' said Smithy. 'It might make you feel a bit better.'

Even though I wasn't in the team I knew I shouldn't be drinking the night before the game, because I was still a member of the squad and it was something I wouldn't normally have done, but in the end I took Jim's offer of a glass of wine and then had another. Instead of making me feel better the alcohol only made me feel worse and when I got back to the room I was sharing with defender Paul Miller, I told him I'd had enough and was going home. Like Peter Shirtliff the previous day, Paul managed to persuade me to stay and not walk out, but on the morning of the match I certainly didn't feel any better about the situation.

We were due to play Blackburn in the final and it was a big day out for both sets of fans. Rovers had yet to reach the dizzy heights they later enjoyed when they went on to win the Premiership. This was before the days of Jack Walker and his millions, they were still in the Second Division and we were struggling to make sure we didn't join them there the following season. It wasn't exactly a sell-out, but the 43,789 fans who were there that day eventually saw Blackburn chalk up a 1–0 win thanks to a Colin Hendry goal in the 85th minute, although by that time I was back in my house in Essex.

After taking my place on the pitch for the pre-match photograph I went back into the dressing room with the rest of the team. Lennie gave his team talk and as the players went through the door and prepared to go out for the kick-off, I went in the opposite direction. I walked out of Wembley Stadium, down to the underground station and headed home on the Tube. It was a miserable end to what had been a miserable few days.

The rest of the season was really nothing more than a struggle for me and for Charlton, but while the team eventually managed to stay up with that play-off win against Leeds, I was never fully able to recover from the operation I'd had and ended the campaign playing for the reserves at Bromley's ground. Not exactly what I'd hoped for twelve months earlier when we had gained promotion and everything looked so rosy.

There was very little I could do except carry on and hope that things would improve for me. I did the pre-season training in the summer of 1987, but never really got a look-in when it came to playing in the first team. It wasn't Lennie's fault and it wasn't mine, it was just one of those things that happen in football. Happily, I managed to get a lifeline from an unexpected place when the Brighton manager, Barry Lloyd, made an enquiry for me. It wasn't quite the glamour move you'd love to get, but it was the chance to play regular first-team football, even though it was in the Third Division.

Brighton had been relegated and Barry was trying to put a side together that would be able to challenge for promotion. There was no money in it for me, but footballers like to play football, and a move to Brighton meant I would be doing that in someone's first team once again.

Lennie wanted me to do the pre-season with Charlton and see how things worked out, but I knew that at nearly 30 years old I still had a lot left in me and I wanted to play regularly. Brighton were willing to give me that chance and so I made the move to the south coast. On the face of it, signing for Brighton may have seemed like a backward step. After all, within the space of less than three years I'd gone from being a First Division player with Villa to signing for a club who had just been relegated to the Third.

In the end I made my decision and signed for Brighton in a £30,000 move, just £8,000 less than Charlton had paid for me when I left Villa. I went from playing a dozen first-team games for Charlton the season before, to missing just a handful of matches in a Brighton team that gained promotion. The only real downside for me in that season was the amount of travelling I had to do. I was still living in Essex and it was a round trip of 160 miles each day for me.

Despite the travelling, I enjoyed my time with Brighton but

still took an interest in Charlton, watching some of their mid-week games at Selhurst when I could. Although I hadn't left the club on the best of terms, it didn't take long before I was talking to Lennie again and he told me how they'd had me watched at Brighton and knew I was doing well for them.

'We should never have let you go,' he told me once.

I stayed with the Seagulls for almost three years before a call from Lennie signalled a new chapter in my career. I had always been interested in the coaching and management side of the game and knew even when I was at Villa that one day I would like to move in that direction. The call I got from Lennie gave me the chance to do just that. He told me that he'd like me to return to the club as player/reserve-team coach, and the more I thought about it the more I liked the idea.

I think Lennie realized that although we'd had the odd run-in, I always tried to go about my business as a player in a professional way. There's no way he would have wanted me back if he thought I couldn't do the job, or if he believed he couldn't get on with me. Barry Lloyd was very good about the situation and didn't try to stand in my way, and I think he probably appreciated the fact that I'd always conducted myself well while I was with Brighton. I was never late for training and always gave everything I could. Barry recognized that and I think he also saw what a good opportunity it was for me.

From my point of view, it wasn't just the chance to coach and manage the reserves that appealed to me, I also thought I would be able to force my way into the first team. Charlton had just been relegated from the First Division after four years in the top flight and, as ever, Lennie was working on a shoestring budget. It was remarkable that the club had survived in the First Division for as long as it had done, and I knew it was going to be a struggle but it was a job I really felt I could get my teeth into.

Lennie gave me a pretty free rein and he also encouraged me to get involved in things like scouting the opposition and looking at players who we might want to try and buy. From day one I enjoyed it and I liked working more closely with Lennie. I'd always liked him and thought he was a good manager. He did an amazing job during his time at Charlton. He was very cool under pressure and I always thought his tactics were very good. Lennie was excellent with his players and he was usually spot-on at half-time, when things needed to be talked about and sorted out quickly. From the day he took over he had a massive job on his hands and when you think of the sort of things he went through, like the club nearly going out of business, the move from The Valley and coping with playing in the First Division while sharing another club's ground, it makes his time in charge even more amazing.

I replaced Peter Eustace, who had been looking after the reserves, and Lennie had Mike Flanagan working alongside him with the first team, but not too far into the season all of that changed. After one of the early matches that season, Flan was a guest on a local radio programme the following day and apparently voiced some opinions about the team and how they were playing. When I got to the training ground on the Monday morning Lennie came in asking where Mike was and if anyone had seen him. He told me that as soon as Flan came in he wanted to see him in his office and although I don't know exactly what happened in the meeting, I do know that pretty soon after it Mike Flanagan left the club.

It was October 1990 and I'd only been back at the club a few months, but after Flan's departure Lennie called me one day and asked if I fancied taking over as first-team player-coach. He admitted that it had all happened a bit quickly for me, but at the same time said he wouldn't have asked if he didn't think I could do it. He also told me that he intended making Steve Gritt the reserve-team player-coach.

Like most things in football it was a case of being in the right place at the right time. I realized it was a great opportunity for me and the good thing from my point of view was that I knew most of the players and had played with quite a few. I was also still able to run around a bit myself, which I think helped to gain their respect from the start. It was great for me because not only was I coaching and getting involved with the players, it also gave me the chance to observe the way Lennie worked and to see from close-up just what it was like to be the manager of a football club. The strange thing was that not only was I coaching, but I also played for Gritty's reserve team and one day Lennie told me he wanted me playing in the first team because he needed my experience and know-how in the side. I ended up playing 21 matches for the first team that season, so I got well and truly involved both on and off the pitch.

The season wasn't easy and we finished it well down the League, eight places above bottom club Hull. One of the pluses was getting Middlesbrough defender Alan Kernaghan in on loan at the beginning of 1991, and his form while he was with us prompted Lennie into believing it would be worth making the deal permanent during the summer.

As soon as the season ended, I was ready for a break and headed off to spend a week at my brother's house in Spain, happy in the knowledge that Lennie was trying to bolster the squad by talking to Middlesbrough in an effort to bring Kernaghan to Charlton for the following season, but it didn't quite work out that way.

He certainly spoke to Middlesbrough, but instead of Kernaghan heading south, Lennie ended up moving to the north-east.

5 Chance of a Lifetime

When I heard the news about Lennie I thought there must be some mistake. He'd had a bit of stick early in the season and there had been some talk around October time that he might be sacked, but in the end the whole thing blew over, and that summer I just assumed that the only changes might be among the playing staff.

When I got back to England after the summer break, I tried to get hold of Lennie to find out exactly what had happened, but I couldn't contact him. Apparently it was while Lennie was talking to Middlesbrough over the possible Kernaghan transfer that their chairman decided to offer him the manager's job. I think the whole thing had taken everyone by surprise, especially Chairman Roger Alwen and Vice-Chairman Mike Norris, who were left wondering how they were going to get a replacement.

It's always difficult for a club when they change managers, but for Charlton it was made even more complicated by the fact that they had left Selhurst Park and were looking to return to The Valley early in the new season. With all that going on off the field, the last thing they wanted was to have their manager walk out.

When I eventually did get to speak to Lennie it was clear he felt he'd been offered an opportunity that was just too good to miss out on. He'd had to go through a lot as Charlton's manager, and perhaps the thought of battling on and not really knowing what was around the corner was too much for him. Middlesbrough offered Lennie the chance to take over a club with some money to spend, who had made it clear they wanted him to lead them to promotion.

Having been brought back to Charlton by Lennie and worked alongside him as first-team coach, I asked the obvious question. Was he going to want to take me with him? Lennie explained that he thought it was too early for me to do that, which seemed to leave me in no-man's land, but he also said he'd recommended that the club should promote from within.

The reality of that meant the field was pretty narrow because apart from Gritty and me, the only other real candidate was Keith Peacock who'd come back to Charlton and done some scouting after parting company with Maidstone United as their manager. Keith was a Charlton legend, having played for the club for 17 years in the 1960s and 1970s. He'd then gone on to coach in America with the Tampa Bay Rowdies, and managed both Gillingham and Maidstone. In terms of experience he was obviously in a strong position if he wanted the job and he was also a firm favourite with the fans.

I spoke to Arnie Warren about the situation and he basically told me that the club were skint, so I knew that whoever got the job would have real problems from day one, but despite all of this I knew that I had to apply and so did Gritty. Keith also threw his hat into the ring and the three of us were left waiting, while we got on with all the pre-season preparations. By this time Keith was looking after the youth team, while Gritty and I took the senior professionals. The three of us weren't the only people to apply, of course, and there were several names bandied about after the club advertised the post, including some other ex-Charlton players.

From my own point of view there was nothing more I could do other than to get on with the coaching and let matters take their course. On the one hand I wanted the job of manager, but at the same time I was under no illusions about the task the new man would face. There had been talk throughout the summer of a move back to The Valley, but the reality was that nothing had been finalized. In effect we had no ground, the team had struggled in the previous season and, even by Second Division standards, we had a very small squad.

While everyone waited for an appointment to be made it was clear that Steve and I were the real outsiders, but despite what was being said in the press I always thought the two of us had a chance, and I actually thought we could have that chance together. In my own mind I thought that realistically neither of us had enough experience to be given the job outright, but we'd been coaching alongside Lennie, knew the club and, more importantly, we knew the players. The more I thought about it the more I believed that together we had a chance, and in the end that's exactly what happened.

When the announcement came it took a lot of people by surprise and certainly raised a few eyebrows. Obviously Keith was very disappointed. He had a lot more experience than Steve and myself but only chairman Roger Alwen and his board can really say why they decided to give the job to the two of us. We were called in by Roger, and told that the job was ours and that we would be called joint first-team player-coaches. The whole thing was sorted out in a meeting at vice-chairman Mike Norris's office in London, where he said that he would back us and that he wanted us to give it our best shot. We were being thrown in at the deep end, but I think both Gritty and I saw it as the chance of a lifetime in many ways and we had to take it.

The joint player-coaches role was a new concept at the time but in the period leading up to the announcement Arnie mentioned to the two of us that it was something the board was definitely thinking about and, as the club's general manager, I can imagine that he probably had quite an influence when various options were floated at board level. So many things seemed to be up in the air at the time and, although the decision surprised people, I think it was a very sensible thing to do, because I don't really know how anyone else coming into the club would have got to grips with the job quickly enough, and we were also still players.

Steve and I got on with things straight away and decided to lay down some ground rules for ourselves with regard to the way we would tackle the job of being joint managers. We were breaking new ground and we took the sensible view that if we had some rules for us to abide by we would save ourselves a lot of aggravation in the future. The first of those rules was to make sure we would never contradict each other in front of the players or the directors.

We also decided to share the training and when it came to team selection we would discuss it together and give our opinions, but if we had different ideas about who should play and who shouldn't, nobody outside of our office would know about it. Whoever won the day with regard to a particular selection, the other person would back him up. When it came to post-match press conferences we would take two at a time, because by doing that it usually meant you would face the media at home and away, instead of one of us just getting the home or away fixtures. They were all little things but I think we both felt that adhering to them would have a really positive impact on what we were trying to do.

We were in the middle of pre-season when the appointment was made and before he left Lennie had already sorted out a trip to Scotland as part of the lead-up to the big kick-off; he'd also arranged to sign midfielder John Bumstead on a free transfer after 14 seasons with Chelsea. Poor John didn't know whether he was coming or going for a time after Lennie moved on. He lived locally and playing for Charlton was a good move for him. Certainly from our point of view, having been left with such a small squad, both Steve and I were grateful to have someone with the experience and know-how of John signing for the club.

We took a squad north of the border that included some experienced pros but also some youngsters, and I'd noticed that some of the older players weren't really mixing with the kids in the way that I thought they should, while the youngsters were a bit cautious about pushing themselves forward. I felt that although the squad was small we still had the nucleus of a decent side, but we had to be a team on and off the pitch, so I told the experienced players to start showing more of an interest in the youngsters and include them more. At the same time I told the kids to be a bit more forceful in the way they went about things. One of the young players we took with us on that trip was Anthony Barness, a left-back with a lot of promise who was only 18 years old at the time, and he probably cursed me for giving my little speech to some of the older players.

One day after training, defender Stuart Balmer pulled Barney to one side and told him he had to give everyone a song that night in the bar of the hotel we were staying at. I think Anthony must have worried about it all day, because he kept telling everyone that he couldn't sing, but Stuart wouldn't let him off the hook and on the night insisted Barness stand up and give us all a song. It was silly but just the sort of thing that actually does help build team spirit and in the end Barney was forced into a compromise.

'I don't know any songs but I can recite a poem,' he said nervously.

'Alright then, but you'll have to sing it!' insisted Balmer.

The incident seemed to break the ice and I think the senior players came to terms with the fact that with our small squad we just had to get on with it as best we could. The Scottish tour wasn't the best in terms of performance and worse was to follow both on and off the field as the new season approached. General manager Arnie Warren was an important part of the new structure at the club and obviously his know-how and experience in the game was something both Steve and I saw as being a real help as we got to grips with our new job. We'd had a poor game in a friendly match less than two weeks before the start of the season when we lost 4–1 at Leyton Orient and we knew that we had to try and bring some players in.

Richard Murray and Martin Simons had joined the board towards the end of the previous season and they had started to take more of an interest in what was going on. They were asking us who we might be looking at in terms of bringing players in, and for Steve and me it was one of the first tests of our ground rules. We were having conversations with Roger Alwen and Mike Norris on a regular basis so you can imagine how important we felt it was to make sure we got things right and presented the same story to them. The last thing we needed was for me to say one thing and Steve to say another.

I told Arnie that I thought we needed a couple of new faces

and asked how much money might be available. He basically said there wasn't any and we'd just have to soldier on, but I couldn't understand where the £300,000 Lennie was apparently going to pay Middlesbrough for Kernaghan had gone. One minute the club looked as though they could afford a fee like that, and now we were being told things had changed and there was no money.

Everything was further complicated by the fact that the proposed move back to the Valley was now on hold. We were due to kick-off the season sharing another club's ground once again, but instead of Palace and Selhurst Park, it was going to be West Ham and a stadium I knew well, Upton Park. When we were first given the job we were told that a move back to The Valley was probably only a matter of a few matches away, but as things turned out our time at Upton Park proved to be a lot longer than anyone had anticipated. I think both Gritty and I felt a bit like sacrificial lambs at the time, because we knew the way we wanted to play, but we didn't quite have the right people in place, and if our hands were going to be tied in the transfer market, how were we even going to get any plans we had off the ground?

We needed an experienced defender and a forward with pace who could worry an opposition defence. I decided to phone Barry Lloyd at Brighton because I knew that defender Steve Gatting was a possible free transfer, and I also knew striker Garry Nelson had fallen out with Barry. After quite a bit of negotiation we managed to agree a free transfer for Gatts and we got Barry Lloyd down to £50,000 for Nelson. The good thing was that I knew both players from my time at Brighton and felt they would do a great job for us. The board were adamant that they had no money, but somehow they found the

£50,000 – I think they thought they needed to show a bit of backing after giving us the job and we were certainly grateful that they did.

It was getting closer to the new season and, with just over a week to go, the club had to deal with a real shock off the field when Arnie collapsed and had to undergo emergency heart-bypass surgery. At the time Arnie had been dealing with the transfers, so I don't know whether the thought of the club having to spend £50,000 helped to bring on his problems! Happily the operation was a success and although he insisted on being involved as soon as he could, it meant that we could only really speak to him on the telephone. So with our first two signings looming large, we had to make sure we got the job done properly. I probably took the deal on board a bit more, simply because I knew Barry and had been at Brighton. So on the Tuesday before we were due to start the season, we signed Gatting and two days later we brought in Garry Nelson. The effect in training was immediate, and their presence gave everyone a lift at a very vital time.

Gatts looked cool and composed as he brought a ball down in a practice game and then calmly laid it off to Balmer, while at the other end Nelson showed his pace and awareness as he picked up a flick from Carl Leaburn and got in on goal. Two little instances, but exactly the sort of thing we had been lacking and the other players knew it as well.

I've been pleased and proud of a lot of things I've done in the years that have followed, but getting those two players in like we did was some of the best business Charlton has ever done as a club in my opinion, because the whole atmosphere changed and everyone got a lift from it just at the right time. As if to emphasize the point we went out at Upton Park for our first

League game and beat Newcastle 2–1 with goals from Robert Lee and Carl Leaburn. It was the start of what proved to be a tremendous season for us and one that helped both Steve and me establish ourselves as a credible partnership.

After getting Nelson and Gatting I always felt we had a very strong spine for the division. We had people like Bob Bolder in goal, Simon Webster at the back, Colin Walsh and Andy Peake in midfield, with Leaburn up front to add some physical presence. We also had Robert Lee who gave us such quality and was a real talent, but what pleased me most was that I genuinely felt we had a very good group of players.

We lost only one of our first six league matches, which gave us a base and helped to get us started. From being the obvious choice for relegation as far as many people were concerned, we suddenly found ourselves getting some attention for all the right reasons. Things went well for us and near the end of October we were in third place.

The only sour note came in a game at Southend which we drew 1–1. Steve Gatting was booked for a foul on Andy Ansah that gave them the lead through a penalty. I let my feelings be known over the incident and got ordered from the touchline for dissent and was sent to sit in the stand. Dave Webb was the Southend manager and was someone I knew very well. When I got up into the directors' box after being ordered from the touchline, Dave pulled me to one side and asked me why I'd been so stupid. He could see I was still fuming and told me I should go into the boardroom, have a drink and not bother watching the rest of the half while I calmed down because nothing I did was going to change a referee's decision. I didn't actually take his advice and instead sat and watched the game from the directors' box, but I did learn a valuable lesson that day.

Dave was right, you can rant and rave at referees but once they make their decisions they are not going to change them on the day.

To make matters worse Gatts was sent off four minutes before the break for another foul. The good thing was that we battled on with ten men and grabbed a point thanks to a Carl Leaburn goal in the second half.

I later had to go to the FA because of what had happened and they took my previous good record as a player and the fact that I'd never been sent off into consideration. They gave me a suspended fine and told me in no uncertain terms that if I ever went before them for a similar offence I would be in a lot of trouble. I'm glad to say that I never repeated the incident and to this day I have always remembered Webby's advice when it comes to referees and their decisions during a game.

Although we had no money I managed to catch Arnie in a good mood after he'd returned to work following his heart problems and he persuaded the board to give us some cash so that we could take the squad away for a few days' break because they had all done so well for us. We decided to go to Bournemouth, but while we were there trying to foster a better team spirit I got a call from Arnie that put our team-building work to the test. He told me we'd had a bid from Lennie who wanted to take Andy Peake to Middlesbrough.

It was just the sort of news Gritty and I didn't want to hear but at the same time it was no surprise Lennie wanted him. As a manager going into a new job you like to surround yourself with players you know and feel comfortable with. Lennie had brought Peaky to Charlton and knew he could rely on him. He had a very high regard for Andy and so did we, because he was our captain. With Middlesbrough pushing for promotion he obviously wanted to bolster his squad and saw a midfielder like Peake as the ideal man to bring in. The fee on offer was £150,000, which was derisory in my opinion, but Lennie knew the finances of Charlton inside out. However, as the two of us were being told that we couldn't have any of the money to spend, I felt we were in a no-lose situation and we should have held out for more. But Arnie made it pretty clear that the club had to do it and that it had to be done immediately. I think it was an indication that we were in a worse financial state than I had thought. There was some talk that the fee from Peake's transfer would pay the wages for the next three months. There was no question of holding out and getting more money for him – it was just a question of getting Andy up the M1 as quickly as possible.

Although the move to West Ham was initially talked about as only being for a couple of home games, that clearly was not the case. With the winter approaching it seemed as though we were going to be playing at Upton Park for a lot longer than people had thought

Having Andy leave was going to mean we had a big hole in our midfield to fill and, having spent £50,000 in the summer on Nels, it didn't look as though we were going to have any more cash to spend and we certainly weren't going to get any of the money from Peake's move. We had to do something and do it fast.

I'd always liked Alan Pardew at Palace. He seemed the sort of midfielder who would fit in nicely with us and we'd had him looked at quite a lot. Gritty and I also went to see him play for Palace in a reserve game against Queens Park Rangers at Loftus Road in a midweek afternoon kick-off. We went there, watched the game and then travelled to Upton Park on the underground because we had a first-team home match that night, stopping off for a McDonald's. It wasn't just transfer fees where you were expected to watch the pennies at Charlton! The press got hold of the story and had a field day with the fact that we'd travelled to a game on the tube, but it was also probably an indication of just what a precarious financial position we were in, and to be honest, it never really occurred to us to do things any other way.

We were both heavily committed to the job and spent hours travelling around the country scouting teams and looking at players. We'd shocked Lennie once by travelling up to Middlesbrough for a midweek game after taking training that same morning, and then driving back after the match so that we could be there at the training ground the next day. We were putting a lot of hours in, but there was no other way of doing it and, despite all the problems, we were enjoying our first taste of management.

The good thing from our point of view was that Pardew was on a free transfer from Palace, so it was just a case of negotiating his contract and settling on the wages. It's amazing to think how different things are these days. When I sit down with a player now we are often talking about a wage structure that will mean he gets paid thousands of pounds each week. Back in 1991 we sat in a pub near our training ground in New Eltham haggling with Pards over whether we could afford to pay him an extra £15 a week.

Happily the deal was done and he joined us, while Andy went to Middlesbrough soon after. Signing Pardew proved to be another piece in the jigsaw for us. He was what I call a 'proper' player. He was good on the field and off it, with just the right sort of personality and, in a way, added a new dimension to our game. I also think that he flourished as a player while he was at Charlton. We gave him the opportunity to get forward and score goals from midfield, while Bumstead sat in there and held things together. We also had Robert bombing up and down on the wing, with Nels and Carlo up front. Alan coming in kind of pulled everything together.

That first season was a real learning experience for us, and Arnie was a great help right through it all. On a personal basis, he had been instrumental in getting me to the club in the first place when I was at Villa, and I also think he had an influence in helping Steve and me get the job at Charlton.

I've always liked him right back to the time when he used to jokingly slip a schoolboy registration form under the expenses sheet I had to sign when I trained at QPR as a kid. He was always desperate to get me to sign for Rangers when he was there, but my heart was set on playing for West Ham. It was good to have Arnie around in that first season with all of his experience to call on if we needed it. Both Steve and I knew we had to give the job our best shot; we realized what a great opportunity it was and knew it might not come along again.

Apart from the signings like Nelson, Gatting and Pardew we made that year we also made use of loans, which, for a club like Charlton at that time, was vital. Chris Wilder from Sheffield United, Leroy Rosenior from West Ham and John Hendry from Spurs all played for us, and on transfer deadline day in March 1992 we signed David Whyte from Palace until the end of the season.

It was the first but not the last time we were to get a glimpse of David, who a couple of seasons later joined us on a perma- nent basis. He had great talent as a striker and made an imme- diate impact during his loan spell with a goal on his debut in the 2–1 win at Portsmouth. That result came at the end of March, and the saga of The Valley rumbled on, with us playing out the season using Upton Park as our home ground. Incredibly, we ended up being involved in the race for a possible play-off place right up to the last match of the season. After all the pre-season talk of a relegation struggle we found ourselves in a position of being a few points away from a play-off place and a possible return to the top flight.

In our last three games of the season we had Leicester and Tranmere at home, followed by a trip to play Bristol Rovers at Twerton Park. Leicester were flying when they arrived at Upton Park and were contesting an automatic promotion place. We had our best home gate of the season, with 15,357 turning up, and I think about 10,000 of those fans were Leicester supporters. They even had to delay the kick-off by 15 minutes to allow the away fans time to get in, but the afternoon turned out to be a big disappointment for them as we ran out 2–0 winners with goals from Robert Lee and David Whyte.

Three days later we went into the Tranmere game knowing that a win would give us a real chance of securing a play-off place in our last game of the season. But instead of the win we wanted, they beat us 1–0 with a John Aldridge goal in front of just 7,645 fans. I must admit thinking at the time that the chance of a possible play-off place and getting back into the big time would have generated more interest, but things like that were a fact of life for us and all part and parcel of the job we had.

We went into the game at Bristol Rovers as one of four teams who still had a chance of securing the final two play-off places, the others being Cambridge, Blackburn and Swindon. All four of us had to play our final match of the season away from home. At one stage during the game with Rovers I thought we were in pole position, because we knew that Blackburn were drawing and I thought Simon Webster had given us the lead with a header only to have it disallowed because David Whyte was in an offside position. We eventually lost the match 1–0 but, with Blackburn winning and Cambridge getting a point, even a win that day would not have been enough for us. Blackburn, backed by Jack Walker's millions and with Kenny Dalglish as their manager, claimed sixth spot and went on to get promoted by winning the play-off final against Leicester at Wembley.

It was a disappointing end, but looked at overall we had to be pleased with what had gone on. At the start of the season we were no-hopers according to a lot of people. Everyone said the joint manager thing wouldn't work and it was only a matter of time before we lost our jobs. People joked about us and we were called Pinky and Perky, or Tweedledee and Tweedledum. I'm not sure how the fans took the whole thing about us getting the job, but results are results and we finished seventh.

The season had been vitally important to the club. We'd been favourites to go down and once again we had to play all of our home games at another club's ground. Before the start of the season there was talk that we might end up going from First to Third Division in a couple of years. If that had happened it would have been a disaster. As we started our new job in the summer of 1991 the club was basically on the floor, still with no ground and no cash, but what it did have was incredibly loyal supporters, a great bunch of lads playing in the side and a fantastic group of directors who seemed prepared to throw money into a black hole.

To get from that point to where the club is now never ceases to amaze me.

6 No Place Like Home

Despite finishing seventh, Gritty and I suddenly found ourselves managing a First Division team as we looked forward to the start of the new season in 1992.

It was the year in which the Premier League came into being and as a consequence there was a restructuring of the Football League, which meant the old Second Division becoming the First. The club seemed to like what Steve and I were doing and in the summer the two of us signed new contracts, with the official title of joint player-managers, instead of player-coaches. Arnie Warren had retired following his heart problems, and we were more heavily involved in all the day-to-day things that went on, which he would normally have dealt with.

Having got so close to the play-offs the previous season it was important that we kept the momentum going, but as usual we knew it wasn't going to be easy. Once again the hope was that the club would move back to The Valley, but the money needed to make it happen still wasn't in place that summer and we kicked off the season playing our 'home' games at Upton Park once more.

There was no real hope of making any signings, because there just wasn't the money for us to spend, but we did at least

manage to get Carl Leaburn to put pen to paper on a new contract, which was important for us and the way we wanted the
team to operate. Carlo had taken some stick over the years
because he didn't score as many goals as people thought he
should. He had got into the side under Lennie when he was just
a few days short of his 18th birthday and had played a lot of
his early football in the top division. He always worked hard
for the team and with his height and physical presence Carl was
important to us. We were also aware that in his first season with
us he'd managed to finish top scorer with 14 goals, so having
him settled and in place as the season started was important,
and he proved that point in our first game of the season.
Leaburn along with Garry Nelson and Alex Dyer were all on
target as we beat Grimsby 3–1 at Upton Park.

That win was the first of a ten-game unbeaten start to the
season, which at one stage took us to the top of the League. It
was also during the course of the run that we had to sell two
players, giving the club some much-needed cash in their bid to
get back to The Valley.

When I first got the job with Gritty I remember Lennie
Lawrence telling me that no matter how important it was for
the club to get back to The Valley, I would do well to steer clear
of all the off-the-field manoeuvrings. I think he knew from his
own experiences that getting too involved could prove to be a
distraction, and we would have enough problems to occupy us
on the playing side of things without getting bogged down with
all the talk about a return to The Valley. It wasn't that Steve and
I didn't care about going back, because we both realized that
the club needed its own home and we couldn't go on sharing
grounds indefinitely.

The effort put into getting back to The Valley was tremendous and the part played by the fans can never be underestimated. They were right there throughout and never lost hope that one day the club would get its own ground back again. Every club has loyal supporters, but when you think about what Charlton fans had to endure when the club moved from its home and the depth of feeling and determination they showed, I think it's remarkable. From the moment the club left in 1985 there was always a push by the fans to get back to The Valley, and one of the most emotional moments came in 1989 when Roger Alwen announced his plans to take the club back. In April of that year the fans actually rolled up their sleeves and began to clean up The Valley, clearing the weeds and sorting out the terraces which had pretty much been left to rot following that last home match with Stoke. Suddenly there was real optimism about returning but there were stumbling blocks to be overcome, not least the cost of a return and a battle to get permission from Greenwich council.

In a unique move the following year supporters formed The Valley Party and, backed up by a brilliant poster campaign emphasizing Charlton's importance to the area and the history of the club, they contested 60 of the 62 seats in the council elections, gaining an amazing 14,838 votes. The whole episode was incredible, particularly when you consider they were campaigning on a single issue, which was getting permission for Charlton to move back to The Valley. In the process the chairman of the planning committee was unseated and the club's bid to return gathered further momentum. Charlton finally got their planning application approved in 1991. But although we all thought it was just a matter of time after that before we played at The Valley again, the whole thing dragged on for longer than anyone thought and after that first season at Upton Park we all knew how important it was that the move happened sooner rather than later.

Apart from the cost the club were incurring every time they played at Upton Park, there was also the practical side of things to consider as well. The fans had been incredibly loyal and supportive ever since Charlton had moved out of The Valley seven years earlier. Although a lot of them had vowed never to go to Selhurst because they were so bitter about the move, we also had a hard core of support that turned out for the home games.

They had done the same for a season at Upton Park even though the ground was on the other side of the Thames and really inconvenient for the majority of them. It was alright for me because I lived in Essex and had played for West Ham. I knew Upton Park, and the surrounding streets, like the back of my hand but there was no doubt it wasn't the best place geographically for a lot of people. There were always horrendous traffic problems on match days and it wasn't just the fans who were affected. I think I lost count of the number of times poor Johnny Bumstead had to abandon his car and run to the ground in order to make sure he was on time for the kick-off!

When we started the season it was hoped that we were going to be able to make a quick return to The Valley but, with the cost of the move and sorting out the money needed, it soon became clear that wasn't going to be the case and in fact we played four of our first five League games at Upton Park, which included a 1–0 'away' win against West Ham.

Our early season form was good. One of our best players the previous season had been left-back Scott Minto, who had attracted the usual attention from some of the bigger clubs, including Chelsea. They wanted to check on him as soon as the new season started, but Minto was injured and instead we played Anthony Barness. Chelsea were impressed by what they saw and it didn't take them too long to follow up with an enquiry. By the end of August we knew we were likely to lose one of our best young players for a fee of £350,000.

It was the sort of money a club like Charlton at that time just couldn't turn down, especially as the cash would go towards getting us back to The Valley, but despite what was on offer I almost succeeded in killing the deal stone dead because I didn't feel Chelsea were generous enough to the player.

At the time of the bid we were actually top of the First Division, and as the team travelled up to Sunderland on a Friday in September, Gritty and I, along with Barney, went over to Chelsea's ground at Stamford Bridge to finalize the deal. We met Anthony's dad there and I could see them looking around the stadium, obviously excited at the prospect of joining Chelsea and playing in the Premier League, but for whatever reason I got the feeling that the West London club weren't really doing their best to sign him. When Barness came out of the room after talking to the Chelsea people, I asked him what sort of deal they were offering him. When he told me I was really surprised. It wasn't good, not good at all, but the problem was Anthony desperately wanted to sign for them.

I decided to take matters into my own hands. I told Chelsea that the deal simply wasn't going to happen if they didn't give the boy at least something like what he deserved. I could understand a club wanting to get a player on the cheap when it came to paying his wages, but what they were offering was not on. I think if Roger could have heard me in that room he would have had kittens. But Barness was a young boy, and it was really before the days of agents. I just felt he was worth more then Chelsea were offering.

In the end the £350,000 transfer went through after Chelsea

had a re-think about the money they were offering Barness, leaving Gritty and I to make our way to Sunderland on the train. As soon as we arrived at the team hotel we had another problem to deal with in the shape of a very disappointed and upset Robert Lee.

Throughout the early weeks of the season there had been speculation that Robert would be leaving the club. Everyone knew we were strapped for money and, as Lee was our most valuable playing asset, it didn't take too much working out that sooner rather than later we would have to cash in on him. From my point of view I hoped that it wouldn't happen, but in reality I always expected that it would. The directors were doing their best to raise the money needed for a move back to The Valley, and once again the fans got heavily involved by pledging cash, but there were still stories of a shortfall. By the beginning of September an actual date for a return had been set. It was going to be 5 December, and the opposition was Portsmouth, but it would only happen if the funds were in place. Selling Anthony Barness had obviously given those funds a major boost. Like everyone else Robert was well aware of all the speculation surrounding his position at Charlton and that was why he was waiting to see Gritty and me when we arrived at the hotel.

'What's happening?' he asked us. 'You sold Peaky last season, now you've just sold Barney and I'm still here. What's going to happen with me?'

I told Robert to calm down and not get upset about things. We had a big game against Sunderland the next day and I wanted him in the right frame of mind for that. I know a lot of fans might find it hard to understand how Robert felt at the time, and probably see it as the player being disloyal, but I had a lot of sympathy for his position.

I'd known Robert for a long time, ever since I coached him when he was a kid and I was playing for West Ham. He was 26 years old but had been playing in the first team for nine seasons. He'd been a great servant for Charlton and nobody could blame him for wanting to try and move to a bigger club in order to improve his career. I also knew that no matter how he felt about things off the field, once he was on the pitch Robert could only play one way, and that was by giving 100 per cent to the cause.

Robert played the next day and we won 2–0 to make it five wins and a draw from our first six games, but I knew that we were going to lose him. Roger had confirmed after our win against West Ham that Lennie had already been asking about Lee, so, instead of waiting for it to happen and then reacting, we decided to try and get someone in first.

Lennie's initial offer of £250,000 was derisory, but it was also clear that Robert would be on his way and the most important thing from the club's point of view was making sure we got as much money for him as we could. I phoned West Ham manager Billy Bonds and told him that we were going to have to sell Robert. I told him what a good player he was and also that he was a West Ham fan having been born a couple of miles from the ground. Billy had heard that Middlesbrough had offered only £250,000 and he didn't seem that keen to come in with the sort of offer we were looking for, neither was Kevin Keegan at Newcastle, but when he did make his bid at least it was a big increase on Lennie's.

In the meantime we set our sights on a youngster I knew from my days at Brighton. His name was John Robinson, he was 21 years old and was the sort of wide player we would need if we were going to try and fill the gap left by Robert's eventual departure. He was out of contract at the time and we knew the fee would have to be decided by a transfer tribunal, but it was a risk we had to take. Little did I know at the time that the move would turn out to be one of the best bits of business Gritty and I ever did. I also had no way of knowing that John would go on to play such a big part in the development of the club in the years that followed.

Soon after Robbo joined Charlton I was at my friend Pat Willis's house on a Sunday afternoon when I was told that Keegan was trying to get in touch with me. I went upstairs to Pat's bedroom, phoned Kevin and got a taste of his transfer negotiating style. He told me he was prepared to offer £700,000, not a penny more, and there would be no 'add-ons' like extra money for appearances or England caps. I told Keegan that Robert was worth more than he was offering.

'You can't offer us that,' I said.

'Yes I can,' Kevin insisted. 'Nobody else is in for him.'

I was basically left with a take-it or leave-it situation and it was obvious Kevin wasn't going to be swayed. I've heard from other people in the game that it was the way he went about things. He'd offer you what he thought was right, but wouldn't change his mind or budge on things. It wasn't too long before I was on the phone again to Billy Bonds to see if he would put in a bid, but all he was prepared to offer was £500,000 and in a last-ditch effort Lennie came back and made an offer to match Newcastle's, but never got the answer he wanted from Robert.

'In the absence of a yes, we agreed on a no,' was Lennie's typical quote in the press.

Robert travelled north, spoke to Keegan and we never saw him again. Looking back on the situation, it was probably the best thing he ever did. He went from strength to strength up there and quite rightly got the international recognition with England that his talent deserved.

As managers Gritty and I had done what was right for the club, but in terms of the team, it certainly didn't do us any favours. When Robert went to Newcastle we were top and Newcastle were second. We'd effectively sold our best player to our biggest promotion rivals at the time. On a slightly different scale it's kind of like Arsenal letting Thierry Henry go to Chelsea or Manchester United, but at the time it had to be done.

We were left with the prospect of hoping Robbo could come in as an adequate replacement, but things didn't get off to the best of starts when John picked up an ankle injury in his first game for us, a 3–1 home defeat to Portsmouth in the Anglo-Italian Cup, and had to be substituted early in the second half. The tribunal ruled that we would have to pay £75,000 for Robinson, with Brighton also getting thirty-three and a third per cent of any future transfer fee. I thought the sell-on figure was too high and couldn't help letting everyone in the room know how I felt.

'That's a bit much, ain't it? Firty free and a fird!' I blurted out in my best Cockney accent to the tribunal chairman.

'Yes, Mr Curbishley,' he replied without batting an eyelid. 'Firty free and a fird!'

So in a matter of days our new signing was injured and we lost our best player, but the fact remains that the money gained from the sale of Robert Lee and Anthony Barness got us back to The Valley. The big day was fast approaching, we all knew there was no place like home and when the team ran out to play Portsmouth on that memorable Saturday afternoon in December, I felt Charlton Athletic became a club again.

7 Partners

Portsmouth manager Jim Smith just about summed things up when he told me after that first game back at The Valley, 'It was always a match you were going to win.'

The whole atmosphere and emotion that went into the club's return was incredible, but what a lot of people might have forgotten was the fact that Colin Walsh's historic goal after just seven minutes not only won the match it also earned us only our second victory in eleven league matches.

From being genuine promotion challengers at the start of October, we fell like a stone, losing nine matches and drawing one game before we met Portsmouth. While most of the attention was understandably focused on going back to The Valley, I can honestly say that I wondered whether the club's return might also be the cue for changing managers. It was a terrible run for us and no matter what we had achieved in our first season, I knew that it was all about results and we had been getting the wrong kind.

We had done everything right for the club, by selling players and getting on with the job of managing, but I think both Steve and I knew it would count for nothing if we didn't turn things around. The game against Portsmouth signalled the start of a new era for Charlton and The Valley went wild when we scored.

The last-minute work that went into making sure everything was ready on the day was amazing. There were literally bits of the ground that still had paint drying as the fans started to come through the gates. We had a crowd of 8,337 for the match, which was all we could get into the ground at the time, but we could have sold out many times over. It was a day to remember and a really special occasion for all of us, even though it probably didn't mean too much to anyone outside the club.

It was certainly a big day for Roger Alwen who had worked so hard to make sure the club returned to its home, and for someone like Derek Ufton who was on the board and had played for the club. He was so emotional on the day that every time he gave an interview I think he burst into tears. I also think it was a big day for people like Richard Murray and Martin Simons. Once we had a home again they could see we were pushing forward. We may have been losing money as a club, but we had our ground back, and even if we hadn't beaten Portsmouth that day, we would still have ended up as winners, because after more than seven years we were back where we belonged.

I had drifted away from the playing side of things and even in the previous season, I'd only managed one league game. I think it was just a natural consequence of becoming a manager and the role I started to adopt. I was still fit and if needed I could still run about, but we had players in the squad who could do a job and when that's the case it's right to let them get on with it. I actually played my last game for Charlton the next season when I came on as a substitute at Portsmouth. I was only on for 15 minutes, just to help shore things up in midfield.

The game at The Valley with Portsmouth was particularly memorable for Gritty as well, because he actually played in it. I think it was important that he did, because emotions were running high and we needed the kind of steadying influence he was able to bring to our team. Steve had also had to deal with a horrible family problem a couple of months earlier when his little daughter, Hayley, was found to have a brain tumour. She was rushed to hospital for an operation which resulted in the tumour being successfully removed, but it was a stressful time for Steve and it said a lot for him and his character that he managed to cope with it all really well.

Despite the fact that going into that game it was almost eight years since I had first signed for Charlton as a player, I suppose I was still classed as a bit of an outsider, and in many ways I think that was how I felt as well. To be honest, that feeling probably never went until we reached the Premier League after our play-off final with Sunderland more than five years later. I think many people saw me as a West Ham man. They were the team I supported as a kid and first signed for, but by the time we played Portsmouth I'd actually spent longer at Charlton as a professional, and there was no doubt the club had grown on me.

After the terrible run of matches we had going into that Portsmouth game we managed to stop the rot a bit with six straight draws, but we were never quite able to recapture the early season form and finished halfway down the table in 12th place. In many ways I suppose the position was overshadowed by the fact that we finally managed to get back to The Valley, but as a club both Steve and I felt we needed to make progress on the field if we were going to be able to do the same off the pitch.

Who knows what would have happened that season if we had been able to hold onto Robert Lee? We may have ended up in exactly the same place, or he might have given us that little spark that meant we could have challenged at the top. All I do know for sure is that we had to sell our best player and it was not a nice feeling. It was something I hoped would never happen again, but in 2004 I had a similar situation when Scott Parker was sold to Chelsea. When such influential players as Lee and Parker are sold it can have a big effect on the team. The player gets his move and good luck to him, but it's the people left behind who have to try and cope without them.

By the end of the season I suppose both Steve and I had packed an awful lot into two years, in terms of experience and having to cope with the sort of problems a club like Charlton at that time threw up. Playing on someone else's ground, selling your best players, moving back to The Valley, finishing just outside the play-off places, having to deal with a bad run, trying to maintain and even strengthen the squad on a very small budget – it was never easy but we both learnt a great deal because of it.

The two of us had a good relationship and I suppose our roles within that relationship developed naturally as we went along. Perhaps I was getting more involved in the managerial sense, because Gritty was still playing in the odd match and maybe I was taking a more forward role. It wasn't something that was planned, it just seemed to happen. I thought the dual role worked well and there was never a cross word between us. Outside of the job we didn't socialize together, but I didn't see that as a big thing and when it came to work I think both of us felt very comfortable with each other, and we genuinely believed we were doing a good job.

As well as trying to bring players into the club for relatively small fees, we also tried to give some of the promising young-sters a chance in the first team – people like Shaun Newton, Darren Pitcher, Paul Linger, Linvoy Primus and Paul Sturgess all got a chance to show what they could do. They were desper-ate to take that chance, as were some of the people we brought in from the outside like Pardew and Robinson.

At the end of that second season in charge with Steve we both knew that we had to try and build on what we had done. We'd probably exceeded everyone's expectations in that first season by finishing in seventh place, and even though we'd fallen from the dizzy heights of first in the table early the next season, we'd still finished in a steady mid-table position and, as I've said, the big thing was to get back to The Valley.

Now that we were there again it was obvious the club had to make the most of it and start developing the ground. An increased capacity means more revenue and without that sort of money no club can hope to grow and become successful. I felt we had been really lucky to have a team that contained players like Simon Webster, Pardew, Gatting, Leaburn, Walsh, Bumstead and Nelson. They epitomized a lot of what Charlton stood for in the early days of our management. You knew exactly what you were getting and they would never let you down.

Those players and the rest of the squad in the years Gritty and I were in charge together helped lay the foundation for what has gone on at the club since. None of them earned any-thing like the huge wages players earn these days, but it didn't matter. Of course they wouldn't have said no to more money, but it simply wasn't there and they knew that. I think we had a tremendous spirit within the team, and that rubbed off on the youngsters coming through the ranks and breaking into the side.

Although we never actually sat down and talked about it, I think both Steve and I were very much aware that there was a certain type of player who fitted the bill when it came to signing someone for Charlton. I'd describe them as hungry and angry. Hungry in the sense that they desperately wanted the chance to show what they could do, and angry because maybe they hadn't been given that opportunity elsewhere. They could be players from teams in your own division or higher who maybe weren't getting a look-in at their club, or they might be lower-League players really keen to grab their chance.

Shortly after the end of that second season we managed to sign defender Alan McLeary from Millwall on a free transfer. Alan was a tried-and-tested performer with the right sort of character and we also realized that Simon Webster looked likely to leave the club, having come to the end of his contract. Webby had been magnificent for Steve and me, but it was obvious that he wanted to move on after catching the eye as one of our best performers. In the end it was West Ham who came in for him and the fee was settled by a tribunal because he was out of contract. They wanted to pay £300,000 and we wanted £800,000; in the end we had to settle for £525,000, but once again it was a much-needed boost to the club's coffers to help develop The Valley, and it also meant we were on the bargain-hunt trail once again if we wanted to bring anyone in. It wasn't too long before we found the kind of bargain we were looking for in Phil Chapple from Cambridge United. He was a big defender who was good on the ball and we got him for around £100,000 in all, which also avoided the hassle of having to go through the tribunal route.

We started the season well again and were top at the beginning of September after six league games, going into a home derby with Millwall at The Valley that ended goalless. The match still managed to make the headlines for a couple of unsavoury incidents, one on the field and one off it.

Derby games between the two sides always have a bit of spice to them and this one was certainly no exception. Right at the start of the match Shaun Newton appeared to be elbowed by Millwall defender Pat Van Den Hauwe, and up in the stands during the second half of the game Roger Alwen had a punch thrown at him by a Millwall supporter sitting in the directors' box as a guest of Millwall. There were also two players sent off, Peter Garland for us and Millwall's Alex Rae, as well as three others booked. A quiet afternoon at The Valley!

The elbow incident went unnoticed by the referee, but when we looked at the video of the match you could clearly see what had happened, and the club made a decision to let the authorities know about it. Gritty and I watched the whole thing at the training ground on the Monday after the game and then phoned Millwall manager Mick McCarthy to let him know what Charlton were preparing to do about it. Milwall's training ground virtually backed onto our own and when we phoned Mick he had just got back from a run.

'Don't bother getting changed Mick,' I told him. 'Just jog around here and have a look at this video we've got.'

Mick duly arrived and looked at the tape we had. 'Oh, f**k,' he said, shaking his head as soon as he saw it. Until that moment I don't think he'd realized exactly what had happened in the incident and how bad it looked, but there was no doubt in his mind after that, and because we pursued the matter Van Den Hauwe had to go before an FA disciplinary hearing, where, amazingly, he was cleared.

As well as signing Phil Chapple in the summer, the only other player we paid money for that season was Mark Robson who arrived from West Ham in November. We got him for an initial £75,000 with a further £50,000 to be linked to appearances. That transfer was sandwiched in between Charlton getting a taste of Europe and me getting the chance to leave the club.

The European football came in the form of the Anglo-Italian competition that was played each year. We got through the domestic stage and then went on to meet Brescia and Ancona in Italy, before taking on Ascoli and Pisa at The Valley. We lost 2–0 to Brescia, drew 1–1 against Ancona and then lost 3–0 to Ascoli and Pisa, ending our little European adventure. It was good fun and a nice experience for the team and our fans, but in many ways I could have done without the whole thing. We had to play midweek games that could often get quite heated and then come back and play a League match at the weekend. It obviously wasn't as important as the League, and there was no doubt that the extra games and travelling involved were disruptive.

The day after the Ascoli game Mark Robson joined to give the squad more attacking options, and soon after he came into the club I found out that Birmingham were keen to have me as their new manager. Terry Cooper had resigned and it seemed they wanted me as his replacement. They were in the same division as us, but having played for them I knew just what a big club they were and the potential they had. Charlton had broken the mould by appointing joint managers and Birmingham had done the same when they appointed a woman, Karren Brady, as their chief executive. Brady along with David Sullivan, who lived near me in Essex, and the Gold brothers were trying to transform Birmingham and help them realize the club's potential. When Roger found out about them wanting me he was very good about the whole thing.

'You have to do what you think best,' he told me.

In the end what I thought best was to stay at Charlton. As I've said, although I might have been seen as more of an outsider to a lot of people connected with the club, the fact was I had been at Charlton for quite a while and had become part of the place. I also felt that I just wasn't ready and didn't have the right experience. I knew that at some stage Gritty and I would have to go out on our own, but December 1993 wouldn't have been the right time for me. If I'd pushed things and insisted that I wanted to leave, I'm sure that would have happened and my career would have taken a different path. I suppose Steve's career might have been different as well, and I don't know if he would have been appointed as Charlton manager had I gone. Having decided that I wanted to stay at The Valley, Roger and the board responded by offering a new contract. Not just to me, but to Steve as well.

December also marked the first anniversary of our return to The Valley, and it was nice to be able to do it in style because we'd managed to maintain our good form right up to the beginning of the month and, almost a year to the day after our return, Phil Chapple came up with the goal that saw us record a 1–0 home win against Luton. There was a bit of a wobble in form after that match, but we recovered quite well from suffering three straight defeats and by the time the FA Cup came around in January we were third in the table.

We beat Burnley 3–0 at The Valley and earned another home tie against Blackburn. Since just missing out on a play-off place to them in our first season in charge, Rovers had gone from strength to strength with the help of Jack Walker's money. They'd gained promotion in 1992 under Kenny Dalglish and by the time they arrived at our place for the Cup game, they were second in the Premier League behind Manchester United, a position they held onto for the rest of the season, before going one better the next year and winning the title.

The contrast between the two clubs in terms of finance couldn't have been more stark, and one newspaper highlighted the difference by saying we'd put our team together for about £350,000, while Blackburn's side had cost £22 million. It was a great chance for our side to have a go against a team that included the likes of Alan Shearer, David Batty, Tim Sherwood and Graeme Le Saux. It was a big game for us and it attracted a lot of publicity, but I couldn't help feeling a bit embarrassed that we were still getting changed in portakabins and I wondered what it was like for the board to be entertaining multi-millionaires like Jack Walker in a portakabin as well. We also only played to three stands, because the new East Stand was boarded up and still under construction, but because the TV cameras were positioned there, the ground looked a lot better than it was when the game was seen on the box. But the fact was we'd still come an awfully long way since getting back and I remembered that first game against Portsmouth when the tarmac was only just dry, and I'd given a press conference a couple of days before the match standing under a roof that was still leaking.

After the game ended 0–0, most people thought we'd had our moment of glory and hadn't quite managed to pull off the kind of shock result the FA Cup is renowned for. How wrong they were!

With everyone expecting us to be lambs to the slaughter when we went up to Ewood Park ten days later, exactly the opposite turned out to be the case and we managed to beat them with the only goal of the game, scored after just 15 minutes by Darren Pitcher. Pitch was another one of the youngsters who had come through the ranks and progressed to the first team. He'd been in the side for quite a few years and was a very competitive player. He certainly wasn't afraid to put his foot in as a midfielder, and was just the sort of character you need in an away Cup tie against a team like Blackburn. The goal not only saw us hit the sporting headlines, it also helped propel Darren into the spotlight, and soon after that match there was a lot of talk in the papers about teams being interested in signing him, including Kenny Dalglish at Rovers. It was a typical case of how one match can sometimes transform a player's fortunes and, although Pitcher stayed with us for the rest of the season, it wasn't too long before he got his wish to play in the Premier League.

After the game we already knew our opponents in the next round would be Stockport or Bristol City, who were playing the following night at Stockport. So as the players headed back to London, singing all the way, the team bus dropped me off at our hotel in Manchester, and I stayed up to watch City win and go through to meet us in the next round. We needed another replay to get through against them, drawing 1–1 away before winning 2–0 back at The Valley, and suddenly we found ourselves in the quarter-finals of the FA Cup. If getting drawn against Blackburn had caused a stir for the club, our sixth-round opponents couldn't have been bigger: Manchester United at Old Trafford, a dream tie for a club like Charlton and its fans.

The game at Old Trafford was worth at least £250,000 to the club and I asked the board if it would be possible to have some of the money to freshen up the squad by bringing someone in, but I was flatly refused and told that every penny we stood to make would be ploughed back into the club. It was disappointing because we were going well in the League and I knew that a little lift at that stage might have given us a better chance for the run-in to the season, but it wasn't to be.

We took around 10,000 supporters up to Manchester on the day, which was a great occasion. The turning point in the game came near the end of the first half with the match goalless. Kim Grant was in on goal and keeper Peter Schmeichel came charging out, handling the ball outside his area, which resulted in him being sent off. Les Sealey came on as the substitute keeper and Paul Parker came off to make way for him. We actually found the switch in personnel and the fact that they were playing with ten men harder to cope with and we ended up getting beaten 3–1. The match was a chance for the fans and the club to have a big day out and anything other than a defeat would have been a bonus. We held them in the first half but then Mark Hughes got a goal just after the break, and they scored two more goals late in the game before Carl Leaburn grabbed a consolation effort for us 13 minutes from time. It was the first time Charlton had reached that stage in the FA Cup since 1947, and I think it was a great experience for all of us. It was disappointing that we didn't manage to get to a semi-final, but at the same time we knew that what really mattered was maintaining our form in the League.

When we went to Old Trafford we were fourth in the First Division and, despite a couple of hiccups along the way, we'd managed to stay in there with teams like Crystal Palace, Leicester and Nottingham Forest. Steve and I knew how important a game like the United one was but, whatever the result, it wasn't going to get us promoted. Maintaining and improving our League form was what concerned us most, but unfortunately the quarter-final match was to be the start of the sort of slump that seems to have blighted different Charlton teams over the years that have followed.

The United match took place in March and at the time we had 55 points from 32 matches in the First Division. By the time the season ended we had dropped from fourth place to finish in eleventh, and managed to gain just 10 more points from another 14 matches. We couldn't really work out what had happened and why we fell away in the way we did, but it was a really disappointing end to our third season in charge of the team. In many ways the side had over-performed for two-thirds of the season, and then having got themselves into such a good position, they just weren't able to take full advantage of it. Perhaps the squad just wasn't strong enough and if we'd been able to use some of the money from the Cup run things might have turned out differently, but we'll never know.

Overall, though, it wasn't a bad season. We'd had the Cup success and towards the end of the campaign the new East Stand was opened, showing just how much progress the club had made in the time it had been back at The Valley, but for Gritty and me it ended on a frustrating note. We wanted to make sure the same sort of thing didn't happen again next time, and as soon as the season finished we began to plan for the new one, little knowing at the time that it would turn out to be our last in charge of the team together.

8 Whyte and Wrong

After three seasons in charge of the team I don't think anyone could deny that Steve and I had done a pretty good job, and at the same time proved a lot of people wrong.

When we took over in the summer of 1991 few thought we would be in charge of the team for very long. The idea of joint managers was something not many people believed could work. It was seen by many as a stop-gap measure on Charlton's part as a way of getting them through until the club could find a new manager, but I honestly don't think that was the intention. Right from the word go, both Roger Alwen and Mike Norris had given us encouragement and support, and I think they were probably delighted that their decision had worked so well when we just missed out on the play-offs in that first season.

From our own point of view, both Gritty and I worked really hard at the partnership. Having established those ground rules we stuck by them and the whole thing seemed to work naturally. We shared everything, presented a united front and never had any real disagreements. We got on with the job and got on well together without ever being bosom buddies, but we weren't the only partnership that was starting to have an influence on things.

Just a few months before we were appointed as joint player-coaches, Richard Murray and Martin Simons had joined the board of directors and it was their commitment and financial clout which eventually had such a big say in helping the club make its move back to The Valley. They had very different characters and personalities. Richard was fairly quiet and thoughtful, while Martin was extrovert and always the life and soul of the party, but both men had dipped into their own pockets when it mattered and thrown money into what was basically a black hole at the time. There were some months when the club couldn't even afford to pay the wages and it was down to the directors to put up the money. I'd heard that Martin was asked on one occasion if he could provide money for the monthly salary bill and came to the rescue of the club by providing the funds – this was about the time of the Andy Peake transfer so the sort of money they were asking for doesn't take too much working out – but then 28 days later he was asked if he could do the same again, which was perhaps a bridge too far for Martin!

If there was commitment and passion being shown by the team on the pitch there were certainly the same characteristics being displayed off it by the directors. I knew when we took over that we were in a unique situation. It wasn't just the fact that Steve and I were going to be jointly in charge, it was also about where Charlton were as a club.

In that first season we'd started off thinking our situation at Upton Park was going to be temporary, and as it turned out we were there for all of that season and nearly half of the next. During that time we had to sell our best player, Robert Lee, and then rely on bargain buys or free transfers to try and build a team that would not only survive in the division, but also try and compete. The way we just missed out on the play-offs meant we had gone from being no-hopers at the start of the season, to possible promotion candidates by the end of it. In short, we'd over-achieved and because of that some expectation levels were raised. It was something that was to become quite a common feature of Charlton teams in the years that followed, and in many ways existed until the day I left the club.

The second season may not have been as successful on the pitch, but as a club we'd taken a massive leap forward because of finally getting back to The Valley and having a proper home again. There was no way we were ever going to progress as a club if we didn't get our own ground back, and when Roger Alwen led the crowds through the gates on that December Saturday in 1992 we became a club again. It didn't matter about a leaky roof in the North Stand, or the fact that parts of the ground still had paint drying. It didn't matter that the players had to get changed in portakabins and the capacity of the ground was so small. We all knew we were home again and playing at a ground so many people had fought so hard for. We were back at The Valley and the second season was an important stepping stone as the club continued to progress.

While the third season had ultimately ended in frustration for us with the way we fell away in the league, you could still make a case for calling it a success. We'd challenged near the top of the League for a good two-thirds of the campaign, beaten Blackburn in the FA Cup, before going out in the quarter-finals at Old Trafford to Manchester United, and opened the new East Stand.

When I sat down and thought about things I realized we had made progress and moved forward in each of the three seasons we'd been in charge, but that didn't stop the two of us feeling, at the start of the 1994–95 season, that we had a really tough job on our hands. Along with some of the good times in the season that had just ended, Steve and I also came in for a bit of stick because of the poor run of results after the United game. Instead of ending on a bit of a high, we were both left believing it was going to be harder than ever to keep the progress going.

That feeling wasn't helped by the fact that at the end of May another one of our best youngsters was sold. Chelsea finally got their man when they came back and took Scott Minto to Stamford Bridge for an initial fee of £775,000. It was a lot of money, but we knew that it was going to have to be used on the ground instead of transfers, although there was a twist.

Richard Murray was quoted as saying that he would let Gritty and I have £400,000 of his own money to spend on transfers if we needed it; he also said that we would be able to use money from any future sales, such as Darren Pitcher. The reality was that the club incurred some extra costs, and so the figure that Richard mentioned got reduced and there was only about £40,000 cash adjustment when Pitcher was eventually sold.

Since his headline-grabbing performance in the Cup against Blackburn, Pitch had been the subject of quite a few newspaper stories that had him being the target for all sorts of Premier League clubs around the country. In the end it was a bid closer to home that saw him move across South London to newly promoted Crystal Palace. Not a move that endeared him to the Charlton faithful but, instead of any straight fee, we decided to try and get a couple of Palace players in a swap deal. Pitcher was one of those players who always gave 100 per cent when he played for us, and like any other player I would never begrudge them the chance to play at the highest level if they got the opportunity and the circumstances were right for everyone involved. That was the case when Pitch left, and as far as I'm concerned he should always be welcomed back at The Valley.

Paul Mortimer had been at Charlton and played under Lennie Lawrence before moving to Villa and then Palace, but it hadn't worked out for him at Selhurst Park and manager Alan Smith was willing to let him go. He was also happy to let David Whyte come to us as part of the deal. Gritty and I obviously knew Morts from his days at the club, and we'd also got a glimpse of what David was capable of when we'd had him on loan during our first season in charge. He had natural talent and a real eye for goal, but it wasn't too long into the start of pre-season before we began to wonder if we'd made an almighty mistake.

We knew from our previous experience of David that he was a little bit laid-back, and perhaps needed to work on his fitness. We also knew that in training and in a match situation he could do things nobody else could do and we felt he'd give us something we'd been lacking in the previous season because he was such a great finisher. The deal for Mortimer and Whyte was done in late June and the first day of pre-season was scheduled for Monday 12 July. On the day we signed David I sat down with him and explained exactly what we needed him to do during the summer, so that when he came in at the start of pre-season he wouldn't be in a position where he would be trying to catch up with everyone else. Having had him on loan before, both Steve and I felt that his overall fitness could be improved and that if he didn't put the work in he might suffer when it came to the actual pre-season training period. After having a chat with him I went away feeling happy that I'd made my point and David would want to use the opportunity of playing regular first-team football after having a bit of a frustrating time at Palace. I thought he could see it as a stepping-stone in his career, and from our point of view I believed his goals and ability would help the side become a stronger outfit.

I've always thought the start of pre-season is a great time at football clubs, particularly if you've got some new players coming in. And there always seems to be a buzz about the place. Pre-season is important for all sorts of reasons. Obviously you have to get the players fit and you want to get your ideas across as to the way you want them to play and the overall approach to the coming season. Any day lost can be a problem because there are only six weeks to get it all done and you need everyone on board and raring to go. As well as Mortimer and Whyte, we'd also signed goalkeeper Andy Petterson from Luton, but as the players arrived for that first day of training it soon became clear that someone was missing. David had not turned up.

We got on with the training and asked the physio to try and contact Whyte, assuming that by the time we got back to the office we shared at the training ground in Sparrows Lane, Steve and I would have a message waiting for us explaining his absence, but we were wrong. Not only had nobody heard from David, we weren't able to contact him and all we could do was assume he would turn up the next day, but we were wrong. Although we tried, we couldn't get him on the phone either. It wasn't long before Gritty and I decided the situation demanded a more direct course of action, and so after training on that second day we got in my car and headed for an address in South London that the club had for Whyte.

It turned out to be a council estate and the address was in a block of maisonettes. They weren't in the best of condition and the estate itself was quite run-down. I could see Steve looking a bit surprised and perhaps a bit disturbed by it all, but I didn't think anything of it because I'd been brought up on a council estate and it was nothing new to me. We eventually found the place we were looking for and the first thing I noticed was a box of empty beer bottles by the side of the door. We rang the bell, which someone finally answered, and asked if we could speak to David. Before too long Whyte shuffled down the stairs after being woken up, and it soon became clear that there had been nothing wrong with him – he'd just not turned up. He stood there in his dressing-gown looking totally oblivious to the fact that he was supposed to be a professional athlete preparing for the start of a new football season. We let him know in no uncertain terms that if he didn't turn up the next day for training we'd have to take some serious action.

'David,' I said, 'you've got to turn up for training tomorrow. Do you understand?'

'I will, I will,' he mumbled and we left hoping we'd made our point, but at the same time wondering what the hell we might have got ourselves into. He was our new signing and a lot of our hopes were resting on him, but either he didn't want to train or couldn't be bothered to report for the first couple of days of our pre-season programme. As far as we could tell there was nothing wrong with him, but his disregard and lack of respect for the club that had just signed him was something that worried me.

I think we both breathed a sigh of relief when the next day he turned up for training as we'd asked him to do, but it was soon pretty clear that he was way behind everyone else when it came to his fitness. We did some running that day and he died on his feet. To be fair to him, he did try but just wasn't physically up to it and looked a sorry state. Both Steve and myself felt that he probably needed a bit more help to get to the required level of fitness. When he came in 24 hours later ready to get on with the training we started to feel a bit more encouraged about his attitude. Although once again he struggled, in a funny sort of way he lifted everyone's spirits by the way in which he went about things.

Towards the end of the second week of pre-season training David was once again on the missing list. This time we received a call from one of his friends telling us that Whyte had been admitted to Lewisham Hospital. After training that day Gritty and I drove to the hospital and both of us were shocked to see David lying in bed in a distressed state. We were told that he hadn't been very well, had taken some medication to try and make him feel better, but had a bad reaction and was taken to hospital. I think perhaps all the effort he'd put in to try and get himself fit had taken its toll, so instead of working with the rest of the team on the training pitch that day he'd found himself in a hospital bed.

We spoke to him at the hospital and he seemed confident that he'd be able to resume training with us soon, but I wasn't quite so sure. We were pinning a lot of our hopes on David Whyte, but it seemed as though from one day to the next we just didn't know what to expect. The next day we were due to play our annual pre-season friendly at Welling, a game we always enjoyed because it's a good way of saying thanks to a club who helped us out when we had no ground of our own, and allowed us to play our reserve games there. There were a lot of our fans looking forward to seeing David in action in the fixture, but there was no way he could play having just been in hospital, and we had to make some excuses without ever revealing the real reason for his absence.

But he did join us for our trip to the West Country and a couple of days after the Welling game he showed his quality in another friendly at Bashley, when he played 45 minutes and almost scored with a spectacular 30-yard effort. It was typical David, he had so much natural talent and was a lovely boy really, which was probably why both Gritty and I felt that, despite all the early problems, we just might have something a bit special.

He scored on his League debut in our first game of the season at Oldham. That was the good news; the bad news was that we got done 5–2 and it was the beginning of a poor start which saw us fail to record a win in our first four matches. We got off the mark at the beginning of September with a 3–2 win against Bristol City at The Valley, but there was something not quite right about the side and we knew we needed to strengthen the squad even though we thought we had a decent bunch of players. We had the experience of people like Pardew, McLeary and Nelson, and there was a good mix with some of the younger players like Steve Brown, Shaun Newton and Paul Sturgess, but we needed a midfielder.

The player we went for was Keith Jones from Southend and he turned out to be one of the easiest and best buys I've ever made. I'd always liked Keith and could remember playing against him. He could pass the ball and was a good athlete; I also remembered him kicking me a few times and knew he liked to tackle. After agreeing a fee with Southend, I arranged to meet him at a hotel in Dartford and to say I had to negotiate with him would be a bit of an exaggeration. Keith walked into the hotel lobby, shook my hand and came straight to the point.

'I don't want this transfer mucked up,' he told me. 'I want to play for you, so just give me what you give the others and I'll be happy.'

It couldn't have been easier and it was a good example of just what a genuine person he was. The fee was £150,000 and it turned out to be a real bargain. Keith went on to be a major part of what Charlton achieved in the years that followed, and he was one of the nicest players I've ever come across in the game. He loved to play and he loved to train. He was very straight and not at all flashy.

One of the most vivid memories I have of Keith is seeing him turning up for training each morning in a Nissan car that had seen a few miles and had a dent in the side. He never did get the dent fixed, and the thought of that made me smile sometimes when I arrived at our training ground in recent years. Some of the cars in the car park these days probably cost as much as a lot of people earn in a couple of years. I'm not criticizing the players – they're just reaping the rewards that are on offer to Premiership players. Keith did make it into the Premier League with us and played a major role in helping Charlton achieve that success, but he missed out on the real big money that is now on offer. It seems a shame for someone who, like so many others, did so much for the club, but never quite got the financial rewards they maybe deserved.

Another player who was to have such a big influence on the team also emerged that season. He was a big, tough-tackling defender who was as brave as they come and fast with it. He could also play football and, as soon as he got in the side as a 19-year-old, Richard Rufus looked as though he'd been playing centre-half in the first team all of his life.

Richard came into the side for his full debut in our game at Sunderland on a Tuesday night in November. It finished as a 1–1 draw but the most memorable thing about the match as far as I was concerned was the way Rufus performed. I remember going up into the Sunderland boardroom after the match and being cornered by one of their directors.

'I'll tell you what,' he told me. 'I've just seen a future England centre-half tonight – that Rufus is one hell of a player.'

He was spot on as far as I was concerned – Rufus was one hell of a player – although he got it wrong about England. Richard never did get a full cap even though they have been handed out like confetti in some of the friendly matches in recent years. Rufus wasn't the only young player to break into the first team for us that season. Early on in the campaign we gave midfielder Lee Bowyer a run in the side. He was only 17 years old at the time, but he was good enough to go straight in and just like Rufus he looked the part. Bowyer lived, ate and breathed football and his dad was equally enthusiastic. Bowyer senior was a big influence on his son's career and I can remember that when Lee signed a contract with us his dad had made a hand-written list of what should go in it and had put right at the top of the piece of paper, 'Bargain of the century!' He knew, and we knew, that Charlton had a real player on its books. He was a joy to have around the place because not only was he a great footballer, he also had so much enthusiasm for the game.

If we were having a finishing session and his shot missed he would run and get the ball himself and then try and push in the line so that he could have another go before some of the other players. He had a great engine in terms of the work he could get through during a game and would be up and down the pitch all day long. He never shirked a tackle, and if he did have a bit of aggression in him on the pitch, it was something I liked because he was a born winner and wanted others to be just as committed to the cause as he was. He also had that special quality that all managers are searching for in a midfielder – he could score goals. His idea of a perfect move during a game would be to receive the ball in midfield, play it up to the centre-forward, get it back and then have a shot. Another favourite ploy was to get the ball, play it wide to a winger and then race into the box to try and score with a header. He was that sort of player.

I had a lot of time for him, not just because he was such a good player, or that he came from the same sort of area in East London that I came from, but because I thought he was such a decent kid who just lived for football. That's why I got the shock of my life in March 1995 when Bowyer and another one of our promising youngsters, Dean Chandler, produced positive drug tests. The pair of them had traces of cannabis in their systems following a random test at our training ground early in the month.

It wasn't the first time the club had to deal with a drugs problem. About 18 months earlier a young Geordie kid named Craig Sloan had tested positive. He frequently went back to the north-east and I think it may have been there that he dabbled with drugs but it was a situation we knew nothing about at the time. He was never charged by the Football Association, but we were given the task of rehabilitating him and I know the club spent £30,000 trying to sort out the 18-year-old at a time when the club were hardly flush with cash. He spent four months in a clinic attempting to kick his cocaine habit, but then dropped out of football, although in a TV programme a couple of years later it was reported that he'd managed to beat his addiction problem. He also did a Sunday paper article some time later which tended to sensationalize the whole incident and at first glance seemed to lay the blame at Charlton's door, but it also showed the club as responsible and concerned employers, which of course was exactly what we were. I don't know where he is now, but I hope he's OK and living a full life.

When the drugs people came to the training ground that

morning in March I didn't see it as a problem. It was something that all clubs have happen to them from time to time. The testers arrive unannounced, ask for a list of the names of players who are on the premises that day, and then all of the names go into a hat. It's a bit like the FA Cup draw. Four are pulled out at random and they are the ones who have to be tested that day. The manager is informed through the physio which players the testers require and that they will need to give a urine sample after they have finished training.

In those days it was up to the player to give a sample when he was ready and it could sometimes cause problems because dehydration might mean a player was unable to give an immediate sample. You might also get a similar situation to the controversy caused when Rio Ferdinand missed a test. A player might train, come in and shower and then go home, forgetting that he needed to give a sample to the test unit.

These days the procedure has changed and the players are accompanied by a member of the unit as soon as they stop training until the moment they produce a sample. Personally, I've always thought a better way of going about it would be to pull four players out and test them at the start of the day, but apparently they don't do that because it might disrupt a club's training. The test unit takes a sample away for analysis, and part of the same sample is given to the club. On that particular day they did the test with the minimum of fuss and went away again.

When I was told some days later that Bowyer and Chandler had tested positive I was totally shocked. Don't get me wrong: drugs have long been a problem in society and I know that it's a fact of life that kids from all walks of life dabble and experiment with them. It's a problem for any parent and nobody should be complacent enough to think it couldn't happen to their kids. Drugs are readily available to youngsters if they want to get them. The hope is that they will be sensible enough to steer clear of them.

It's probably even worse today than it was then, but drugs were very much part of the scene in pubs and clubs in 1995, and when you're young the temptation is there. I've never smoked in my life and the strongest thing I ever took when I was playing was a pint of beer or a glass of wine, but I can remember drugs being around 25 or 30 years ago. I was having a drink in a pub in London at the time I was playing for Villa, and someone called for a whip-round, where everyone in your group puts money into a pot which I thought was going towards the cost of a round of beers, but it turned out they wanted it to buy some drugs! Call me naïve, but I was shocked and made sure I got out of the place as quickly as possible

The reason I was so totally amazed by the results on Bowyer and Chandler was because I couldn't imagine someone like Lee doing anything that might put his football career at risk. It meant too much to him; he lived for football. When we tried to unravel what had gone on we learned that the two of them had played in a midweek reserve game at Welling, and then on the way home from the game had decided to go for a drink in a pub. That was apparently where the whole thing happened. I got the impression after talking to both of them that they really didn't think they had done anything wrong, and probably in their own misguided way imagined that taking the stuff was no worse than having a couple of pints. They honestly didn't seem to understand the seriousness of their actions.

That was the day we decided as a club that we would have to try and do everything we could to educate and make our players aware of the dangers of drugs and the threat they posed to their careers. Because of the work put in by the FA and the authorities we are in a much better position today, but unfortunately for Charlton the Bowyer and Chandler episode was not the last experience of drugs we would have.

The FA was very good about the situation and very supportive in trying to make sure that the right action was taken and a suitable period of rehabilitation took place. The two of them weren't addicts; they'd done a very stupid thing and got caught. They had done the wrong thing, but it was important that they learned from the incident and never did it again.

Interviews took place to find out how it had happened and what the truth was. Dean Chandler was still protesting his innocence at one stage and came up with the excuse that other people in the pub had been smoking and he must have got it into his system passively. It wasn't an explanation that really held water, and an expert pointed out that he would probably have needed to have his nose over a chimney full of the stuff to clock up the test results he'd produced.

The fact of the matter was that we had two young footballers in the club who had taken drugs, but I felt it would be wrong for anyone else to crow about it. As I've said, it may be sad but drugs are part of the society we live in and to suppose that football clubs are immune to having some of their employees straying is unrealistic. We all make mistakes, particularly when we're young, and all clubs can do is to make sure they educate players and warn them of the dangers and consequences if they do get mixed up in drug taking.

For Bowyer and Chandler it turned out to be a tough lesson to learn, but they came through their rehabilitation period and, after getting clearance from the FA, they both played in our final game of the season when we lost 2–1 to a last-minute goal at Reading. Chandler actually scored for us that day as part of a team that was the youngest side fielded by the club for a first-team game.

I think both Gritty and I were pleased to see the back of the season, because it turned out to be such a difficult and disappointing one in so many ways. We finished 15th in the League, our lowest position since taking over. We got knocked out of the Coca-Cola Cup at the first stage by Swindon. Having won the first leg at their place 3–1, we were in the driving seat, but got outsmarted in the return game, losing 4–1 in extra-time. We also got knocked out of the FA Cup at the third-round stage when Chelsea beat us 3–0 at Stamford Bridge.

On the bright side we had found ourselves a new goalscorer in David Whyte. After all of the early season problems we had with him, he'd shown the sort of quality we knew he had and ended up with 21 goals for the season. Some of those goals were exceptional, so he became a favourite with the crowd and also attracted a lot of transfer speculation. Another plus for us was the fact that we had a batch of good young kids coming through, as the average age of just over 22 years in that last game against Reading showed.

Overall the club was still moving in the right direction and, considering it was less than three years since we had returned to The Valley, I still felt Gritty and I were doing a good job as joint managers and that the partnership was working well. However, not everyone thought it was the right way forward and in the summer of 1995 my career took a whole new direction.

9 Going Solo

The influence that Richard Murray had on the club took a giant leap forward at the beginning of 1995.

After being a director for almost four years he took over as chairman of Charlton Athletic plc, while Martin Simons became the new football club chairman, with Roger Alwen stepping down but remaining on the board. It was a move that meant little in the wider world of football, but down at The Valley it was to have far-reaching consequences.

As I have already said, the two men were becoming much more heavily involved in the club and its day-to-day running. Richard in particular was keen to know what was going on when it came to the footballing side of things, without ever appearing pushy. Although he was an extremely successful businessman, it was clear that he was still feeling his way when it came to football and it was also clear that he had a genuine interest as a fan. As well as being the plc chairman he was also the club's managing director, and as such was really the man running things.

It must have been very frustrating for him at times when he phoned up the training ground and spoke to either Steve or me. Quite often it was to ask a question about whether a player was in the team or not for a particular match, and if we hadn't quite decided ourselves I'm afraid Richard must have felt as though he was being fobbed off.

Gritty and I would sometimes spend ages talking things over before coming to a final decision on team selection, and it was often the same when it came to deciding on a player that we might want to have a look at with a view to a possible transfer bid. Sometimes Richard might phone up at the training ground and Gritty or I would answer, but because we hadn't come to a final decision on whatever it might be that he was asking us about, we would never commit ourselves.

If he asked us, 'Is player A going to be in the team tomorrow?' and we hadn't yet made a decision, we'd say exactly that. It was all part of the fact that we wanted to stick to having the united front we'd decided on in the ground rules right at the start of our partnership. We didn't want to contradict each other, even if we had different views on the same subject. It may have been a case of me saying I wanted a player in the team, and Steve thinking he shouldn't be included. We used to thrash things out and whoever won the day would never let anyone else know about it. All of our decisions stayed between the two of us, and there was never a case of one of us being upset, or trying to undermine the other.

As far as we were concerned we were as much of a team off the field as the players were on it, but it must have been murder for Richard sometimes, because I'm sure he thought we were deliberately trying to keep him at arm's length, even though that was never the case. Steve and I were joint managers and as such we shared everything, took the rough with the smooth, the good with the bad and got on with it.

Although the previous season had not been the best, I think

we had to cope with quite a few problems on and off the pitch that contributed to where we actually finished in the League. I still believed that as a partnership we were making progress, but I subsequently found out that Richard felt otherwise. He eventually used the word 'plateaued' to publicly describe the way he felt the partnership had gone that season, but neither of us had any idea that was the way he was thinking as the final whistle blew in that last match at Reading. As the summer break approached the biggest thing I had on my mind was getting ready to move house, but it wasn't long before I found out about a far more sweeping move that Richard was about to propose.

Just as Carol and I were packing in preparation for our house move in the first week of June, I got a phone call from Richard asking me to come and have a chat with him. I had no idea what he wanted to talk to me about and it was clear he didn't want to elaborate on the phone, but when I saw him face to face it didn't take him long to come straight to the point.

'I don't think the joint-manager thing works,' he told me. 'I'm going to give you the opportunity, if you want it, to be manager on your own.'

He went on to tell me that it would obviously mean Steve would have to leave the club, that I wasn't going to benefit financially from a better contract although it might be extended if I did well and because it was a decision he was making, he didn't feel he could change the contract at that time. Richard said that Steve's contract would be honoured in full and that the club would look after him. I have to admit I was shocked and surprised by the whole thing, because there were no real signs that it was going to happen. We both dealt with Richard, although perhaps I used to have the slightly longer conversations with him when he phoned the training ground, but neither of us thought anything of that. The decision still came like a bolt out of the blue and I knew I needed some time to think the whole thing through.

It was a very awkward time because I realized Steve knew nothing about what had gone on. I decided to phone up Jim Smith, who by this time was in charge of the League Managers Association. As well as being my old manager, Jimmy had always been a good person to talk to when I had a problem and I felt happy confiding in him, just as I had done more than eight years earlier as a player on the eve of that Full Members Cup Final. The first thing he asked me was whether Gritty was going to be looked after and I told him he was.

'In that case, Curbs, you can't do anymore and you've got to take it,' said Jim. 'Unless you go out on your own nobody's ever going to recognize what you can do.'

I kept telling Jimmy that we'd both done a good job and surely people could see that.

'It doesn't matter,' he insisted. 'Unless you're out there on your own, making all the decisions as a manager, it counts for nothing.'

The more I thought about it the more I realized I wanted the job. Both Gritty and I knew that at some stage we'd both have to go out on our own if we wanted to continue our careers as managers; it was just that neither of us would ever have believed the opportunity would have come at Charlton. If there was going to be a change I think we both thought it would happen either by us being sacked, or one of us getting the offer to manage another club. Probably the one thing that had stopped me from saying yes straight away was the fact that Steve would be shown the door as a consequence.

After a lot of thought I phoned Richard up and said I'd take the job. The first thing to be done was going to be the hardest part – letting Gritty know. I told Richard that I wanted to be there when it happened. I was adamant that I was going to sit in the room with my head up. It was an uncomfortable situation but as bad as it was for Steve, I didn't feel I'd done anything wrong, and it was something I had to do.

I suspect that once Richard had said what he wanted to do there was no way Steve was going to still be at the club for the next season. Suppose I'd said no? I doubt whether he would then have gone to Steve after asking me. The more likely scenario would have been for Richard to have looked outside of the club for a new manager. Of course it was hard on Steve – he was Charlton through and through, and had been at the club for 18 years. The fans loved him and rightly so, but we both found ourselves in a situation that had not been of our own making.

Both Steve and I were asked to go to the training ground for the meeting and I have to say that Gritty somehow managed to make what was a very uncomfortable situation bearable by the way he reacted. Perhaps he knew or at least had some idea of what was in store but, whatever the reason was, he took the whole thing incredibly well. I couldn't help thinking how I would have reacted if the boot had been on the other foot, but it was hard to contemplate what must have been going on in his mind. Richard made it clear to Gritty that he didn't agree with the joint-manager thing, and that he didn't think it could work if we were going to continue to progress as a club. He'd made the decision to offer the job to me and I'd accepted; then he asked if I could leave the room so that he and Steve could talk privately.

I waited outside for Gritty and shook his hand. It was important for me to make sure that he understood how sorry I was about the whole thing, and I made a big point of telling him that it had nothing to do with me. Richard had made the decision and it was then up to me to say yes or no to the job. I think Steve knew that and also appreciated how awkward it was for me as well. He handled the situation really well but later admitted in the press that he had been shocked by what had happened. Typically of Gritty, he went out of his way to let people know how difficult it was for me as well:

'In a way the person I felt really sorry for was Alan Curbishley,' he said. 'He was put in a very difficult situation by the whole thing. I think we both knew it could quite easily have been the other way round and he just had to get on with it.'

Having taken the job I knew that I wasn't going to come out of it looking great when the announcement was made public. I knew there were going to be whispers and snide remarks suggesting I'd engineered the situation, but nothing could have been further from the truth. All I could do was give my honest version of events, and I knew I'd done nothing wrong or underhand in the whole affair.

There was a press conference I held at The Valley when the official announcement was made and Richard gave his reasons for wanting to change things:

'I've come to the conclusion that a joint-management partnership is flawed in its conception,' he told the media. 'I recommended the move to the board. I've had this in my mind for some time and I think that last year the joint-manager thing plateaued and I have to say that when I spoke to Steve about it there seemed to be one side of him that was relieved. I think the partnership has worked but I also think that now is the time for a change.'

After the press conference I sat in the stand with Gritty and told him that, whatever anyone might think, I believed the partnership we had did work and I think he felt the same. We had both been landed with a difficult situation, but we also knew that we both had to move on. For me that meant going solo as a manager for the first time, and the next year Steve got the chance to do the same when he took over at Brighton. He did a brilliant job there keeping them in the League, while at the same time having to battle against the sort of financial problems that he was so familiar with during his Charlton days.

Having said yes to the job and left poor Carol to deal with all the problems of moving house, it was time for a family holiday in Spain, but I soon realized that it wasn't exactly going to be relaxing. One of the first things I wanted to get sorted out was the appointment of a first-team coach. It had been decided to advertise for the post, but Richard was going to leave the actual selection down to me, and I already had someone in mind.

We were staying at my brother's house but I wanted a bit of peace and quiet for the telephone call I was going to make, so armed with a bagful of coins I headed off to a Spanish call box and eventually tracked down the man I wanted. David Kemp was on holiday in America at the time, but I'd managed to get a number for him and must have spent a fortune that day as I pumped the coins in for long enough to have a decent conversation with Kempy. He'd been at Palace as assistant to manager Alan Smith, but the team had just been relegated and the two of them had left Selhurst Park. Dave had a lot of good experience in the game and had been a manager himself at Plymouth. He was a good coach and I thought he would be right for the job. When I finally got through and asked Dave if he fancied joining me at Charlton he said he did, but then explained it wouldn't be possible because he'd already given his word to Smithy that he'd go with him as his assistant at Wycombe Wanderers. So it was back to square one for me but getting someone in as coach wasn't the only problem I had while I was in Spain.

Although I was on holiday I was still very much in contact with Richard as I started planning for the coming season. I was hoping that I might be able to bring some players in, but it was soon clear that there wasn't too much money in the kitty and if there was going to be any summer transfer activity it looked as though it might involve players leaving The Valley rather than coming in. I knew that was a possibility, but I wasn't prepared for the news that Richard hit me with one day.

'Coventry have come in for Richard Rufus,' he told me.

It struck me that Richard Murray was quickly making a habit of shocking me. First the manager's job and now telling me the club might have to sell one of my best young players. After playing in that Sunderland game, Rufus had gone from strength to strength. He had always been a good player and there was never a doubt in my mind that he would make it as a first-team player. The fans could also see what a good player he was, and he ended the season with 27 full appearances in the team and got voted player of the year in his debut season.

Richard had looked so good during the season, and was probably my best player at the time. I soon began to feel I'd been set up a little bit. Here I was in sole charge of the team for the first time, a lot of people were waiting to see what sort of job I was going to make of it, and now there was the possibility that the ground would be cut from under my feet. If there wasn't going to be very much money to spend on players and bringing people in, the one thing I needed to do was make sure we held onto the bunch of promising kids we had.

I told Richard that whatever money was on offer I really didn't want to sell Rufus. When I'd said yes to the job I thought I had half a chance of having a good first season and building a decent side. I saw Rufus as such an important player for me in what I wanted to do, and that's why I thought it was so important to keep him at the club. To be fair to Richard Murray he decided that he'd fend off the offer and told Coventry Rufus was not for sale. If a deal had gone through then I think I would have had serious doubts about my future even though my new role had only just begun.

I got back from Spain a few days before we were due to start pre-season training, but despite all the applications we had for the job of first-team coach, I still hadn't settled on anyone I really wanted. I was getting a bit of pressure from Richard and the board to name the person I wanted, and I think that maybe some of them were hoping I would go for someone who might be quite well known and a bit of a 'name' in the game. After getting a no from David Kemp, I had to rethink things, and in the end I went for someone that virtually nobody outside of the game had heard of, but whom I'd known since I was about 18 or 19 years old.

When the name of Les Reed was announced by the club as the new Charlton first-team coach it inevitably prompted the kind of 'Les who?' headlines you might expect. Nobody really knew his name or his background, but I was very comfortable about appointing him and I knew that I'd managed to bring a top-class coach to the club.

I'd first met Les almost 20 years earlier when I was a young player with West Ham and he was a regional coach with the FA. I had decided to take a coaching badge which involved me doing six consecutive Sunday-morning sessions at Leytonstone, and Les was the coach in charge. I did three of the sessions but didn't turn up for the fourth because I had been injured playing for West Ham's first team the day before and had to go in for treatment. When I went along the next week and said hello to Les he just looked straight at me.

'You've failed,' he said.

I couldn't believe it, but he was quite adamant. I'd missed one of the sessions and because of that I'd failed. It didn't seem to matter to him that the reason I had missed the session was because I was injured, and he wasn't about to enter into any discussions about it either. Despite that first unhappy encounter, I began to get on well with Les over the years that followed whenever he was involved in any of the coaching courses I went on, and I got to learn more about him as a person. He was a good coach and had a very professional approach to the way he went about things. I'd also got to know him better a few years earlier when Gritty and I went on a two-week coaching course at Lilleshall which Les was helping to run, just before we got the joint player-coaches job at Charlton.

I had thought about Les when I first got the manager's job, having had a conversation with Martin Hunter who was with Chris Kamara at Bradford, and had been at the FA as one of their coaches before leaving to try his hand at the professional game. He suggested Les, but I thought he might be too heavily ensconced at the FA. In the end it was Carol who prompted me into making an approach, because I think she could see I liked the idea the more I talked about it.

Les was very different from me: in many ways he was much more studious and would do things by the book. For example, if I was teaching someone to drive I'd soon be crossing my hands over as I turned the steering wheel, which wouldn't affect where we were going, but it wouldn't be a great help to the learner driver. I knew Les was the sort of person who would turn that wheel just the way it was supposed to be turned, and anyone copying him would pass their test.

Once I'd decided that Les was the man I wanted to come in as coach it was a case of trying to persuade him to leave the comfort and security of the FA to join Charlton and the uncertain world of professional football. I found out that Les was running a course in Aldershot as part of his job as regional coach for London and the south-east, and decided to drive down one day after pre-season training to see if he'd be interested in the job.

The timing could not have been better from my point of view, because Les told me that he was a bit disillusioned with the whole set-up at the FA, and thought the chance to get into day-to-day club football with Charlton would be something he'd really like to try. I had a good feeling about the whole thing as I drove back from Aldershot, and the only real downside for me was that Les had to give a month's notice, meaning he wouldn't officially join us until 25 August, which was a couple of weeks after the season started. I'm sure there were some people wondering what I was doing. First I'd got someone in who nobody had ever heard of, and then he couldn't even start the job until after the new season had begun, but as far as I was concerned, it was worth the wait because I knew I'd got the right person.

I think to many people in the professional game there's still a bit of stigma attached to someone like Les, who had not played professionally and had coached as part of the FA set-up. But as far as I'm concerned, not playing as a professional doesn't mean a thing: coaching is a different world and I knew Les had the sort of qualities I was looking for.

I liked the fact that he was very different from me in the way he approached things. When I'm coaching I might start at A, but jump forward to E. Les would start at A and go through B, C and D before he got to E because that was the way he had always done things at the FA. I knew it would be a change for him, because you can't always go through routines as methodically in a club situation, but at the same time I thought he would be a good foil for me. We did things differently, but I believed we complemented each other well.

I had no doubt that Les would soon gain the respect of the players because they would be able to see just what a good football coach he was, and I also knew that he was excellent on a one-to-one basis, improving someone's skills and their understanding of the game.

The one thing I didn't want Les to do was get in any kind of confrontation with players, because I thought that would spoil his relationship with them. If there was any kind of problem with a player, it would be me and not Les who dealt with it. In many ways it was similar to what had happened with Gritty when we first took over. There were ground rules and I thought it was a good thing if they were decided on early and we stuck to them.

Les is a very intelligent man, extremely knowledgeable when it comes to football, and is very considered in the way he approaches the game. He and I seemed to click from day one and knew exactly how we wanted the team to play. We knew the players we had, knew what they were capable of and had a 4–4–2 system that we believed suited them.

10 Making a Stand

I'm sure that fate can sometimes play a big part in what happens to a football team over the course of a season, and I think it was certainly the case as I took charge of the team. Having finally sorted out the situation with Les it was nice to get the season started with an away game at West Bromwich Albion. It wasn't a good result for us because we lost 1–0, but it was what happened three days later that was to have a significant effect on the team and our season.

As always at the start of a season the games come thick and fast, with hardly any breathing space for teams. After that defeat at West Brom we had the potentially tricky task of overcoming Barnet in a two-legged encounter in the Coca-Cola Cup. In typical cup fashion we were a shock waiting to happen, because Barnet were two divisions below us in the League and we were due to play at their place first. They also had a familiar face playing for them in the shape of Alan Pardew, who had gone to Barnet on a free transfer, and I knew that he would love to pull one over on his old club.

When it came to the transfer market I hadn't exactly made a big splash, due mainly to the fact that there just wasn't the money for me to spend. Instead, John Humphrey had rejoined us on a free transfer from Palace five years after going to Selhurst Park in a £450,000 move. He was 34, but still as fit as a fiddle, and I knew his experience and enthusiasm in the side could prove to be invaluable. I had a young team and having someone like Humph around, both on and off the pitch, could only help.

After just 22 minutes of the game at Barnet's Underhill ground I was forced into making a change when Richard Rufus picked up an injury and had to come off. It was obviously a blow to lose one of your central defenders so early on in a game, and it meant I had to reshuffle things. John Robinson came on for Rufus, with Steve Brown having to move back from midfield to partner Stuart Balmer in the middle of defence. Robbo came on and played wide. The game ended in a goalless draw, but I was more concerned with what I'd seen on the pitch.

After John had come on we looked a more balanced side, and what happened that night set the pattern for the way we played as a team that season. We had two wide midfield players who could get forward with pace, but also worked hard at getting back and defending; Keith Jones worked really hard in midfield in the holding position, while Lee Bowyer switched to a more central role, getting forward and into the penalty box whenever he could. I knew I had to have Bowyer in the team because he was just too good to be left out, but the trick was finding the right role for him and that night helped to do just that. During the pre-season period I was playing him in wide positions and asking him to get in the box, but the Barnet game changed things for us. It was very similar to England's problems in the 2002 World Cup when they were playing Paul Scholes wide left, and Owen Hargreaves in the middle. Then Hargreaves got injured and Scholes moved inside, with Trevor Sinclair coming in on the left. Suddenly, because of injury, England had their shape, and the same sort of thing happened to us at the start of that season.

At the back we had the defending of Rufus alongside either Balmer or Phil Chapple, and the experience of John Humphrey. Obviously the team changed personnel slightly during the course of that season, but fate had played its part and that Barnet game set the pattern.

The match was also a sign that not everything was rosy as far as some of the supporters were concerned, even after just two games. We actually got booed by a section of Charlton fans during the game and at the end of it, which seemed incredible but perhaps had more to do with me and what had gone on in the summer than the match itself.

I think it's true to say that there were some Charlton supporters who didn't like the idea of me taking over. Maybe they thought Steve should have got the job instead of me, or that we both should have gone and made a clean sweep of things. There was also that element of doubt with some people as to whether I had instigated the whole thing in order to get the job, but that was simply not the case. As I've said before, Gritty was Charlton through and through, and I think some of the fans questioned whether I was as committed to the cause, which was ridiculous. If they had stood back and thought about things a little more they would have seen that I'd been at the club as a player for almost three years before going to Brighton, came back and was a player-coach for a year, and then did four years with Steve as joint manager. So I'd been involved with the club for eight of the previous 11 years. I'd also turned down the Birmingham job and I don't think anyone could question my loyalty, or the fact that I desperately wanted Charlton to do well. We hadn't played brilliantly at Barnet, but I had a young team and it was the start of the season. Fans have always got a right to voice their opinions, but I thought the reaction of those supporters who booed that night was a bit over the top to say the least.

We got off the mark in the League four days later with a 3–1 win against Birmingham in our first home game of the season, and followed that up by knocking Barnet out, with a 2–0 win in the second leg at The Valley. Both goals came from Bowyer in that game and he'd got his first senior goal for the club in the win against Birmingham. It was a sign of things to come, because he went on to finish top scorer for us that season, with 14 goals.

Bowyer may have only been 18 years old but it was very clear he was going to be a major part of things for us that season, and even in the first few games the young side that we had was already beginning to attract attention. After the win against Birmingham we lost just once in our next eight games, which helped to push us up the table. We also had two incredible South London derby games in the Coca-Cola Cup against Wimbledon, who were a Premier League team at the time. It was Wimbledon who were known as the Crazy Gang, but it was the match at Selhurst Park which was crazy that night. We got a 5–4 win over there and Bowyer got a hat-trick. The home leg was almost as mad and we finally went through to the next round when the second match ended 3–3 after extra-time.

By this time Les had been with us for a few weeks and I could already see that he was having the right kind of impact on the players. He gained their respect with the way he went about his job and he was very good when it came to having a quiet word with a player and working on a particular aspect of their game. I seemed to have a good working relationship with him from the very first day he walked into the training ground, and it was nice to have someone like him around. With Keith Peacock there as reserve-team coach and Les as first-team coach I felt I had people around me who would make a good team off the pitch. I didn't really know Keith until that first season Gritty and I were in charge, but since then I'd obviously worked with him and there was no doubt his personality, experience and ability played an important part in what was happening to the club. Keith had not only played for Charlton for all of those years, he also had experience as a coach and a manager. He worked well with the players, and during the pre-season period before Les joined the club, all the coaching was down to me and Keith.

Having Les and him around when it came to deciding on things like team selection was also helpful to me. Of course I had the final say in who was in or out of the team, but I've always been the sort of person who is open to the opinions of other people I'm working with, and the three of us quickly got into the routine of discussing anything I thought was important with regard to the team, and I always took their views on board.

The side continued to do well in the League, but there was no repeat of the sort of high-scoring game we had against Wimbledon when we travelled to play Wolves in the next round. Instead, the match ended goalless but we failed to take advantage in the replay at The Valley, going out 2–1 after extra-time.

We finished November with a 2–2 home draw against Port Vale. It was the sort of result we had become used to by then, because of the 19 games we had played, nine of them had been draws. We had only lost four matches, but if we could have turned a couple of those draws into wins, we would have been in there challenging for the play-off places. As it was we were halfway down the table but the good thing was that there was not a big gap developing. I knew that if we could put a few results together we could be right in there as we went into the New Year. We started December well with a 2–1 win at Grimsby, never an easy place to go to, and three days later on a horrible winter's night we went into a game that I think proved to be a real turning point.

Millwall have always been big rivals of Charlton and the derby matches between the two clubs mean an awful lot to the respective sets of supporters. I can remember taking the first-team squad out on a run near our New Eltham training ground one day when it was freezing cold and there was snow on the ground. As we ran back to do our warm-down there was a group of teenage boys hanging around, and once they saw who we were they started jeering and shouting abuse at us. It was soon obvious they were Millwall supporters, and they weren't exactly holding back with the verbals. As we stretched off they kept up the abuse, and I decided the time had come to have a bit of fun of our own.

'Right,' I told my players. 'On the count of three we're going to run over there and get that lot. One, two, three!'

The entire squad charged at the startled bunch and within seconds we were pummelling them with snowballs. It was light-hearted enough, but it certainly had the desired effect and we didn't hear too much from them after that. Steve and I actually had a very good relationship with Millwall manager Mick McCarthy, and although their training ground virtually backed onto ours, they certainly didn't have the same kind of quality when it came to pitches. Their ground was quite often water-logged when it rained, while our pitches were perfectly playable. I know that on a few occasions when we had a day off and weren't training but Millwall were, Mick and his players would run to our ground, jump the fence and use our pitches because theirs were too muddy.

The rivalry wasn't just confined to the supporters either. I can vividly recall Gritty getting really worked up when we played Millwall. He let the team know in no uncertain terms just how important it was to beat them, but the trouble was we never could. For whatever reason, we just never seemed able to get the better of Millwall, and although we'd beaten Grimsby on the Saturday, I don't think there were too many Charlton supporters who thought we were going to be able to change things as we travelled to meet the Lions at the New Den the following Tuesday.

It wasn't a great night for playing football. It was bitterly cold and there was snow on the pitch. Millwall had done well under Mick and at the time sat at the top of the First Division. Everything seemed set up for another Millwall win, but we had other ideas and the players were desperate to go out and show what they could do against a team who were not only one of their biggest rivals, but were also leading the pack in the First Division. One of the reasons we hadn't done well against them during our time in charge was because Mick had built a good team, but I think the night ended up being a bit of a turning point for both sides.

The New Den wasn't as intimidating as the original Den where you had to run the gauntlet of their fans just getting into the ground. When you had 14,000 in the old Den the atmosphere was intense and it felt as though the fans were right on top of you. The new ground was different and the same crowd left plenty of empty spaces. But the rivalry was always in evidence and sometimes it was over the top. A few years ago I went to watch a game at the New Den and asked a Millwall-supporting friend of mine if he'd like to come along and see the game from the directors' box. I was waiting outside for my mate when a group of Millwall supporters spotted me.

'Curbishley,' one of them shouted, 'I hope you die of cancer!' Not the nicest of greetings, and I did think at the time that when Mick McCarthy watched a game at our place all he got was a cup of tea in the boardroom.

That night, although Millwall had done well and were League leaders, we played some great football in very difficult conditions and won the match 2–0, with a goal in each half from Kim Grant, who was on the transfer list at the time, and left the club three months later when he was sold to Luton. It was our first League win over them for 17 years and, as an added bonus, it came on the day the club celebrated the third anniversary of our return to The Valley. The win gave us new impetus, while Millwall began to drop down the table.

The three points did come with a bit of a price. Phil Chapple had to come off just before the break with a leg injury that had to be so heavily strapped that I ended up driving him home to Cambridge after the game, and Bowyer got his marching orders after 21 minutes of the match for a second bookable offence. He'd been wound up a bit by Alex Rae and got carried away with the emotion of the whole thing. Lee was, and still is, the sort of player who wears his heart on his sleeve and sometimes his will to win gets him into trouble. Although we had to play with ten men, things were evened up after 57 minutes when Millwall's Keith Stevens whacked Jamie Stuart in the face and was also sent off. We'd spoken to Lee before the game and said that he might be a target, but then he got involved early on before clashing with Rae.

After the game it was nice to go into Mick's room and have a drink with him and his assistant Ian Evans. Winning against Millwall was so rare for us that I was determined to enjoy the moment. It was also good to hear Mick congratulate us on the way we'd played and I think he realized that we had a decent team. I got on the team bus knowing that a lot of our supporters probably didn't go to the game. Firstly because they didn't fancy our chances and secondly because they just didn't like going to the New Den. I knew they must have been gutted that they weren't there the night we finally turned the tables.

Bowyer wasn't just receiving attention on the pitch either. His performances since becoming a regular in the team were earning him rave reviews in the papers and I knew there were several clubs keeping tabs on him. There were stories saying that Arsenal manager Bruce Rioch and Sheffield Wednesday's David Pleat were keen on signing him, but we never got anything like an enquiry from another club during the course of the season, despite all the rumours.

Pleat got a chance to have a first-hand look at Bowyer in January when we beat Wednesday 2–0, and knocked them out in a third-round FA Cup tie at The Valley. It was a really good performance and the thing I remember most about it was the atmosphere we had in the ground that day. It was really upbeat because a lot of people thought we might pull off a shock, and not only did we take the game to Wednesday, so did our fans. They didn't stop urging us on from the first whistle until the last and, in fairness to them, it became a feature of The Valley in the years that followed. The win came in the middle of a really good run by us in the League and we had got ourselves into second place in the table. I wasn't about to get carried away by what was happening and actually went out of my way to try and play the whole thing down. I also didn't want to talk up any of my young players like Rufus and Bowyer, even if they were becoming major factors in the side. It's a policy that I've always tended to adopt. The only time I didn't really stick to it came in more recent years when Scott Parker got into the first team and I started singing his praises, only to see him transferred midway through a season.

After the Millwall game and going into the New Year I began to feel that we had a chance of staying in the promotion play-off places. The side had worked well as a unit and although there were some youngsters in the team we also had some very good experienced players as well, like Humphrey, Nelson, Balmer, Chapple, Leaburn and Mortimer. We played with a lot of pace and had people in the side with great attitudes. If they got knocked down, whether it was physically or mentally, they tended to be able to get back up again, and they really worked hard for each other.

After beating Wednesday we defeated Brentford 3–2 at home in the next round, but then drew Liverpool away. It was a great tie for us and it reminded me of what had happened two years earlier when we got to the sixth round of the Cup and lost against Manchester United at Old Trafford. I knew there would be similar excitement about playing a club like Liverpool and going up to Anfield, but win, lose or draw, the one thing I didn't want was for us to fall like a stone in the League the way we had after playing United. We wanted to go up there and give a good account of ourselves in the hope that we might be able to pull off a shock result. As nice as a Cup run is, I knew that our main focus had to be trying to maintain what we were doing in the League.

We weren't the only team in decent form and Liverpool went into the match against us on the back of an unbeaten 14-game run. Robbie Fowler scored after about 12 minutes and Stan Collymore added another for them in the second half. Kim Grant maintained his knack of scoring against Premier League teams in the FA Cup that season, and added a late consolation effort for us.

In those days when we travelled to an away game our coach driver, together with the club's press officer, Peter Burrowes, would pre-order fish and chips for the players to have on the bus. By the time we were ready to leave the chips would usually be cold and the fish would be sticking to the paper it was wrapped in. It's all light years away from the re-fuelling drinks and nutritional guidelines we have for the players these days after a game. When we got on the bus that night after playing at such a great stadium, none of us fancied the idea of eating what was inside the greasy packages that had been left on the seats, so instead of cold fish and chips we opted for hot burgers and got the driver to stop at the first McDonald's on the way out of the city. I think the local customers were a bit surprised to see our bus turn up and the entire Charlton party eating burgers. We finally got back to our training ground at about four in the morning. It's sometimes hard for me to believe just how things changed at the club in a relatively short period of time, and I have a quiet little chuckle to myself.

These days not only would the players be able to tuck into well-prepared food and healthy drinks which helped them recover properly from the physical demands of the game, they would also have flown up to Merseyside for the match and flown back afterwards and most of them would be in their own homes by 1 am. Not all the money in the Premiership goes on players' wages, as things like travel and correct preparation and recovery are so important now.

We came away from Anfield as the losers, but we still managed to earn praise for our performance and soon had to get back to the bread-and-butter business of chalking up League points. Unfortunately, we didn't do too well on that front in our next couple of games, losing 2–1 at Portsmouth and then 3–0 in a home game against Southend. We suddenly looked a bit jaded and, although some of the key ingredients of our season had been the spirit and aggression we'd shown, I suddenly started to feel as though there was a tired look to the side. I knew I had to get some players in because we already had a small squad and any injuries we might pick up during the vital run-in period would hit us hard.

I wanted to bring in a striker to give us more up front and hopefully score some goals during the last couple of months of the season. I thought I'd found the right man when we spoke to Millwall and made a bid for Chris Malkin, who, when he played for Tranmere, always caused us problems with his power, pace and aggression; he was also a very good finisher.

Ironically, the transfer negotiations all started to happen in the week leading up to our home League match with the Lions at The Valley. It was probably one of the few transfers to be conducted between the two clubs. It looked as though it would all be settled in time for us to play Chris against his old club in the derby game, but the deal started to fall apart the day before the match because Chris had struggled to get through the medical due to an old knee injury that he had had for some time, which was probably down to wear and tear.

Jimmy Nicholl had taken over as Millwall manager from Mick McCarthy (who had gone on to become the Republic of Ireland manager), and I had to phone him the night before the game and say that it didn't look as though we were going to be able to go through with the transfer. The medical problem with Malkin meant a bit of a change of plan for us because I was probably going to play him the next day if he'd signed, but it also screwed things up for Millwall as well and he didn't play for them either. Jimmy was very good about the situation, but because he'd already planned his team thinking Malkin would be gone, Chris didn't play for them and in some respects I suppose the whole transfer saga had more of an effect on their team than it did on ours.

I felt sorry for Chris because I had to phone and tell him that the transfer was off, so mentally he must have been in turmoil after thinking he was going to be transferred and then seeing everything go wrong because of a medical opinion. He'd had the knee problem for some time, and he told us about it during the medical, but it hadn't stopped him going to Millwall from Tranmere. However, once a surgeon flags up a problem during a medical it's virtually impossible to get a player insured and that's why we couldn't go ahead with the transfer.

I've always been very aware during the course of a transfer to make sure I have the player's interests at the forefront of my thoughts in case he fails the medical. That's why I've always tried to keep any transfer I do out of the media until after everything is signed and sealed. I've had other players fail medicals but the fact that it's happened never got out. If I went for a player and he failed a medical I didn't think it was fair on him to have that tag following him around and maybe putting other potential buyers off. It's also true to say that a player can play for a club regularly and yet fail a medical when it comes to a possible transfer

It can often come down to medical opinion or whether a club is prepared to take a calculated risk, even if a player isn't 100 per cent when it comes to passing a medical. Some players can go through their careers with a slight weakness in a knee or ankle from an old injury and it won't have any effect on the way they play, but if they go for a medical as part of a transfer deal that same injury may show up and put the buying club off. It's a shame but it happens and that's why I always preferred to keep transfers quiet if I could. Unfortunately for Chris, that particular deal got into the papers before it was actually completed.

Once again that season a match against Millwall proved to be something of a springboard for us and it also made a mark in the record books. The win we got provided our first League double over them for 61 years and the first at The Valley for 19 years. Perhaps more importantly it was also our first victory in six matches and it was just the sort of boost we needed.

I may have missed out on Malkin but I did manage to bring in one new face that week when I signed Chris Whyte on loan from Birmingham. Chris was a big experienced defender, but I knew I needed a striker after realizing that the Malkin deal could not be resurrected, and by the end of the month my search came to an end when we paid £350,000 for Bradley Allen from QPR. Bradley was a consistent scorer for Rangers and was coming to the end of his contract with them, so it was a question of whether they wanted to get some money for him, or face the prospect of not getting anything at a later date. I also got defender Matt Jackson in on loan from Everton and began to feel happier about the strength of our squad as we approached the final few weeks of the season.

We had ten matches to go and Bradley made an immediate impact by getting the only goal of the game as we won at Norwich on his debut, but we then made things hard for ourselves. We only lost two of the remaining matches, but at the same time won only once and drew six times as we crawled across the play-off line on the last day of the season, just two points ahead of Ipswich. We managed to get a 1–1 draw with Wolves at The Valley, while Ipswich could only manage a goalless home draw with Millwall. Ironically, on the day that we got into the play-offs, Millwall were relegated. If they had won at Ipswich then Portsmouth would have gone down. It was probably one of the few occasions where our fans were actually willing Millwall to do well. The fact that they did a good enough job to help us out, but failed to escape relegation, seemed to add a special note to the afternoon.

We were through to the play-offs, but having finished sixth we had to play the team that had finished third and had been the form side of the division going into the final phase of the season – Crystal Palace. Palace had been transformed since the arrival of Dave Bassett as manager in February of that year and had put together a tremendous run. I realized it was going to be a tough task to get through, but it was going to be over two legs and I knew my side would be desperate to upset the odds against another one of our biggest local rivals.

The first leg was at The Valley on a Sunday afternoon and we played well in the first half but failed to get a goal. Palace were on the back foot for long periods and if we had made the breakthrough I think we could have gone on and taken a lead to Selhurst for the second leg. We did score first just before the hour, but didn't manage to build on it, and Palace started to have more of a say in things, scoring twice and putting themselves in pole position for the return game. Despite trailing after the encounter at The Valley I still felt we were in with a chance at their place three days later, but the game had barely started when Ray Houghton scored in the fourth minute and in effect put the match beyond us.

It was disappointing because we had done so well right through the season and had to contend with quite a lot of injuries in the final phase, including the play-off matches against Palace, but at the same time I think if we had managed to get promotion that season it would have come along too soon for us. We weren't ready to make that big step and I don't think the infrastructure of the club was ready to cope with the leap that we would have had to take.

The team had done really well for me in my first season in charge on my own, we had surpassed expectations and I knew we were heading in the right direction. I think the sort of season we had helped to answer a lot of the questions some people might have had about me as a manager, and I was pleased with the way Les had come in and done such a good job. We also had a lot of promising youngsters at the club, with some, like Bowyer, Rufus, and Newton, already showing what a vital part of the team they were. I knew it was important to keep hold of the kids we had if the club were going to continue making progress, but I also realized the realities of life as manager of Charlton. The club were still losing something like £700,000 or £800,000 per year, but at the same time I knew we weren't in the sort of position we'd been in when we had to sell someone like Robert Lee a few years earlier. We were trying to build for the future both on and off the pitch, and the important thing was for all of us to be pulling in the right direction.

There had been almost constant rumours that Bowyer was going to be sold to a Premier League club, with Arsenal's name popping up time and again, but when the season finally came to an end for us following that play-off defeat against Palace it wasn't the Gunners who were interested in signing Lee.

Coventry, West Ham and Sheffield Wednesday were the clubs showing a real interest and, although we didn't actually need to sell, I think both Richard Murray and I soon realized that the player and his agent were keen on a move. When a situation like that arises there's really very little you can do to stop it, and the main thing as far as the club is concerned is to hold out for the right price. Bowyer still had a year to run on his contract and even though I thought staying with us would have benefited him, the fact remained that he wanted to get away and play in the Premier League. Richard knew exactly what he wanted as a transfer fee, with a guarantee of £2.5 million and an overall package worth around £3 million. It was the biggest ever fee for a teenager, but I knew that at 19 years of age, whoever got Bowyer would be getting a bargain – just like his dad had told me in that handwritten contract. He had got into the side because he was simply too good to keep out and having him in my team and around the place was a real pleasure. He played like he trained and he trained like he played. He was a 'proper' footballer and a player I knew we were going to miss.

Although we offered Lee a new contract, he and his agent, Jonathan Barnett, were determined to go ahead with the move and it was up to them to talk to all the interested clubs, the only criterion for us being that any club they spoke to had to meet our valuation first. Just when most people thought it was going to be a straight fight between Coventry and Wednesday, a new bidder entered the scene when Leeds manager Howard Wilkinson showed an interest.

Howard had done a tremendous job with Leeds and had taken them to the League title in 1992, the last year before it became the Premier League. It was no surprise to me that he was interested and I remembered an incident at Huddersfield in February that probably had a lot to do with his decision to go after Bowyer.

We drew the game up there 2–2 on a cold Tuesday night, but it was Bowyer and the way he played that probably stuck in Howard's memory. The Huddersfield manager, Brian Horton, was always a lively character on the touchline and he was screaming at his side to get stuck in to us. One of their players seemed to take it a bit too literally and clattered into Bowyer with a tackle that shook him to the bone, but he just got up and carried on playing. Not only that, he really started to run the game and got the first of our two goals. Just after that bone-cruncher on Bowyer I happened to turn around and look into the stands. Howard was sitting there watching the game along with quite a few other managers and anyone who saw that match couldn't have failed to be impressed by Bowyer's performance.

The story I later heard was that Howard, on returning from a holiday that summer, had bought a newspaper at the airport and found out other clubs were interested in Bowyer, and then immediately set about trying to sign him. He must have done a good job because in the end Lee opted for Elland Road and Leeds ahead of everyone else and headed off to Yorkshire.

I had a sneaky feeling that, at 19 years old, he might have stayed in London and gone to West Ham, but I think he wanted to get out of the area and start to grow up in a completely new part of the country. We were left with a massive hole to fill in the side but, at the same time, the club had some much-needed money.

In my earliest conversations with Richard after he had given me the job, he had said that he felt the immediate future for Charlton was to become a decent First Division club who would probably need to sell a player every now and then in order to help balance the books. Maybe we could have a decent cup run from time to time and get our hard-core support up to the 12,000 or 14,000 mark. We mentioned clubs like QPR as examples of where we would like to get to, but it was seen as a long-term plan. If you are going to build your support a club needs to be successful, and unless someone comes along with a load of money to throw at the whole thing, success takes time. Part of the plan was always going to involve improving The Valley. I had been used to spending only about 10 per cent of any money the club received through transfers and I knew things weren't about to change just because we'd got a record fee for a teenager.

At that time the West Stand at The Valley consisted of green seats on green boards and it used to be partly dismantled during the summer when the seating was planted around the greens and used at the British Open for spectators to sit on. It was clear something had to be done about the 'golf' stand and most of the money from the Bowyer deal went towards just that – a new stand. Richard said there would be some money available to me for transfers, but he also said the vast majority was going to go into ground development. The idea was to increase the capacity of the stadium and in doing so help the income of the club; once that was achieved then more money would be released to me for team building. I could see the sense it made and in the years that followed Richard was as good as his word.

Over a period of time the money did come back out for me to use in the transfer market. We may have lost one of our best players, but we were about to make a stand!

11 Sharon, Tracey and Clive

There was no doubt that the departure of Bowyer was a big blow for us and I still believe that the move was probably one or two years too soon for him and for us. It would have been nice to have seen what would have happened had we managed to keep him but it wasn't to be and we had to move on. Apart from his overall play in midfield, I knew one of the things we would miss most was his ability to score goals. Losing a midfield player is bad enough, but losing a midfield player who was your top scorer as well was a double blow, especially to a club like Charlton.

I wanted to try and get someone in who could do a job for us in midfield and, at the same time, might be able to chip in with a few vital goals during the course of a season. I knew I didn't have loads of money to throw around and because of that I realized I would be shopping for a replacement in a limited market. In the end I went for Brendan O'Connell at Barnsley, an experienced midfielder who consistently scored a few goals – he cost us £125,000. I knew I also had some more cash available if I needed it. Defensively I felt we could do with someone who I could use in more than one position if I needed to, and I went for a player I knew well, re-signing Anthony Barness from Chelsea for £165,000.

Brendan and Barness weren't the only new faces in pre-season training that summer; we also had a little Irish midfielder on trial from Colchester named Mark Kinsella. It was pretty obvious from his first training session with us that he was a good player; the surprising thing for me was that nobody had tried to buy him. He'd played something like 200 games for Colchester and I'd heard that quite a few clubs had looked at him during that time, but decided not to take a gamble. It was Keith Peacock who recommended Mark, having seen him on several occasions, and was very persistent. I think a lot of people had perhaps been put off buying Kinsella because of his size and lack of real pace, but he could pass the ball, link up play, had a great strike and was a tremendous worker.

After having him around for a while it was obvious that he'd have no trouble making the step up to the First Division, but although I would have liked to have signed him, we really didn't have any money. We haggled with Colchester but they were set on the sort of fee they were after and we couldn't give them what they wanted. Mark's agent was Jonathan Barnett, the same person who had represented Lee Bowyer in his transfer to Leeds, so we had a decent relationship but just couldn't get the deal done. Kinsella had scored a couple of goals in pre-season for us and when I called him into my office I think he was expecting us to make an attempt to sign him. I had to explain that nothing was going to happen, not because I didn't want him to come to us, but because we simply didn't have the money at the time. Although he took the news well I could see the disappointment in his face, and I did tell him to keep us informed if anything happened and another club came in for him, just in case we might be in a position by then to do something ourselves.

That summer also saw the end of the road for Colin Walsh, who had to retire because of injury. He had a testimonial at The Valley against Tottenham and more than 10,000 turned up to pay tribute to the man who scored that historic goal against Portsmouth when we returned in 1992.

I think this was another indication of how the club was changing. There had been instances in the past where well-deserved testimonials for players had not been supported in the same way. Two that spring to mind are the games for Derek Hales and Steve Gritt. Derek got about 2,000 people for his match against West Ham, and Gritty had a turn-out of just 1,762 for his game with Spurs. Quite a few players had benefit matches in recent years and happily the crowds seemed to get better as each one came up.

Colin had a great left foot and was one of the players who did such a vital job for the club when we were going through some pretty tough times. You could always rely on him and he had the ability to produce that little bit of magic during the course of a game that would excite the fans and possibly win the match. He was another 'proper player' both on and off the pitch. He was someone who was always reliable when it came to his performances, but he contributed in other ways, especially when it came to team spirit.

The testimonial also acted as one of our pre-season matches and the 3–1 defeat was a bit of an indication of what was to come in the League. Three of our first four fixtures were away from home and we lost all of them, while only managing to pick up a point in the home game with West Brom. The third of those away defeats came at the beginning of September at Wolves on a Friday night, with the home side scoring the only goal of the game in what was the first Charlton match shown live on Sky, but the real drama came in the build-up to the game.

We had just finished our last training session at Sparrows Lane on the Thursday, before preparing to leave for the match, and Les was out on the pitch collecting some footballs. He apparently bent over to pick up a ball and then collapsed. I was actually in the main building at the training ground, but some of the players carried Les into the treatment room where our physio, Jimmy Hendry, was packing his bags for the Wolves game. The good thing for Les was that Jimmy was around at the time. He was one of the old-school physios who had been in the game all his life and he had a tremendous network of contacts. Jimmy was soon on the phone making sure Les was in the right hands, and it wasn't long before Les was in the Wellington Hospital in London, where the initial diagnosis was that a blood vessel had burst in his brain. It must have been a frightening experience for Les and it later emerged that he could quite easily have died. Happily for him his condition was treatable but at the same time I think we all realized that he'd had a lucky escape.

We may have lost at Wolves but with poor Les lying in hospital and not knowing what was going to happen, somehow the result didn't quite seem so important in the cold light of day. I remember visiting him on the Sunday after the game and we were all mightily relieved that he was going to be alright and, even though it was a shock to everyone at the club, it was good to know he was in such safe hands.

The result against Wolves sent us to the bottom of the table and the danger signs were there. I think there was maybe a bit of a hangover from the previous season's play-off games against Palace – teams that lose in the play-offs generally have it tough the following season because such a big effort has been put in. The fact that we had sold Bowyer didn't help either, but I just started to get an uneasy feeling about the team and how we were playing. There didn't seem to be the usual spark or aggression to a lot of our play, and I knew that without it we would struggle.

We got off the mark in our next game with a 2–0 home win against Southend. The League table still wasn't looking too healthy from our point of view, but it soon emerged that the chairman of another club wasn't put off by the poor start.

QPR had just been relegated from the Premier League and parted company with their manager, Ray Wilkins. Chris Wright was the Rangers chairman and one of his directors was Nick Blackburn. Both men had links with the music industry, because Chris was head of Chrysalis and Nick ran Ticketmaster. I'd come across them in the past because of my brother Billy's involvement in the rock industry, and word got to me that if I was at all interested in the QPR job they would be interested in talking to me. It was all very loose and very tentative, but it was clear Rangers wanted a new manager to help get them back into the Premier League at the first attempt. They certainly weren't a big club in the Manchester United or Arsenal sense, but they were bigger than Charlton at that time, with some decent players and good support, and there were a lot of people who thought it wouldn't be long before they were back in the top flight. I suppose it might have been an opportunity for me to jump to the next level in my career.

Unlike the Birmingham situation a few years earlier when I was with Gritty, the whole Rangers thing wasn't 'full-on'. I knew that if I had made the right moves and noises I would probably have got the manager's job at St Andrews had they got as far as being able to talk to me. The QPR thing was never really like that, and to be honest it never got much further than some press speculation, although I think Richard was realistic enough to know that it wasn't all talk and there was some substance to all the stories floating around at the time. He was certainly never formally approached, so I got on with the job I had at Charlton and QPR eventually appointed Stewart Houston.

September turned out to be quite an eventful month. Happily Les began to make steady progress, but I knew it would be some time before he would be able to get back to coaching again. Not long after all the speculation regarding Rangers we heard that Mark Kinsella was about to sign for Gillingham. I'd always hoped that a deal for Mark could be resurrected and we literally managed to step in and nick him just before he was about to put pen to paper. Just as before, the big stumbling block was finding the money for the transfer. I was under the impression then, and still am to this day, that Richard paid for Mark Kinsella. He somehow quickly agreed a deal paying more up front to Colchester and then giving them extra add-ons that brought the fee to around £200,000. The main thing was we had got our man and over the years he came to epitomize everything Charlton were about. Having managed to come up with the money for the transfer, it has to rank as one of the best pieces of business Richard has ever done for the club when you think of the impact Kinsella had on the side during the time he was at Charlton.

Although Mark fitted in well from the start the team was still struggling to put a decent run together and pull away from the bottom places in the league. We seemed to win a game then lose a couple and maybe get a draw in the next match. We just weren't firing on all cylinders in the way we had done the year before, and because of that the last thing I needed was to have my team selection disrupted for any reason, but I was faced with just that prospect because of the rules governing international call-ups – this was before we had clear international breaks. It was a crazy situation for us and we actually managed to get the rules changed when we demonstrated how we were being unfairly penalized. The problem was that you could only get a game called off if a team had three or more full internationals missing from its side. The fact that we may only have had one full international called up, but still had another couple of players missing because they were on Under-21 duty with their country, counted for nothing. We weren't allowed to get the game postponed even though we had three of our first-team players missing. It was a silly rule and thankfully because of our persistence as a club the authorities finally saw sense and agreed with our case, allowing us to have a game against Barnsley called off because John Robinson was on international duty with Wales, while Richard Rufus and Shaun Newton were with the England under-21s.

By the time the end of October rolled around we were still struggling to break free of the bottom places even though we hadn't played that badly; we also had the prospect of another meeting with Liverpool, this time in the Coca-Cola Cup at The Valley. Getting drawn to play Liverpool again in a cup match wasn't the only thing causing excitement with the fans. There was a lot of press speculation regarding Rufus and a possible move to Tottenham. He had become a big part of my team and was also in the Under-21 England set-up, so he was always likely to be a target for a bigger club. I knew it might be difficult to keep him at Charlton, but despite all the press coverage we hadn't received any real enquiry and I was more concerned with strengthening my defence rather than weakening it by selling someone like Richard.

The Liverpool game ended in a 1–1 draw and we played well, with Newton almost scoring a winner late in the match. We took more than £160,000 in receipts, which was a record at The Valley, and it was just a shame that we didn't quite manage to produce a cup upset for the 14,796 fans who packed the ground. A couple of days before the replay I was able to sign defender Gary Poole for £250,000 from Birmingham. He was a good player who Steve and I had wanted when he was playing for Barnet some years earlier, and I knew he could do a really good job for me at full-back or central defence if he had to.

We were beaten 4–1 at Anfield but it was no disgrace and once again it was the League and our form week-in, week-out that I was more concerned with. We did get a good win straight after the Liverpool match with Gary Poole scoring for us in a 2–1 victory at QPR. It was our second away win on the bounce and suddenly our form on the road started to look very different, having started the season by losing all of the seven matches we played away from The Valley. But just when things start to look good football has a habit of kicking you in the teeth and in the space of a few days we were beaten at home by Bradford and then hit the headlines for all the wrong reasons again.

Jay Notley was an 18-year-old central midfielder who hadn't quite managed to make an impact. He wasn't the sort of youngster you felt might be pushing for a first-team place in the way that someone like Bowyer had, and he was unlikely to be kept on when his contract expired. It was because he wasn't really making any great progress with us that we agreed to let him go out on loan to non-League side Dagenham and Redbridge. He had played for them on the Saturday and got injured, so turned up at our place the following Monday morning in early November to get treatment on the same day that the drug-testing unit arrived at Sparrows Lane. Since the incident with Chandler and Bowyer we had gone out of our way to make sure nothing like it ever happened again, and I'm convinced that no club was doing more than us to combat any possible drug problem. We had the police in to talk to the senior players, the youth team, the schoolboys and even their parents about the dangers of drugs, and they came out with an incredible statistic saying that something like 80% of kids would sample one form of drug or another before they even left school. The players were well aware of the harm they could do to themselves and how it would affect their careers, but no matter what you do it seems there are always going to be people who choose to ignore the advice. When Notley was one of the names chosen by the drug-testing people, I didn't even know he was at the ground and had no reason to believe the whole thing would be anything other than routine. How wrong I was.

We later learned that not only had Jay tested positive, he was found to have a cocktail of drugs in his system with traces of cocaine, ecstasy and cannabis in his body. We had done so much as a club to make sure players were aware of the dangers of drugs, but once again one of our lot had produced a positive drugs test. I seriously began to wonder whether we did have some sort of problem with drugs within the club and I wanted to find out for myself whether that was the case. Not surprisingly the young players at Charlton knew the other young players at some of the other London clubs, and the story we were told was that some of these kids were actually serving the stuff. We had been the club who had someone positively tested, but I just couldn't believe we were an isolated case and I remember phoning a couple of other managers from London clubs at that time and warning them not to be complacent. One of our youngsters had been caught, but I told them they might have a similar problem on their doorstep as well.

Notley's age was taken into consideration when the FA commission met in December and he was given three months to try and rescue his career after they deferred sentence for his drugs offence. He appeared before the commission again in March 1997 and was allowed to restart training, but his career at Charlton was unlikely to have carried on even if he hadn't taken the drugs and at the end of the season we released him. Once again we'd had another positive test and it wasn't exactly the best sort of publicity for the club.

We finished the year having managed to pull ourselves away from the bottom rungs of the table but we still weren't in great shape and it seemed to often be a case of taking two steps forward and then one step back. At least we knew we had something to look forward to in the New Year when the third-round FA Cup draw gave us a home tie with Newcastle. The game was given a bit of added spice by the fact that Robert Lee would be returning to The Valley and also because rumours were flying around concerning the future of Kevin Keegan. Robert did the predictable and opened the scoring in the first half, but Kinsella got us back on level terms 12 minutes before the end and earned us a replay at St James's Park. On the morning of the game there were stories that Keegan was leaving Newcastle and the 1–1 result was completely overshadowed by all the speculation regarding Kevin. By the time the replay came around the picture was a lot clearer. Keegan had left and Kenny Dalglish was appointed as the new manager the day before our replay with them.

We put in a great display up there, taking the match to extra-time, before Alan Shearer got the winner in the 100th minute of the game. It was a real shame for Richard Rufus who had played brilliantly against Shearer right through and had the better of the England striker for virtually the whole game. Les Ferdinand, who came on as a substitute during extra-time, actually came up to me at the end of the match and said Richard was the best centre-half he'd played against all season. The match also stands out in my memory for another reason.

David Whyte had not been having the best of times in front of goal, but on the Saturday before the match at Newcastle he found his scoring touch again, getting one of our goals in a 2–2 draw at Reading. It was obviously a relief for David and he naturally wanted to carry on where he had left off when we started the match at St James's. Everyone knew David was capable of producing the unexpected during the course of a match and sometimes he could even take his own team-mates by surprise. When we were awarded a free-kick on the edge of their box during the first half of the match, the team knew exactly what to do because we'd rehearsed a similar situation in training the previous day. Brendan O'Connell got ready to take it, only to see David decide to have a go himself and whip in a shot. It was easy to see Brendan wasn't too pleased at what had happened and he quickly made David aware, in no uncertain terms, just what his feelings were.

I usually like to take my time before going into the dressing room at the break, because I'd sooner think about what has just gone on in the first half and get things clear in my own mind. It also allows the players time to settle down, which makes the atmosphere better, but when I walked through the door I could see all hell had broken loose. There seemed to be blood all over the place, including the dressing-room wall, coming from a cut over David Whyte's eye after Brendan had apparently lashed out at him. O'Connell was still upset by the free-kick incident from earlier in the half and it seemed the two had come to blows as things had boiled over. Instead of the nice calm atmosphere that I had hoped for, it was all we could do to keep the two of them apart and we had to quickly patch up David's eye to make sure he could go out for the second half!

The whole thing was eventually forgotten and everyone just got on with the job of trying to beat Newcastle. There are quite often flare-ups between players, and it is all just part of life as a footballer. When the nature of the business is all about being so competitive emotions can often boil over, but the incidents go as quickly as they arrive and there's never usually any lasting problem.

The Cup defeat was a bit hard to swallow because we'd played so well, but I think it left a bit of a hangover a few days later when we were beaten at The Valley by Stoke. We also lost our next game, which was an away match at Grimsby. It's the sort of place that is never easy to go to and they had a striker playing for them who always seemed to cause problems for defenders. His name was Clive Mendonca and I'd always thought he had some great qualities as a forward, with the ability to hold the ball and bring others into play. Clive seemed to have the ability to scare you whenever he got the ball, because there was always a feeling that something was going to happen. In later years I used to have the same sort of feeling about Paolo Di Canio when he played for West Ham against us at Upton Park. Mendonca also had a great eye for goal and was a deadly finisher. We lost the game up there 2–0 and Mendonca got his 13th goal of the season when he scored from the penalty spot. The defeat was bad enough but I also had Rufus and Kinsella sent off, making it a really costly afternoon. Our lack of punch up front was becoming a concern to me and I knew we needed to get someone different in to allow me some options in attack and give us the kind of energy we lacked.

Garry Nelson had left in the summer and gone to Torquay after giving Charlton five magnificent years. He was another player who simply seemed to epitomize what the club was about and he had the ability to really inject some life into our play because of his pace and directness. I believed we needed that type of player in the squad and I thought one of my old clubs might have just the man for the job. Steve Jones was a bit raw and had come through at West Ham after playing non-League for Billericay Town. He'd also had a couple of years playing lower down the League with Bournemouth before going back to Upton Park, but he wasn't really getting a look-in and I knew that West Ham manager Harry Redknapp needed to get some money into the club in order to help him buy strikers John Hartson from Arsenal and Paul Kitson from Newcastle. Jones had pace and an enthusiasm to work hard in a game. He would run the line and go into the channels for you. It was something we'd been missing since Garry Nelson departed.

We paid £400,000 for Jones and he went straight into our side for the 2–2 home draw with Barnsley, but in the next game which saw us draw 4–4 at home to Norwich he did his cartilage and never played again that season. So the new option that I thought I had to see us through the last part of the season was suddenly gone. There was still some talk of us having an outside chance of getting into the play-offs, but that would have required the sort of run Palace had the year before when they'd beaten us and lost in the final to Leicester. In my own mind I just couldn't see that happening because we weren't consistent enough. If our form on the pitch was a bit stuttering that certainly wasn't the case for the way things were going off the field. The club got their listing on the Alternative Investment Market with a fully subscribed share issue that really gave us a financial boost. A lot of people contributed and it also gave Richard Murray a chance to increase his investment in Charlton. It was mainly due to Richard's success with his own companies that investors were willing to back his lastest venture.

Our young players were still attracting interest and Shaun Newton was a target for Joe Kinnear over at Wimbledon. They sniffed around and were keen to do something but nothing came of it in the end, and I was more than happy to see the whole thing die because I knew Shaun could be important for us. We were lucky to have such a good little crop of young players in the squad. People like Shaun, Richard Rufus, Steve Brown, Jamie Stuart and Kevin Lisbie. But there is also no substitute for quality and experience, which was what I knew I would get from a player like Mark Bright.

Mark had done brilliantly at Palace forming a great partnership with Ian Wright and then went on to play at Sheffield Wednesday, but at the age of 34 David Pleat had decided to let him go and Brighty signed for the Swiss club Sion early in 1997. It turned out to be a bad move for him and I got to hear that he desperately wanted to come back to England.

After quite a lot of hassle because of his contractual situation with Sion and a dispute they had with Wednesday, I finally managed to sign him on transfer deadline day until the end of the season. It was a good move for us and I knew how much he wanted it to work out, because if things went well there was the possibility that we would offer him a permanent deal. Mark looked the part from day one when he trained with us. He brought professionalism, know-how and a bit of steel. All things that I could only see as a plus, and I think it was quite good for some of the other players as well because Brighty was a bit of a 'name' and as a club we were still hoping to try and get to where he'd already been as a player. When you sign players of that age the last thing you want is for them to coast their way through things, but that certainly wasn't the situation with Brighty. From the first day he seemed to be on a mission to prove to a few people that he could still do it, and he had my favourite ingredients in a player: he was angry and he was hungry.

With the last few weeks of the season approaching I started to think ahead and plan for the next campaign. It had been a bit of a frustrating time after all the excitement of getting to the play-offs the year before, and it was clear I had to think about what I needed if we wanted to be challenging for promotion again. One of the big ingredients for any successful team is being able to score goals. After that first season with us the goals had dried up a bit for David Whyte, and he'd also had some injury problems. Steve Jones hadn't really had a chance to make an impact after injuring himself and Bradley Allen had also struggled with injury. I knew Mark Bright had the quality but I still wasn't sure we would be able to get him in on a permanent basis. If we were going to have a chance I thought we needed a proven scorer at First Division level who would frighten other teams, and I believed I knew the player who fitted that description perfectly. His name was Clive Mendonca.

On the Friday after we had lost that game at Grimsby and had Rufus and Kinsella sent off, we played Tranmere at The Valley and came back with a bang, winning 3–1. I decided to make the most of having a spare Saturday and drove up to Oldham to take a closer look at Mendonca. Grimsby won 3–0 and Clive got on the scoresheet again with a goal in the last minute, but it was his overall play that impressed me. The one thing he didn't have was pace, but he more than made up for that with the way he used his footballing brain. His touch, control and awareness was excellent and of course he was a terrific goal-scorer. We made enquires and found out that Grimsby might be willing to sell Clive but it was going to be for a lot of money, and even though Charlton had been making progress and grown as a club, I still wasn't sure he'd want to come to us because we were far from being big time. We still had to watch every penny we spent, so making sure we got things right in the transfer market was very important. Once again, to his credit, Richard Murray was prepared to back me up and started to speak to the Grimsby chairman to see if a deal could be sorted out.

Les and I went on a coaching course soon after the season ended, leaving Richard to try and tie up a deal with Grimsby; we also knew that both Birmingham and Mendonca's home-town club, Sunderland, could be interested in signing Clive. I have to hold my hands up and say that I've never been that comfortable with new technology, and although the mobile phone had been around for some time, the most complicated thing I did with mine was dial a number. Things like picking up messages left by other people were still a bit of a mystery. Richard had apparently been trying to get hold of me while I'd been on the course in order to give me an update regarding the Mendonca situation. Just as Les and I were leaving to drive home, my mobile rang and I soon recognized Richard's exasperated voice on the other end.

'Where have you been? I've been trying to get hold of you to let you know about Mendonca,' he told me.

For some reason I must have sounded less than enthusiastic, even though I was desperately hoping we could sign Clive.

'Look,' said Richard. 'Do you want me to f***ing sign him or not?'

I was so taken aback by Richard's out of character verbal volley that for a second I was a bit stunned.

'Yeah, sign him, sign him,' I managed to finally say and that's exactly what he did, agreeing to pay out a club record fee of £700,000.

Richard has often said that I very rarely used to lose a player. The two of us were pretty good over the years when it came to nailing a transfer deal. There were a few where things did not work out, like the time I tried to sign Steve Claridge when he was at Cambridge, and he went to Birmingham instead. In more recent years we missed out on some potential signings because the competition in the Premier League is so tough and there were a lot of clubs after the same player, but overall my record at Charlton was pretty good when it came to closing a transfer deal.

Once the actual fee and finances had been agreed between the two chairmen on that Friday in May, we made arrangements for Clive to travel down to London a few days later to have his medical. It was a good opportunity for me to speak to the player and to hopefully make sure he had a good idea of what the move would mean for him.

So on the Monday after the transfer had been agreed I found myself parked at the side of King's Cross station drinking coffee from the local McDonald's and waiting for the arrival of my new striker. Clive duly emerged from the station, looking a bit shell-shocked at 9 am that morning, but hadn't brought his wife with him, which surprised me a bit. I still thought it would be a good idea to give him a bit of a tour of London and show him around to give him a better understanding of the place. I knew he was from the north-east and had been playing his football in Grimsby, so arriving in London might have come as a bit of a shock to the system. The size of the city can be a bit intimidating and getting an idea of just where everything is can be difficult, so I decided to give him the Alan Curbishley tour of London. We also had plenty of time to kill because the medical we had booked for him wasn't due to take place until 1 pm that day. I had reservations about the whole thing because he was due to see the same man who had failed Malkin and I didn't want the same thing happening a second time.

Clive was very quiet in the car and hardly said a word to me as I started to tell him all about Charlton and at the same time give him a conducted tour of the capital. We went past Madame Tussauds, then on to Trafalgar Square, along the Embankment and past the Tower of London.

'That's where we are, south of the Thames,' I told him pointing over Tower Bridge. 'We're staying on this side of the water because we've got to go to Woodford for the medical and that's more East London.'

It didn't seem to make too much impression on Clive as he gazed out of the window and at the same time ignored the ringing of his mobile phone. Apparently he knew it would be Alan Buckley on the other end trying to persuade him to stay at Grimsby.

'I'm not answering it,' he said, and almost seemed a bit scared of what might happen if he did.

Buckley had managed Clive at Grimsby but then moved on to take charge at West Brom. He'd since left them and had agreed to go back to Grimsby, but wasn't due to be formally announced as their new boss for another couple of days. Alan must have realized what an important part of his team Clive could be if he got him to change his mind and was desperate to stop the deal, but although Mendonca was having none of it he clearly didn't fancy having Buckley hammering on at him down the phone. I was still finding it difficult to get a conversation going but I kept talking, telling him how many football teams there were in London and how it was always possible to go and watch a game in midweek if he liked doing that sort of thing. I must have told him the location of just about every club in London, just to keep the conversation going. We still had a lot of time to kill and so I thought I'd take him to have a sandwich in Loughton, which wasn't too far from where the medical was going to take place. On the way we went through Chigwell.

'This is Chigwell, Clive, I said. 'It's where Spurs train and a lot of the West Ham players live around here, but it wouldn't really be any good to you because you want to live on the other side of the water near the training ground.'

Clive suddenly perked up and I could see I'd finally got his interest. I thought he must have been a bit concerned about where to live and the housing situation, but I couldn't have got it more wrong.

'Chigwell,' said Clive, suddenly looking more animated than at any time during the entire journey. 'Sharon and Tracey come from Chigwell!'

I might have failed to make any impression on him, but the mention of Chigwell had done the trick. He'd obviously heard of the place because it was where the Sharon and Tracey characters from the TV comedy series *Birds of a Feather* were supposed to live. I had to smile – after all that time in the car with him it was really the first thing he'd said to me.

He passed the medical without any problems although we did know that he had a bit of a history with back problems. But it was a far cry from our last visit with Malkin. True to his word, once the new stand was up and running, Richard had started backing the team with hard cash. It was still May and I'd managed to sign what I believed was one of the best goalscorers outside of the Premier League. He had finished the season with 20 goals and, at 28 years old, I thought we were getting someone who could really make a difference to the team, but I certainly had no way of knowing the impact Clive would have on Charlton and how quickly he would become a legend at the club.

12 Packing a Punch

When the players reported back for pre-season training there was a bit of a buzz about the place. Not only had I signed Clive Mendonca, I'd also brought in Matt Holmes from Blackburn for a fee of £250,000. Something had changed because the other players in the squad recognized the two new faces at the training ground, and they all realized that we'd added quality to the squad.

We also let some people go. Brendan O'Connell went back to the north when he signed for Wigan in a £120,000 deal, Mark Robson went to Notts County and David Whyte was released and later went to Reading. Mark Bright trained with us that summer even though there was still a problem with getting his registration sorted out. It was finally resolved and he signed a contract in time for the coming season. Another new face at Sparrows Lane was Sasa Ilic, an Australian-born Serb goalkeeper, who had been playing non-League football the previous season for St Leonards Stamcroft and who turned up with his boots in a Sainsbury's plastic bag. He was hoping to impress us and get a contract, but initially he only got expenses. In fact, I used to give him a personal cheque each week on a Friday, so that he didn't have to wait for his money, and then I would claim the amount back from the club. It reminded me of the days when I occasionally used to pay for things like meals at hotels or buying players' boots. It was in the days when the club had no money and places like hotels wouldn't give them credit, so I was asked to pay the bills and then I'd claim it back at some later date. Ilic was a big, confident keeper who used to love throwing himself around and was a good shot-stopper, but I had Andy Petterson and Mike Salmon, so it was difficult for Sasa to get a look-in. I didn't know anything about him other than the fact that he lived somewhere in Putney, but I didn't have a problem with him being around the place especially as we weren't really paying him anything.

The season didn't get off to the best of starts when we lost 2–1 at Middlesbrough on the opening day of the season, but despite the defeat I came away from the Riverside Stadium thinking we had a real chance to go up that year. We played really well and it was what Clive didn't do that helped give me cause for optimism. He didn't score that day but he had three great chances. There was just something about the squad, and the mix we had in it, that made me feel confident we could do something. Unlike the previous season when we never seemed to get things together, I felt that I had a pretty decent squad of players who were capable of competing with the so-called favourites in the division.

We got off the mark in our next game, beating Oxford 3–2 at The Valley, and it was a memorable day for Paul Konchesky, one of the youngsters I had in the squad. At the tender age of just 16 years and 93 days, Paul became the youngest player ever to represent Charlton at senior level. It was another example of the fact that pretty much from the time I took over with Gritty, the club had always managed to produce at least one or two really good kids who made it through to the first team. It was always one of the big selling points to parents when we were trying to sign a promising kid. We could honestly say to them that although we might not be Manchester United or Arsenal, we were a club who brought youngsters through and then gave them their chance in the first team. There was another prime example in our next League game, a goalless draw at Bury, when another 16-year-old, named Scott Parker, made his first-team debut after coming on as a substitute.

Having people like Mendonca, Holmes and Bright in the squad gave us a stronger and more balanced look. They were experienced players who were very professional in the way they went about their business, and all three quickly gained the respect of the other players, so when I got the opportunity to sign another player in a similar mould I jumped at the chance.

Mark Bowen had bags of experience with Tottenham, Norwich and West Ham. and had been playing for Shimizu-S-Pulse in Japan. Going to the Far East was a good move for him financially but he was really keen to get back to this country. Although he was 33 years old I knew he was fit, and he had the attitude and qualities we needed; he could also play left or right back. However, I have to admit to being a bit shocked when I saw him – in fact I didn't recognize him because he'd lost so much weight while he was out there, and I almost walked straight past him! With Steve Brown having picked up an injury and Gary Poole still out of action with a knee problem, I knew Mark could come in to do a good job at either right- or left-back. Signing him was another piece of the jigsaw as far as I was concerned. As we moved into the autumn, we were well placed in the League and I felt the team was coming together nicely.

Off the pitch Richard Murray was increasing his team as well by recruiting Peter Varney. He joined in late October as commercial director, but quickly became managing director of the club and in more recent times has been Charlton's chief executive. As far as I was concerned the appointment was spot on. I'd got to know Peter in previous years because he worked for the British Brain and Spine Foundation, and Gritty had been involved with them because of what had happened to his daughter Hayley. Peter had also been involved in helping to organize testimonials for people like Colin Walsh and Bob Bolder. He was a Charlton supporter and I couldn't help being impressed at the way he operated. He had a real knack of being able to organize events and also showed tremendous ability when it came to raising funds. I mentioned all of this to Richard one day and said I thought Peter was someone he should meet, but I think he already knew about him and had made a mental note of what a capable individual he was. Nothing actually happened right away, but some time later when Richard was looking to expand the commercial operations of the club he organized a meeting with Peter and got him on-board. In my opinion it was one of the best appointments Richard ever made, because since that day in 1997 Peter Varney has been a major influence on the way Charlton Athletic have progressed as a club.

As November arrived we were in pretty good shape, well placed in the top six and playing some decent football. Everything was going smoothly and it all seemed pretty settled, but then QPR decided to sack Stewart Houston and 14 months on I found myself in the frame again to become the new manager at Loftus Road.

This time the whole thing was more than just speculation and I have to admit that it took a lot of thought on my part.

Richard was aware of their interest and spoke to me about it. He said that he didn't want me to go and that if Rangers were thinking of taking me they would have to pay compensation. I think Richard was confident that Rangers wouldn't want to do that, but he was wrong. Football is a very close community and it's hard to keep secrets. I know for a fact that they would have been prepared to pay compensation, and I also know that I could have virtually doubled my salary by going to them. Chris Wright and Nick Blackburn were still in charge, but one of the things I didn't really like about the prospect of going there was the fact that the previous manager had spent a lot of money, and it seemed that anyone taking over would have to sell in order to re-build. With all the speculation I started to sense an uneasiness in Les. I think he quickly realized that he was tied to me in many ways and perhaps wouldn't have too much of a say in his own future. Although QPR hadn't managed to get back into the Premier League at the first attempt I knew they still had some decent players, their support was good and the wage structure over there was better than Charlton's. After a week of speculation in the papers I made up my mind about what I wanted to do. I drove over to Richard's house in Surrey on a Sunday morning and made a decision that would have long-term implications for my career and for Charlton. As we sat and drank tea at his house I told him that my future was at Charlton and not QPR. It was a big relief for me because I didn't enjoy the situation, but as with all the speculation over the Birmingham job, I felt it wasn't right and I was better off staying at Charlton. I know the Rangers people were very disappointed when they heard, but it was time for me to draw a line under the whole business and move on.

I knew that in doing so I was turning my back on earning a

lot more money, because I would probably have been between 30 or 40 per cent better off if I had taken the Rangers job, but it just didn't feel right. Richard told me Charlton might not be the biggest or the best in the world, but he was trying to do something at the club and he wanted me to be part of it. He's as straight as they come, and I knew he wasn't trying to flatter me; I also realized that he was being honest when he told me about a new improved contract he was going to give me.

'I can't give you any more money than I'm offering,' he said.

I knew he meant it and, even though the salary increase I was getting was way short of what I might have got at Loftus Road, once I'd made the decision to take myself out of the market for the Rangers job I was happy with it. I had the feeling that we had a decent side and I'd worked long and hard since taking over with Steve six years earlier. The progress of the club during that time had been amazing and I suppose I decided that I wanted to be a part of what was to come. I knew the people I was working with and, more importantly, I liked the people I was working with.

We didn't exactly celebrate in style after I let people know about my decision, because in our next game we got thumped 5–2 at Nottingham Forest and that wasn't the only big disappointment I suffered. At the beginning of the week we had another visit from the drugs-testing unit and as usual they asked for a list of all the players on the premises at Sparrows Lane. One of the names to be drawn at random by the testers was Jamie Stuart, who duly produced a sample at the end of training.

After all the problems we'd had with positive drugs tests in the past the club had decided to do something about it. I've already said that we had people like the police come in and give talks and we also tried to make players as aware as possible about the dangers of taking drugs, but as Jay Notley had proved a year earlier, all the talk and advice can count for nothing. It was because we felt the problem was a social one and that no club could be complacent that we decided to take more positive action ourselves.

With the consent of the players we started to do our own in-house testing and came to the conclusion that if a player refused to be tested it was an admission of guilt. The players went along with the idea and I think they could see that we wanted to make sure we were doing all we could to root out any potential problems and deal with them as a club. The procedure was pretty simple and it just became part of the routine of being a player at Charlton. Obviously we hoped the testing would be nothing more than a formality and that none of the players would come up positive, but we were wrong.

Jamie Stuart claimed it was nothing more than a one-off mistake on his part when we confronted him with the positive result from his drug test with us. We sat him down and went through the whole episode; he got medical help and support from the club, and assured us that nothing like it would ever happen again. It was because of what had happened with Jamie that I wasn't particularly worried when his name was drawn by the FA testers on that November morning at the training ground.

When we got the results and found out that he had tested positive for cocaine and marijuana I felt a mixture of emotions. I felt let down after all the work and encouragement he'd been given by the club, and the fact that he'd promised it was a one-off situation, which it clearly wasn't. I felt sad for Jamie because he was a promising young footballer whose career had gone off the rails, and I also felt guilt because we knew from our own test that he'd taken drugs before. When I started to think the whole thing through I came to the conclusion that we probably couldn't have done any more for him, and Jamie knew that as a club we could not afford to give him a second chance. We'd had problems with players taking drugs in the past, and no club could have done more to prevent it happening again, but the fact was it had. The players all knew that because of what we were doing in-house, on any given day they could be tested. We'd already given Jamie a second chance with us and he'd repaid that faith by taking drugs again.

Ironically, the public announcement that Stuart had tested positive came the day before we were due to play at Reading in the League. The same club who had already tabled a £150,000 bid for Jamie. It might have been easy and convenient for us to have gone ahead with the transfer and taken the money, but instead the club came to the conclusion that Jamie's test was the straw that broke the camel's back. A week after Stuart's drug test became public knowledge the club made the decision to sack him. It was zero tolerance, but it needed to happen.

Jamie was suspended by the FA until the end of April and underwent counselling and rehabilitation during the period. When the suspension was lifted he still had to undergo random tests for two years. He trained with Wigan and then signed a three-year contract with Millwall in May 1998.

While the drugs episode was upsetting for everyone we managed to maintain our form and stay in the promotion pack. I also got linked with the manager's job at WBA, but there was absolutely nothing in all the speculation, although Charlton did feel the need to issue a statement and go on record to say there was no truth in the reports and I was staying at The Valley.

The New Year started well for us: we got a bit of revenge

against Forest by knocking them out of the FA Cup with a 4–1 home win, and in the League we had an emphatic 3–0 victory against leaders Middlesbrough at The Valley. January also saw the departure of Carl Leaburn, who had been on a weekly contract with us for more than a year. Carlo wanted to play in the Premier League and finally got his wish when Wimbledon agreed to a transfer that was potentially worth £300,000. Leaburn had always done a job for me when he was required and although his scoring record wasn't the best, he was a great team man and the players in the side always appreciated the work Carl got through during the course of a match. He was a bit of an unsung hero really who had been at the club for a long time and was in the thick of it through all the bad times, but we had quite a few strikers at the club and there was no way Carl was ever going to be a regular in the way he had been in the past.

We finished the month with three draws, two of them in the League and the other in a home FA Cup fourth-round tie against Wolves. I could have done without the replay and the extra game because the League was our priority and I certainly didn't want the Cup to become a distraction.

As things turned out the game at Molineux ended our involvement in the competition when we lost the replay 3–0. It was a bad result but it was what happened during the course of the match that proved to be far more costly. Mark Bright was sent off in the second half by referee Graham Poll for allegedly stamping on their keeper, Mike Stowell, which meant he picked up a suspension, but the game will be remembered most for a tackle by Kevin Muscat that was to end the full-time career of Matty Holmes.

Matty was a really nice lad and he'd taken a big pay cut to

come to us from Blackburn, who had paid £1 million to West Ham for his services, but he never really got a look in there and felt it was time to get away. He was just desperate to play and was a total professional, who did everything right in the way he went about his job and conducted himself. He'd stayed in digs after signing for us, only seeing his family at weekends, and was a terrific player to have around in training. The day before the Wolves replay I spoke to him about his move south and the fact that it had hit him in the pocket.

'Matty, I know the contract we gave you wasn't the sort of money you wanted,' I admitted, 'but if I can get you an increase and possibly extend the length, would you sign it?'

'Definitely,' he said. 'Definitely I would.'

Within 24 hours of that conversation poor Matty's career was effectively over. The game was only five minutes old when Muscat tackled Holmes and left him reeling in agony on the ground. I instantly knew Holmes had a bad injury as soon as Muscat made contact with him. We later found out that the tackle resulted in Matt sustaining a compound spiral fracture of his left fibula. The one regret I have about the whole incident is that I didn't publicly criticize Muscat for his actions and flag up the fact that Matt had been badly tackled by the Wolves player.

I've always been a firm believer in getting my facts right before I say anything and, although it was little more than eight years ago, there wasn't the sort of TV technology we have available now. I didn't really say anything about the incident on the night because I wanted to see a full video of it, but in my own mind I was sure about what had gone on and so were a few of the other managers who were at the ground that night. After the match they said, off the record, exactly what they thought but when it later came to giving evidence in a court case that Matty brought, none of them wanted to step forward.

Muscat came with a bit of a history for the way he made challenges and I didn't want to pre-judge him, but having looked at the incident I had no doubt that it was a bad tackle. Poll and the other officials were there to make the decisions about fouls and tackles, but they don't see it all and they weren't as wised-up as they should have been. In situations like that a lot of weight is carried by the decision the referee takes, and whether or not he books the player or sends him off for the tackle. We all knew what had gone on but it just felt as if nobody was interested. When we delved into his background and looked at videos of other games, and the tackles he'd made, we realized there were all sorts of challenges that make you wince a bit. Some he got pulled up for, some he didn't.

When you are in the game as a player, manager or coach, you know whether a tackle is reckless or not, dangerous or not, or just purely nasty. Some people say they would have a player like Muscat in their side, others just wouldn't want him. All I know is that to call Muscat's tackle that night 'reckless' is being kind. Matt had to fight long and hard to get any form of compensation for what had happened to him and in February 2004 was finally awarded £250,000 damages; with the addition of costs the overall sum paid out was in the region of £750,000. The club backed him all the way, something that I know Matty was grateful for. When the case was going to court there was talk of both sides bringing in expert witnesses. I often wonder why there isn't an independent body, perhaps using the League Managers Association, that could deliberate in these sort of cases. There are so many former managers out there not involved in football anymore who could be called to look at this sort of evidence. Managers know if someone has been 'done' and also whether the person committing the offence actually meant it.

While February 1998 saw the injury that would eventually lead to Matt's retirement, the month also saw the start of Sasa Ilic's career as a Charlton first-team player. We had a dreadful result in our away game at Stockport, losing the match 3–0 and I decided to make a goalkeeping change for the trip to Stoke four days later. Keith Peacock had been doing a great job with the reserves and his overall help in the way things were run off the pitch was a real bonus for me. I knew I could rely on Keith to do an awful lot around the training ground and individually with players. He was very good at working with players, particularly those who were not in the first-team squad for one reason or another. Our reserves were organized as a proper team and Keith paid a lot of attention to detail with his sides and their pattern of play. It wasn't just a case of having to 'turn out for the reserves' and any player involved knew he was part of a successful team who were challenging for the Football Combination title.

One player who Keith had been working hard with was Sasa Ilic. He had been looking impressive for the reserves and in one particular game against Southampton Sasa had apparently been in outstanding form. I decided that it was worth bringing him in for the Stoke trip and he didn't disappoint me. He let a goal in but did well enough and we came away with an important 2–1 win. From that moment on Sasa became a permanent fixture in the team as we stepped up our bid to claim a promotion place. His confidence grew as he played more games in the first team and he used to love to work on the training pitch. He was really hungry and eager to prove that he could make it as a goalkeeper with us.

The team was beginning to pick itself in many ways. There

was Sasa and then people like Mark Bowen, who had been there and done it as a player, Newton on the right who was so quick and a great athlete, Kinsella and Keith Jones in the middle of midfield and then John Robertson who had become the player I always thought he could be, but was doing it on the left-hand side of the field instead of the right. Up front we had Clive, who had not only made us play in a certain way because he liked the ball passed to his feet and was then so good at bringing others into the match, he was also proving to be the sort of potent goalscorer I'd hoped he would be for us. Mark Bright was also playing his part on the training ground with the way he conducted himself and went about his work, and on the pitch with his overall play and ability to chip in with some important goals.

Despite the fact that we were doing well by the time March came around, with its transfer deadline for signing players, I still felt I needed to get a couple of people in for the final push towards a promotion or play-off place.

At the beginning of March I was asked to take charge of a Nationwide Football League Under-21 team chosen from all the Leagues that was going to take on its counterpart from the Italian Serie B League at The Valley. I already knew some of the young First Division players but didn't really have a clue about some of the lads who were playing in the other divisions, so when I had quite a few players pulling out I called up Peter Taylor who was in charge of the England Under-21 side and he gave me a list of names that he thought would be up to the job. I suppose I suddenly got a taste of what it's like to be an international manager.

The match was due to be played in midweek and on the Sunday before the game the squad assembled at a hotel for Les

Reed and I to have a brief meeting with them. I told the play-ers that although I recognized a few faces, I didn't really know a lot about some of the others and so we asked them to give a written answer to a couple of questions I'd photocopied onto pieces of paper: '1) Where would you like to play; 2) what other positions can you play?'

We got all the bits of paper back, and as Les and I sifted through them we noticed that someone had actually written in answer to the first question, 'I'd like to play for you!' Another one we got back simply said, 'Right-back, left-back, centre-half.' The player who'd written it was Danny Mills.

When the players trained at The Valley the next day in prepa-ration for the match, I noticed that there was a directness and pace about everything that Mills did, and I liked what I saw. I told the players on the night before the match that I didn't really know much about the Italians, and that inevitably some of our lot would draw the short straws.

'One of you is going to get the whippet of the team,' I told them. 'One of you is going to be up against the guy who is four inches taller than you, and someone else is going to be playing against their nastiest player. But you're all going to have to cope and we'll just have to get on with it.'

On the night of the game it was Danny Mills who captained the team as well as getting the whippet from their side to look after, but I couldn't help being impressed at how well he coped with the situation. I decided that I wanted Mills to be one of the players to come in and help us in the final phase of the season even though he wasn't in the Norwich first team at the time, and not too long after the 0–0 draw with the Italians we signed him in a deal that was eventually worth around £400,000.

I think I surprised a lot of people with the choice of my other signing before the transfer deadline. There was speculation about who I might go for and I think some supporters thought it would be another forward, but instead it was Eddie Youds from Bradford who was a big central defender. I knew Eddie had problems with his knees but I liked him as a player and as a character. Everyone I ever spoke to in the game about him always used the same word as part of their description – 'Winner'.

When it comes to trying to get a player in, the first contact is usually between the two managers of the respective clubs. You ask firstly if the player concerned is available and, if so, what sort of fee would be involved and what kind of money he is on. I also liked to do my homework on a player before I made an enquiry. Not only would I watch him play, but I also talked to as many people in the game who knew him and asked their opinions, including what he was like off the pitch and what sort of character he was. Once you get the go-ahead to approach the player direct, I always found it strange that the next step was talking to the player and his advisors, agreeing personal terms and talking about the future, even before a medical had been carried out. If there's a problem with the medical then it can all fall apart, and I could never quite understand why that part of the transfer process can't be done first. In terms of the medical it tends to follow a similar pattern. First the player will be looked at by the club doctor who carries out some of the more mundane tests, and if there are no problems the player goes on to see an orthopaedic surgeon. If he's satisfied with the results he'll pass the player as being in the right condition to sign for the club, but if he doesn't pass him then no insurance company will insure the player for you. If that becomes the case the club has to make a decision about whether they'll go ahead with the transfer, knowing the player may break down at some time in the future and they won't have any insurance policy covering him, or they perhaps try to re-negotiate the fee and the way it is paid relating to the number of games played. If a player comes into a medical having recovered from an injury, it usually means he will have to play 12 consecutive games to allow him to be covered by an insurance policy. Some clubs have taken a gamble on players who they couldn't get insured and the deals have been very successful, but these days with so much money involved in transfers, it's very dangerous for a club to take the risk on a player who doesn't pass a medical.

When we signed Youds, unlike the time the Malkin deal fell through, we did take a bit of a gamble with regard to Eddie's previous medical history. It was reflected in the way we paid the fee, because to safeguard ourselves the payments were linked to the number of games he played for us.

Eddie was also the first player who turned the tables on me as I was giving him my usual chat about the club and where we had come from. I sat with him in the West Stand at The Valley and started to explain about the struggle we'd had to get back to the ground and about how there used to be portakabins all over the place.

'I don't want to know about that,' said Eddie. 'I want to know where you think you're going as a club, because I think you can get into the Premier League and that's why I want to join you.'

Eddie signed for £550,000 on deadline day but not before an awful lot of haggling over his money and the transfer fee. When it was all done I knew I'd managed to get another vital part of the team in place ready for the last weeks of the season. We were looking strong as a squad because a couple of days before getting Eddie, Manchester City manager Joe Royle agreed to let me have midfielder Neil Heaney on loan until the end of the season, and that included any possible play-off matches. Neil was a player who could play right or left side and was another valuable addition to the squad.

Eddie made an immediate impression on the rest of the lads in his first training session with us. I remember he headed the first ball to safety that he had to deal with in a practice match, kicked the next and then kicked the striker he was supposed to be marking. He also made a fair impression on his debut the next day when we beat the division leaders Nottingham Forest 4–2 at The Valley. Eddie was up against Pierre Van Hooijdonk and the Dutchman certainly knew he'd been in a game afterwards.

The Forest match was a bit of a landmark in our season that year, because for the remaining seven League games we didn't concede a goal. We were certainly one of the form teams in the last stages of the season, and Keith's reserve side weren't doing too badly either. In fact, they went on to have a great season and won the Combination title for the first time in 48 years.

It was another sign that the club was moving in the right direction and going into the final match of the League season we were actually in with a chance of gaining automatic promotion. A lot of things had to fall into place for us to go straight up, and realistically I thought it was more likely we would have to go through the play-off route if we were going to get into the Premier League. We had to go to Birmingham for the last game, and they had a chance of getting into the play-offs as well if they beat us and Sheffield United lost. I rated Birmingham as a real danger, because like us they had shown some really good form during the last part of the season, and I certainly didn't fancy having to meet them in the play-offs. It was very similar to the way both Crystal Palace and West Ham won promotion in the last few seasons, with a good run going into the play-offs.

We drew the game 0–0, with Sasa adding to his growing reputation by pulling off some great saves, and it ended their hopes, but kept ours alive by finishing the campaign in fourth place. We also got 88 points, which would have been enough in most seasons to have seen us go straight up. Sunderland finished above us with 90 points, with Ipswich in fifth five points behind and Sheffield in sixth spot on 74 points.

With the way the play-offs worked it meant Sunderland would meet United and we would take on Ipswich. I knew it wasn't going to be an easy game because they had already beaten us twice in the Coca-Cola Cup, and although we had won in the League at The Valley, they were the last team to beat us before we went on a ten-game unbeaten run at the end of the season.

As we had finished above them, the first leg of the semi-final was played at Portman Road, where, as you might expect, the atmosphere was electric. We knew they fancied their chances against us and Mark Kinsella, who lived in Colchester which isn't too far from Ipswich, brought in a local newspaper with a story basically saying they thought they were the better footballing team and were going to beat us over the two legs. It all helped to motivate the players and on the day of the game, we carried the theme on during the team talk, saying that Ipswich probably felt it was their year and that we had to be spot-on in our approach to the first leg and set the tone for the game.

The match was played on a hot Sunday in May and, although they had their fans right behind them as you might expect, we took a noisy contingent of supporters there as well and made our presence known on the terraces. For some reason,

I'd always felt the games against Ipswich were more like derby matches for us and they usually turned out to be really competitive affairs. Right from the first whistle I could see we were up for it and very early on we won some crucial tackles that sent out all the right signals from our point of view. We also got the all-important first goal after 12 minutes, when Keith Jones crossed from the right and Jamie Clapham put the ball into his own goal under pressure from Mark Bright. It was enough to see us win the game, and the only thing that spoilt things for us was having Danny Mills sent off in the second half for a second bookable offence. It came after he attempted to tackle Ipswich's Argentinian full-back, Mauricio Terrico, and even though it appeared he never even made contact, referee Mick Fletcher got the red card out.

It all added to the tense atmosphere and Neil Heaney also had a couple of run-ins with Terrico. When John Robinson had injured himself in the win over Forest, Neil came in and did a good job for us on the left, making sure the side kept its balance. By the time the final whistle blew tempers and emotions were running high and, as the players filed down the tunnel, there was still some ill-feeling flying about. My main concern was to just get everyone in and calm the dressing room down.

We'd had a great result but the job was only half done and it was important that we went into the second leg with the right attitude and focused on that game rather than the one we'd just played. I sent the players out for a warm-down on the pitch not realizing that the Ipswich team were still out there. It was their last home game of the season and I think they were doing a lap of honour and saying thanks to their fans. The timing was a bit unfortunate because it meant the two sets of players bumped into each other again and the needle there had been towards the end of the match between Heaney and Terrico flared up again. That sort of thing can happen after closely fought matches and once the players were back in the dressing room again, I went to speak to the press and then have a drink with the Ipswich manager, George Burley.

I'd known George well for a number of years, going right back to the times when he was playing for the Ipswich youth team and I played against him for West Ham in the FA Youth Cup Final. When I found him he was with a few other people talking about the match and, before I had a chance to say very much, someone came bursting in and told George he needed to speak to him outside. When George came back I could see from his face that he was furious and that there must be something wrong. He told me there'd been a fight in the players' lounge and that one of my players had broken Terrico's nose.

I went back to the dressing room to see if Les or Keith knew anything about it but by this time the players were already on the team bus waiting to leave the ground. I found out that Neil Heaney had been involved in an incident with Terrico, and went straight to the bus to find out what had gone on. Gary Poole got off with Neil and told me he'd been there as well and Neil hadn't done anything wrong, but instead had just acted in self-defence. By the time I got back to tell George he wasn't very happy at all, and said he thought Terrico had broken his nose and probably wouldn't be able to play in the second leg. He actually thought that if that was the case I shouldn't play Heaney either. The whole thing was beginning to develop into a major incident. The police got involved and our bus wasn't allowed to leave because of all the fuss. By this time the Ipswich chairman, David Sheepshanks, had joined us and the atmosphere in the room was pretty sombre while it was decided what course of action should be taken. Eventually someone told us there was a video of the whole thing and we all sat and watched to see exactly what had gone on.

The video showed Terrico in the office area at Portman Road with his wife. Neil and Gary Poole walked into the office, which everyone had to go through in order to get to the players' lounge, and they then had to climb some stairs. You could see something had been said, but it wasn't obvious who had said what, and who they had said it to. Gary Poole started to go up the stairs and Heaney was walking behind him. Suddenly the video showed Terrico rush across the room and shoot up the steps with his arms flying all over the place. He apparently threw a punch at Heaney and Neil threw one back, knocking Terrico back down the stairs.

We all looked at the video footage and then at each other. I wasn't gloating, I just felt relief. I knew how George must have been feeling. I just wanted to concentrate on the return game that was coming up three days later at The Valley. I got on the team bus with Les and Keith and could see the players were waiting to see what I was going to say about the flare-up.

'That's it,' I told them. 'It's over and done with. Terrico tried to hit Neil, and he threw a punch back in self-defence. Mind you,' I added, 'it looks as though it was a great punch, Neil!'

The cheers were deafening and at that moment I knew the first part of my team talk for the second leg had already been taken care of.

13 Wembley Way

There was a great atmosphere at The Valley for the second leg, even though our main stand didn't even have a roof on it. That was because work had already started on the West Stand as part of the continuing development of the ground.

After all that had happened in the first leg I knew it was important that we went about the job in a really professional way against Ipswich. I wanted the team to concentrate on the second leg and make sure we started the game in the right fashion. We may have had a one-goal lead but if we got sloppy, particularly early on in the match, the whole situation could change for us. Because of what had happened up at Ipswich Terrico seemed to get booed every time he touched the ball. We seemed to be in complete control and there never really seemed to be any chance that Ipswich would make any impression on the night. We got control early on and once again scored a goal just at the right time. Mark Bowen took a throw on the right, Brighty helped it on to Newton and he managed to drag it across some Ipswich defenders on the edge of the penalty box, before hitting a left-foot shot into the top of the net nine minutes from the break.

When the game was over the place went wild. Not only had we got through, we were also going to play at Wembley. It was going to be a massive game for the team and for the fans. Little old Charlton, the club that didn't even have a home six years earlier, were one game away from playing in the Premier League. At the end of the match against Ipswich you only had to look at the faces of the supporters to realize how much winning the play-off final would mean to them, and I also knew it would mean an awful lot to someone else who had been watching the game from the stands that night. Mervyn Day had gone to the second leg against Ipswich knowing that if we got through he was going to be a step closer to coaching in the Premier League.

A couple of weeks earlier I had taken a call from Howard Wilkinson who had become Technical Director at the FA. Howard had apologized, but then went on to tell me how things had changed at the FA and that he wanted Les to join him there as Director of Technical Development in charge of youth coaching. It meant Les would be leaving as soon as the season was over, and it also meant that I had to look for a new coach.

I certainly didn't want Les to go, but at the same time it was a great opportunity for him and I got the feeling that having had three years as a club coach he was ready to move back to the FA. Les had done a fantastic job working with me and in many ways probably adapted better to the role than I could have ever hoped, but I think there was still part of him that didn't really like the insecurity of it all. He was also a very big family man and because his wife was a teacher, he had been used to being able to plan things like family summer holidays. The trouble was we were all back at work doing pre-season training just as the kids broke up, and I'm sure a lot of what he had taken for granted in his working life had been disrupted during his time with us. I also suspect that Les felt he was tied to me in many respects. If something happened to me or I went some-where else, where did that leave him?

Les was a superb coach and he did some great things during his time at Charlton. His planning and method of going about things in such a meticulous way certainly helped me after I took over on my own, and he'd played a big part in the success we'd had in reaching the play-off final. The one thing I didn't want was the news of his new job leaking out until our season was finally over, and Les agreed that the matter would be a closely guarded secret between me, him and Richard Murray.

He understood that with the chance of getting into the Premier League at stake I wanted everything to carry on as normal, and that meant I didn't want the players sitting around talking about who their new coach was going to be. I didn't want any distractions as we all focused on trying to gain promotion, but it did mean that I had to try and have someone lined up to take over from Les.

Despite what a lot of people might think, Mervyn and I were never really that friendly when we were at West Ham, and although we got to know each other better at Villa when our paths crossed, we still didn't really socialize that much. When he moved on to Leeds I would usually stay up if ever I played against them for Charlton and we'd often talk about football, but it certainly wasn't a case of me bringing in a mate when I decided to ask Merv to replace Les.

When I'd gone for Les three years earlier I felt I needed some-thing different. The fact that he hadn't played the game profes-sionally and came from an FA background didn't bother me, and I think I was proved right by the success he had as a coach at Charlton and the way he showed he could do the job. Once I knew he was leaving I felt I needed someone else with a different mix. Mervyn had played the game as a professional and been a very good goalkeeper. He had coached and also managed, doing a great job with Carlisle, and he'd worked in the Premiership with Everton. Merv had done the rounds, and had a good knowledge of players from those at the top to others in the lower divisions. He was different to Les, but was a good coach and someone I thought I would be able to work well with. He was also keen to move south again after living in the north for quite some time, and I think he saw it as a great all-round opportunity for him. After watching us beat Ipswich he knew he had another 12 days to wait before he found out exactly what division he would be coaching in, but having got the details of his appointment sorted out Mervyn also had to keep quiet about the whole thing until after the final.

We were going to be playing Sunderland at Wembley, and it was probably fitting that the two teams who had finished with such big points totals and yet not gone up should be battling it out for a place in the Premier League. We gave the players four days off after beating Ipswich because there was such a long time to go before the final. They came in on the Monday, one week before the Wembley game, and we had the whole week mapped out for them. We trained well and planned everything the way we wanted to. Les even got the groundsman at Sparrows Lane to mark out a pitch with the exact measurements of Wembley so that the team could play on it and get used to how it felt. We didn't put any great emphasis on taking penalties, but knowing that the players might have to take them in order to decide the outcome of the match, we made sure they got used to the experience. We even made them walk from the centre-circle to the penalty spot, just as they would have to in a shoot-out situation at the end of the final.

One of the big problems I had that week was seeing whether Paul Mortimer and John Robinson would be fit enough to be in contention for a place at Wembley. I didn't want any last-minute situations when it came to selecting the team, and I always liked to let the players know in advance who was going to be playing and who wasn't. The situation with Morts was pretty straightforward because he really didn't have much of a chance, but Robbo was desperate to play and had been getting back to fitness after injuring himself in the Forest game at the end of March when he'd sustained a hairline fracture at the top of his right fibula.

We arranged a practice match at The Valley just so that we could assess the situation, but it was clear by the end of it that I couldn't afford to have John in the starting line-up. His fitness just wasn't up to it and when I broke the news to him at the training ground later that week he wasn't too happy. In fact, he had a real go at me in my office. It was nothing strange for John to be upset at being left out of the side, and it didn't bother me that he wanted to come and see me and go through all of my reasons for making the decision. John loved to play football and hated not being in the team. I could understand that and it was good to see him so passionate about everything.

He'd done a great job for me since coming from Brighton and had become one of the main ingredients of the side. He'd come a long way from the time during his early days in the team when he was devastated by a comment from Bob Bolder after a game. Bob basically told Robbo that he hadn't done too well in a particular situation during the match, when he'd thrown the ball out to John hoping to ease some pressure, and added that Robert Lee would never have made the sort of mistake John had. The remark hit him hard, but I think Bob was just trying to emphasize the way Robert played and what was expected of Robbo. However, John rightly made the point that although everyone kept going on about Robert Lee, he was a completely different player, and it wasn't too long before John found his feet and he quickly established himself as one of the crowd's favourites.

Whenever he was left out I knew I would be in for a grilling from him. Sometimes it was just a quick couple of minutes after training when he came to see me; other times it was longer than that, and on some occasions it was a case of me shouting out for someone to put the kettle on for a cup of tea, because I knew I was going to be in there with him for ages. When I told John he was only going to be one of the subs for the Sunderland match he went mad and stormed off. It was no more than I expected in some ways, and I remembered how bad I'd felt all those years ago when Lennie left me out of the team for the Full Members Cup Final against Blackburn, but I also knew Robbo would calm down and could still be a vital member of the squad at Wembley.

The players trained well that week and the mood was very positive. I knew we had a good team, but I was also aware how good the Sunderland team was. Their manager, Peter Reid, had done a great job with them and I had a lot of respect for him. The two of us went back a long way and Reidy was a real character. I was once in the same England Under-21 squad with him for a game played at Brighton in 1977 when we beat Norway 6–0. After the match we went back to our hotel for a meal and Peter got me drinking white wine, which I couldn't really handle, but that certainly wasn't the case with Reidy, who managed to drink me under the table that night. With Sunderland having finished the season on 90 points and us on 88, it seemed a shame that one of the two clubs was going to miss out on the Premiership.

The day before the final we travelled to our hotel, The Complete Angler, which Les had used before when he was with the FA. Quite a few teams used it to stay in before playing at Wembley. It was a good location with great facilities and that night we tried to get everyone as relaxed as we could with the big day just around the corner. Apart from being a good coach, Les is also pretty handy when it comes to choosing a bottle of red wine. I don't usually drink it but that night, along with Les, Keith and physio Jimmy Hendry, I probably had a glass or two more than I should have.

I'm a terrible sleeper and if there's any kind of noise in a hotel you can bet I'll find it. I had a lovely room with a waterfall outside which would have seemed wonderful to most people, but because I'm such a light sleeper the noise of the water falling meant I didn't exactly have a peaceful night's kip. The next morning I had a bit of a headache because of the wine and I'd hardly had any real sleep. I decided some drastic action was called for and, instead of the usual traditional English cooked breakfast, I opted for some smoked haddock and poached eggs. Keith and Les encouraged me to try it even though I could see from their faces that they weren't about to join me, but at least it did the trick and I went back to my room to make some last-minute preparations before we left for Wembley.

It must have been strange for anyone wandering into the hotel lobby that day to see about twenty blokes all dressed in the same beige suits. They weren't Armani, Boss or Paul Smith outfits. Peter Varney had managed to do a deal with a local store and got us kitted out with off-the-peg gear. They were nice enough, but with the prospect of a hot day ahead I started to wonder how I'd be feeling in a few hours' time dressed in a three-piece suit. Just to set the whole thing off we were each given a flower to wear in our buttonhole as we boarded the team coach for our journey to Wembley.

As we were waiting to get on the bus Mark Bright came wandering through the hotel clutching a video camera. I wasn't quite sure what he was doing, but Brighty soon explained.

'I've played in cup finals before Curbs and they go by in a flash,' he said. 'You don't really take it all in, but this time I want to make sure I can remember everything.'

The thought struck me at the time that he hadn't even asked if he could do it, but it didn't really matter and I could understand exactly what he was saying. You want to be able to savour the big occasions although, considering Brighty now works in broadcasting with the BBC, maybe he was just planning for his future career!

We had a good journey to Wembley and once we were there it didn't take too long to see what a big game it was going to be. There seemed to be fans everywhere and most of them appeared to be Sunderland supporters who booed us in, because they were congregated at the entrance where the coaches used to park at the old stadium. The gates would open, the coach went in and then the gates closed behind you. The coaches were actually parked at the end of the tunnel the teams used to walk out onto the pitch, and on either side of it were the dressing rooms. The first thing I noticed when we got into ours was that there was a little man sitting in the corner waiting for us. I quickly found out that he was there to help out and do any running around we needed. If we wanted extra towels, water or ice, he was the man. I have to admit it was a bit disconcerting to have a total stranger in the dressing room, especially for such

a big match. We had a bit of a team talk and tried to get everyone settled and it was then that we heard Sunderland arrive.

Their supporters were accommodated at the tunnel end of
the stadium and, with more than an hour to go before the
match, most of them were still outside waiting for their heroes
to arrive. They were loud enough when our team coach arrived
and they booed us in, but the decibel level must have gone up
a notch or two when they spotted the Sunderland players. We
could hear the cheering from inside our own dressing room. It
was a bit like the experience you had at Highbury. They liked
the visiting team to get in first at Arsenal and then, as the visiting side were changing and getting ready, you suddenly heard
all the home supporters cheering their team in as they arrived
at the stadium. It wasn't as if we didn't have any of our supporters at Wembley – in fact we sold out the first 24,000 of our
allocation for the final in a day – it was just that all our fans
were at the other end of the stadium and any noise we heard
was being created by the Sunderland fans.

As soon as they were changed we sent the team out to warm
up on the pitch and to try and get a feel for the stadium. No
matter how many times you have seen Wembley on the television, or gone there to see a match, you can never properly
understand what it's like to play a game there unless you've had
the experience before, and it was only really Brighty who knew
all about the place. Once the players had gone out I followed
them down the tunnel and spotted Peter Reid looking out onto
the pitch as his lads warmed up as well. It must have seemed
funny to all the players as they finished their routine and
trooped back to the dressing room, seeing Reidy and I chatting
away like two old mates who hadn't seen each other for years.

Without going over the top about the whole experience, I

have to say that it's quite a lonely feeling when you're there knowing that one game can be such a turning point for you and the club. Getting to the play-off final was one thing, but it really only means something if you win. Like any final the losers soon get forgotten, but unlike a cup competition we were playing a game to decide whether we were going to be in the Premier League or not. The press had speculated that whoever won would be in for a £10 million windfall because of all the money attached to playing in England's top division. Many would have said that for a club like Charlton just getting to the play-off final was enough and that we'd overachieved, but that wasn't my thought as I stood in that tunnel with Peter Reid.

As far as I was concerned it wasn't just going to be a good day out for little old Charlton and their long-suffering fans. This wasn't the Full Members Cup Final that I'd walked out on all those years ago, this was a chance to play against and compete with the best. During my time in charge, from the early days with Gritty, I had made a promise to myself that we would improve things on the field each season. It wasn't always easy, but I honestly felt that the aim had been achieved. We'd made tremendous progress and we needed to take that extra step. I felt we were ready for it, unlike a couple of years earlier when we'd lost to Palace. Back then making the leap into the Premiership would have come too soon, but a lot had happened to the club since and we'd grown both on and off the pitch. The infrastructure was good enough and so were the team. All that stood in our way were Sunderland.

The clock was ticking down and I had to get on with my pre-match team talk. I wanted to keep it short and sweet and at the same time leave the players in no doubt about how we were going to approach the afternoon. For some reason I kept thinking about all the times I'd seen teams walk out at Wembley and immediately look around them almost in awe of the arena. They would try to pick out friends and family in the crowd and wave at them. I told the players I didn't want any of that. I wanted them to walk out with their heads down or looking straight ahead, because I wanted them concentrating on the game and to be totally focused. This wasn't just a big day out. We were going on the pitch to do a job. It might be Wembley with a massive crowd, but it was all about the match and making sure we won it. This was our big chance and we had to take it.

The walk out of the tunnel and onto the pitch was incredible and something I will always remember. The noise was deafening and the colour just hit you. I was sticking to my plan of looking down or straight ahead, but you couldn't help noticing that the stadium was just a sea of red and white, and as we walked towards the centre-circle the chants from our own supporters got louder and louder.

It's funny the sort of things you recall about a day like that. With all that was going on and the importance of the match, I remember glancing across at Peter Reid and the rest of the people on the Sunderland team bench and thinking how much cooler they looked, and I meant it literally. The suit I had on was already making me feel hot and the game hadn't even started. Little did I know how much my temperature was going to rise during the course of the match, and it had nothing to do with the weather or the suit.

Going into the game everyone was aware of just how important and what an influence Clive Mendonca had been on our season. From the day he first pulled on a Charlton shirt it was clear we had signed a great player who had come our way at just the right time. The way in which the team played had definitely changed because of Clive, and changed for the better. His ability as a footballer became more and more apparent as the season wore on and his goals helped to make sure we maintained our push for promotion. The fans had taken to him from the word go, and apart from being such a good footballer, he was also a lovely guy. Clive certainly wasn't an extrovert, he was quiet off the field and tended to let his feet do the talking for him with the way he played and trained. He had a terrific work ethic and was great to have around the training ground. The other players liked him as a person and knew just how deadly he could be in front of goal.

By the time the final came around, Clive had netted 25 goals, which was more than anyone could have asked for going into the season, but it wasn't too long into the match with Sunderland before he added to that total in classic style, opening the scoring after 23 minutes. It was pure Clive, as he took the ball after a Brighty flick and turned almost in the same movement before hitting his shot into the net.

It wasn't all going our way at the start of the match, and we were screaming at Rufus and Youds from the bench because they weren't picking up the right men. Before the game we'd asked Eddie to look after big Niall Quinn and then wanted Richard, with his speed, marking Kevin Phillips. For some reason the two of them swapped. Richard was marking Quinn, with Eddie trying to take care of Phillips, but we eventually got the whole thing sorted out, and when we went in a goal up at half-time, I felt pretty good about our chances.

When the players got into the dressing room at the break we settled them down and I said we were where I wanted us to be. I let them know that I thought we had given ourselves a real chance, but I also emphasized the fact that I felt Sunderland would start to go long a bit more in the way they played, which meant they would try to hit Quinn and use his ability in the air for little knock-downs to Phillips. I also told them it was important for Eddie to get tight on Quinn and for Richard to be aware of Phillips and his pace. I knew we had a chance of getting more goals against Sunderland because we had the ability to break well from defensive positions and catch teams. If they were going to push on to us in the second half, I wanted us to be ready to break and hit them on the counter-attack. I was pretty upbeat and confident, and then out of the corner of my eye I suddenly caught sight of the little guy I'd noticed when we first arrived. He was the man who had been sitting there in the corner of the dressing room ready to give us a helping hand if we needed it. Whether it was my imagination or not, I couldn't help thinking that, although I might be doing a good job with the players, my half-time team talk didn't seem to impress him too much at all.

When Les and I walked out of the tunnel to take our places on the bench the noise from the Sunderland fans was incredible. For some reason I always felt that the team leading at half-time in the play-off final had a real chance of going on to win, because the other side could feel their opportunity of promotion slipping away and their fans got a bit edgy and nervous, but that certainly wasn't the case with the Sunderland fans. They really got behind their side and I honestly think their support galvanized the team. Within five minutes of the second half starting, our little dressing-room helper must have been thinking 'told you so', because the whole complexion of the game began to change. Quinn equalized for Sunderland with a bullet of a near-post header and about eight minutes later we found ourselves behind in the match for the first time when the other half of the Sunderland striking double act, Kevin Phillips, put them in front, when he got behind us and scored. It was a blow and the goal gave Sunderland a real lift.

I decided we needed to try and give them something more to worry about and so I brought on Steve Jones in place of Neil Heaney. When I bought Steve from West Ham I knew I had someone who had pace, but I also realized he was unpredictable. In many ways Jones was uncoachable, because he was so set in his ways and technically he lacked certain things in his game, but he was direct and, given the chance, could scare defences.

After they scored their second we hit a bit of a sticky patch and had to hang on and make sure the game didn't run away from us. With 71 minutes of the match played we managed to pull ourselves level once more. It was Steve Jones who helped set the goal up, breaking in midfield before laying the ball back to Keith Jones. His long pass over the top found Clive, who raced onto it and took two touches before finishing in typical Mendonca fashion. From the moment the ball was played forward I don't think there was another thought in Clive's head other than putting his shot in the back of the net.

It was a great feeling to be back in the match again after it looked as though we would have trouble breaking Sunderland down, but things changed in the space of a couple of minutes. Sunderland crossed the ball from right to left and when Danny Mills jumped and missed it, Quinn was in behind him to ram a shot past Sasa and we found ourselves behind once again.

With time running out I felt we needed to try and create more, so I brought John Robinson on for the final 14 minutes of normal time. I knew John was bursting to play in the match and he began to do exactly what I thought he would, chasing some lost causes and turning them to our advantage. It was one of those lost causes that led to us scoring an equalizer with just five minutes of the match remaining. Robbo won a corner on the right and when he swung it in I could see their keeper, Lionel Perez, starting to come for the ball; I could also see that there was no way he looked like getting it. I was willing him to go for it and I could feel Peter Reid looking on and saying 'stay', because he knew Perez wasn't going to make it. Sure enough the keeper never got near the ball, and I saw Richard Rufus leaping above everyone at the far post to head over the line. It was his first senior goal for us and he couldn't have chosen a better time or place to score it.

When the whistle blew for the end of 90 minutes and we knew there was going to be extra-time, I thought we might have a slight psychological edge, having scored the equalizer so late in the game, but at the same time I realized there was really nothing in it. The match had gone backwards and forwards all afternoon. At 3–3 and with the extra 30-minute period looming I knew the first goal could be vital, and it didn't take too long for that goal to arrive. It came from the boot of Sunderland's Nicky Summerbee in the 99th minute, who shot home from the edge of the penalty area after Quinn had laid the ball off to him. It was a real hammer blow and at that point I have to admit that I thought we were going to lose the match. We'd come back twice in the game and I just felt that it was asking too much for it to happen again. How wrong I was.

Steve Brown was another player who was Charlton through and through. He was an unsung hero who I knew I could play anywhere across the back and also in midfield. He would always give everything and had been at the club as a trainee, making his debut in the season Gritty and I took over. He was dependable and reliable, a really good professional and he would never shirk a tackle. When I put him on as substitute for Mark Bright six minutes before Sunderland got their fourth goal I was hoping he would stiffen things up and stop them from scoring. That plan quickly fell apart, but four minutes later Steve Brown made one of the most important tackles of his Charlton life. After Brownie threw himself into a challenge in the middle of the park and won possession for us, the ball eventually found its way out to Steve Jones on the right, and his pace and directness once again made things difficult for the Sunderland defence. Steve managed to get round their defenders and pull the ball back. It wasn't an easy ball to control but Clive somehow stuck a leg out and then managed to swivel and hit a shot into the net from close range. I'm convinced that most players in a similar situation would have tried to get their body in front of the ball and maybe try to lay it off, because it was so difficult to do anything else. The ball bounced up after that first touch but once again Clive showed he was a great finisher and knew exactly what he was doing.

Clive's goal not only gave him a hat-trick it also emphasized how important he'd been to our season, because when you've got someone in your team with that sort of ability to put the ball in the net, a side will always feel they have a chance in a game, even if it sometimes seems like a lost cause. The team had shown once again that they had a real fighting spirit to them with the way they refused to lie down, despite going behind three times during the course of 120 minutes of football. After all the excitement and goals, when the referee blew his whistle at the end of the second period of extra-time, it suddenly dawned on me that it could all count for nothing because of a penalty kick.

We had our five penalty takers for the shoot-out and Sunderland had theirs. I looked at Peter Reid and he looked at me, we both knew that in a few minutes' time one of us was going to be the manager of a Premier League team, and one of us was going to be left bitterly disappointed. When I think back now it seems silly but I just felt it had to be our year. Why? Because I thought we needed it more as a club than Sunderland did. I also felt they could recover from losing the game but I wasn't sure that as a club we would be able to. It was a stupid piece of logic really, but having come so far in such a short period of time, I desperately wanted us to move to the next level.

Taking a penalty in a game is never as easy as some people think. You have to be confident and have the bottle to do the job, and that's just during the course of a normal match. So you can imagine what it was like to have played 120 minutes of football in which eight goals have been scored, and then have to take a penalty that could make or break your team's chances of getting promotion.

When I got to the centre-circle to let the players know who was going to be taking the penalties both Eddie Youds and Richard Rufus were looking the other way. They might have been fearless on the pitch when it came to winning balls in the air and making tackles, but it was pretty obvious neither of them fancied taking a spot-kick. The five who took them for us were Mendonca, Brown, Keith Jones, Kinsella and Bowen. For some reason I fancied Sasa to get to one of the Sunderland penalties. He was big and I just thought he would guess right at some stage. Clive knocked the first one in for us and every penalty that followed from both sides hit the back of the net. Ten taken and none of them missed. The teams were still level and it was time for sudden death.

Having nominated the five original penalty takers it was now left to the five remaining players to decide what was going to happen; all I could do was sit helplessly on the bench as they sorted it out. John Robinson was first up and took his kick really well, putting us 6–5 in front. Quinn was next up for them knowing that if he missed or had the kick saved, we were the winners. At that point I think everyone's nerves in that stadium were shot to pieces. It may have been great entertainment and sporting drama but at times it was agony to watch, and the tension was unbelievable. Niall looked like the coolest man around and he made no mistake at all from the spot to level the penalty score at 6–6.

I only found out what happened next some months after the play-off final had taken place. With the scores level the referee, Eddie Wolstenholme, asked the remaining players who was next up. Only Eddie, Richard, Newton and Steve Jones were left and apparently Rufus suddenly pushed Newts out of the centre-circle. That's why, if you ever take a look at the video of the match, poor old Shaun is the only player who runs all the way to the penalty spot. It was because he was so nervous! To his credit, you would never have believed that was the case from the way he took his penalty, because it was a perfect kick giving Perez no chance at all. We were in the lead again, but the whole thing was beginning to get to me.

Michael Gray was already on his way to take Sunderland's next penalty when I turned to Keith on the bench beside me.

'I can't take much more of this,' I told him. 'I've watched all of them and they keep scoring.'

Keith leaned across and told me not to watch the next one and reminded me that Gray was a leftie. We both knew that Gray had a great left foot and was just the sort of player you wanted taking a penalty because he was so accurate. After the way things had gone I couldn't really see Gray missing and I decided to take Keith's advice and instead of watching, I put my head down and placed my hands over my face. All of the penalties were being taken at the Sunderland end of the stadium and for a split second I couldn't hear the cheers I'd expected. Instead, I heard a kind of collective gasp and then an incredible roar from our fans off to my right. The next thing I heard was Keith's voice screeching in my ear.

'He's missed it, he's missed it, he's missed it!'

I stood and suddenly all hell broke loose around me. I remember walking onto the pitch and all of our players who had been on the bench were running past me to get to Sasa. He had dived to his left and saved Gray's kick, bringing an end to the drama and making us a Premiership club in the space of a split second.

They all piled on top of Ilic, congratulating him, and as I began walking I looked across and saw Peter Reid pushing his way through all the mayhem to go and comfort poor Michael Gray. I had to feel sorry for Gray and for Reidy. Once he'd consoled Gray, Peter was straight over to see me and we had a hug, knowing just how much it had taken out of both of us. The only real emotion I had at that time was relief because everything else had been drained out of me during the course of the match. I looked across at Les and he seemed a bit tearful. He'd done so much to make sure we got promotion and I knew what it meant to him. He was desperate to go out on a high, and I realized that sitting at home watching it all on television, Mervyn would have been desperate for us to do it as well. Me? I was just desperate.

I was certain losing would have meant starting again. I would almost certainly have had to re-build, with players like

Rufus and Mendonca being targeted by other clubs and picked off. I didn't want that. We'd slowly built something and I didn't want the result of one match to destroy it all. In the end it was Sasa's save that decided the game, but I knew our season had been about much more than one save or one result. We had been consistent and were always there or thereabouts in the League. The team not only played well but it also had something about it. There was a real spirit and character in the side and when they'd needed it most they had come up with the goods.

It was a strange feeling as I stood on that Wembley pitch after the match. I knew we'd done it, but I didn't quite know what to do next. I'm not by nature the most extrovert of people and I wasn't about to go dancing around or jumping in the air. Instead, I just wanted to take it all in. I didn't want the moment to pass without trying to savour the whole occasion and the satisfaction of knowing we were going to be playing in the Premier League. As I looked around the famous old stadium and watched our players and fans celebrating, I knew it was the start of a totally different era for Charlton Athletic Football Club.

14 Portakabin Mob

It was Sunderland who walked up the steps to the Royal Box first, and you couldn't help but feel sorry for Peter Reid and his side.

They had played their part in making sure the match would go down in history as one of the most remarkable games ever to be played at Wembley. They had given everything and ended up with nothing. It was cruel but football can be like that at times. It's all or nothing and I was just pleased that, after all the things we'd gone through as a club, we weren't the ones who ended up with nothing.

When it was our turn to go up, I was last in line and somehow ended up with the trophy Mark Kinsella had been presented with as captain of the play-off winning team. As I started to walk down the steps my sister Laura shouted to me and I suddenly caught sight of my son Michael wearing a red and white jester's hat and beaming from ear to ear. I called to him to come over and he jumped the wall to join me, but I couldn't see my daughter Claire. I finally managed to spot where she was and I told my sister to get her over the wall as well. Within a couple of seconds there I was strolling onto the Wembley pitch with the cup in my hand and my two kids beside me. It was a great moment and if you look at any of the pictures showing the team celebrating after the match that day, you'll see the two of them enjoying the moment just as much as their dad.

We were all standing in front of our fans celebrating and as I glanced at the huge scoreboard behind me I saw for the first time written confirmation of what we had managed to achieve that day: 'Congratulation Charlton, 1998 First Division Play-Off Winners.' It was a nice feeling and a couple of minutes later I couldn't resist having another sneaky look just to remind myself that we'd done it, but by that time all they had up on the board were the train times for fans leaving the stadium! It didn't really matter because we all knew the job had been done and I wanted to take a look around me as I walked off the pitch, trying to savour the moment for one last time before disappearing into the tunnel and our dressing room.

When I got there I found out that Peter Reid had already been in to congratulate the players and shake each one of them by the hand. It was typical of the way the game had been played and there had been some good-natured banter between the two benches during the course of the match. Neither of us could quite believe the ups and downs that had gone on and I think both sets of management teams knew exactly what the other was going through. I was sorry that I'd missed Peter, but glad to finally be in the dressing room with the players and everyone else. We'd just achieved promotion in such dramatic fashion but although there was champagne in the dressing room it wasn't being sprayed around, and there was no leaping about or yelling. I think we were all drained, mentally and physically. We'd done it and we knew we'd done it. There just seemed to be a massive feeling of satisfaction from everyone involved.

Long before his involvement in Charlton Richard Murray

had already proved himself to be an extremely successful businessman with media-related companies, such as the one that would later give birth to the television quiz show *Who Wants To Be A Millionaire?* For the game against Sunderland Richard had arranged for his television studio near Wembley to be used as a base for all the Charlton staff and players, before an evening reception at a hotel near Heathrow. Earlier in the day there had been a champagne breakfast at the studios with everyone then being ferried off to the stadium on coaches, and the idea was that after the match we would all meet up there before going on to the hotel.

By the time I came out of the dressing room most people had gone off in different directions and some of the players had disappeared upstairs to meet family and friends in the Wembley banqueting hall. Since we all knew we were going to be meeting up at the television studio we'd given our allocation of tickets for Wembley's banqueting hall to Sunderland. Because we had arrived that day before Sunderland their coach was parked behind us in the tunnel blocking our one in. It meant we couldn't drive away until they went and as there was no sign of any movement I decided to walk to the studios. On the way out I saw Danny Mills standing against a wall. Obviously he was happy that we'd won, but it hadn't been one of Danny's best games for us. He'd missed the ball and let it drop behind him for their third goal when Quinn scored, and in the end I felt I needed to bring him off and put John Robinson on. It was just one of those things and everything had worked out well for us in the end.

I told Danny where I was going and we started walking to the studios, which were just off of Wembley Way. Just as we got to the stairs that led up to a balcony and the banqueting suit at the front of the stadium, we saw a smiling Mark Kinsella holding the cup we'd just won. I also spotted Carol, with her sister and my children. They came down and we all just carried on walking in a bit of a daze. By this time there were a few other people with us, including Keith, and as we made our way there were fans everywhere. There were Charlton fans, looking just as happy and exhausted as we did, but there were still a lot of Sunderland fans around as well and they were tremendous. They clapped us, congratulated us, and seemed to want to have their picture taken with us just as much as our own supporters.

When we got to the reception at the studios I had my first real chance to talk to Carol, and found out that she almost hadn't made it to the game. She hates watching matches that I'm involved in because she gets too nervous. It can actually make her feel physically sick, and she's probably only gone to about half a dozen during the time I was Charlton manager. She told me that when they were on the coach making their way through the crowds to the game, Roger Alwen had asked everyone to make sure they had everything they needed for the match. Carol suddenly shouted out that she'd forgotten her ticket, and then said that she would go back to the hotel and make her own way to the ground. In fact, she had no intention of going to the match. She wanted to stay behind because the nerves were getting too much for her. They insisted she stay on the coach and somehow managed to get her into the game as part of the official Charlton party, but by the end of the match it wasn't just her nerves that were in shreds – she had also torn right through her programme as a consequence of all the nail-biting action.

There was champagne at the studios but I didn't really have anything to drink. I think we were still all coming to terms with the match and the drama of the afternoon. Eventually all the players wandered in and it was time to get on the coach for the reception that was going to take place at the hotel near Heathrow. As we sat on the coach everyone was still trying to come to terms with the fact that we had won promotion and were suddenly going to be rubbing shoulders with the big boys of the English game.

I'd heard that after the match Steve Jones had been running around shouting out 'Loadsamoney!' to anyone within earshot. I liked Stevie, he was a good lad and he often used to make me laugh with the way he carried on. I asked him what he'd been shouting about.

'You know,' he said. 'Promotion. We're all going to get pay rises now we're in the Premier League!'

I joked with him that he wouldn't be getting anything, but I also realized that because of promotion players were inevitably going to be thinking about new contracts and earning more money. It was all part of the new world we were going to be entering as a club, but we still hadn't celebrated too much as a squad and although the champagne had been flowing I was more of a beer man. As we went past Wembley station I suddenly shouted out to everyone, 'Who wants some beers?'

There were some cheers and I told the coach driver to stop at the bottom of the hill where there were some shops and an off-licence. The guy in the store must have wondered what had hit him as this huge coach pulled up outside and we all piled in wearing identical suits, choosing beers, crisps and nuts like kids in a sweet shop. We'd just won a Wembley final that was going to be worth millions of pounds to the club and the result against Sunderland was going to transform all our lives, but there we were in this tiny off-licence celebrating with beer and crisps. We bought about three or four crates of beer, but by the time we got to the hotel only about four cans had been drunk. We were still all too full of the match and the excitement of everything that had happened, preferring to talk instead of drink.

When we got to the hotel I went up to my room and unpacked my bag before returning to the main reception which was going on downstairs. When I got there I found out about an incident which took a bit of the enjoyment away from the occasion for me. Something had happened which I thought was wrong. I was told that when Richard Murray had walked in some of the players immediately confronted him asking about bonuses. As a club we obviously weren't big payers, but I always felt we were fair payers considering the kind of money we took in. Richard and the board paid what they could. Money was always tight, but compared to the dark old days at Upton Park, things had dramatically improved. If the players had a problem with money they should have come to me instead of going to Richard on the day the club had just achieved so much. They might have had a legitimate gripe, but that certainly wasn't the time to start talking about it, and Richard didn't deserve to have to deal with it there and then.

Another sad note for me that evening was Les. I looked across at him and although he was really happy at what we'd done he was also tearful. He was leaving but nobody really knew. He wanted to tell the players, but I didn't want him to. It might have been a bit selfish, but the reason I wanted him to keep quiet was because I didn't want people and players coming up to me throughout the night asking what I was going to do about getting a new coach and whether I had anyone lined up for the job. I think Les would have liked to have stood up at some point and told everyone he was going. I think he wanted to say he'd enjoyed his time at the club, tell everyone how well they'd done and wish them all the best in the Premier League. I wanted him to do that as well, but not on that night. I just wanted everyone there to be able to relax and enjoy the evening. Enjoy the moment and realize just how far we'd all come.

One of the first faces I saw when I walked into the reception that evening was Martin Simons. Although Richard Murray was the chairman of Charlton Athletic plc, Martin was the chairman of the football company. Both he and Richard had put so much time, effort and money into the club since they first joined in 1991, and Martin was not only a Charlton supporter through and through, he was also probably one of the most sociable people you could ever wish to meet. He had boundless energy and enthusiasm for anything he did and loved life. Carol and I once went on a trip to Paris with Martin, his wife Leigh, Richard and his wife Jane. As you would expect, Martin knew all the best restaurants and was determined to sample them. After a long dinner one night with some great food and wine, everyone seemed ready for bed. Not Martin. Richard and Jane decided they'd had enough, but Carol and I somehow ended up drinking with him until about five in the morning at an Irish bar he knew somewhere in the city. The next morning I could hardly open my eyes, but Martin was as full of life as ever, and when I saw him he was tucking into his breakfast like a man possessed, but at the reception he looked shot to pieces. Several courses of French food, endless bottles of wine and several beers might not be a problem to Martin, but the Sunderland match had left him exhausted.

I sat there that night at the reception feeling really pleased not only for the people who had been directly involved on the day, but also for the people who I call the portakabin mob.

They are the people who went to Selhurst Park and Upton Park, the Nelsons, Gattings, Bolders, Walshes, Pardews, Leaburns, Websters, Balmers, Lees and Bumsteads of this world. I thought about a lot of little instances during those early years, when we had such a small squad and the players just had to get on with it. I smiled at the memory of the time I gave John Bumstead a real verbal blast at half-time during a game because he didn't go into a tackle and was letting a particular player on the opposition get away from him. Bummers went out and worked his socks off in the second half and it was only after the game that we found out he'd cracked his ankle early in the match – no wonder he didn't fancy going into any more tackles! There had been some great characters who had helped see us through and perhaps they had sat at home that afternoon and watched as we got promotion. I hoped they realized they had played their part as well. It wasn't just about what happened that day, it was about what Charlton stood for as a club and where we'd come from.

When the dinner was over we all went to the bar, but I still didn't really feel like having a drink and neither did anyone else – except for Clive. He had all of his family down for the game and they were all Sunderland people. It was funny seeing them stood there drinking with the man who had destroyed the dreams of a team he had supported since he was a kid. He really was a hat-trick hero that day and will never be forgotten by Charlton people because of it.

I walked out of the bar and up to my room. It had been an unbelievable day and I was exhausted. We were in the Premier League and after all the celebrations and euphoria that went with the win over Sunderland I knew that reality, in the shape of the new season, was only a few weeks away.

15 Getting a Taste

The day after the win over Sunderland was pretty hectic because a civic reception was planned for us and we travelled through the streets in an open-top bus with thousands of fans turning out to see us. Once again it was a great occasion for the club and the supporters, but by this time news of Les going had leaked out.

As I've mentioned, I didn't want him making an announcement the previous night, but one of my big regrets is that because of the way things worked out he was never given quite the send-off he deserved. Les did a great job during his time at Charlton with me and he made the decision to leave for all the right reasons. It was just a shame that things went the way they did because of the circumstances we found ourselves in, and there was no time for him to really go in the way I think we all would have liked. Les has remained a personal friend, he's also been a friend of the club, and was always welcomed back while I was manager. After I left, Les was brought back to the club as part of new manager Iain Dowie's coaching staff. His decision to join the FA back then proved to be a good one to begin with: he was in charge of helping to set up academies at Premiership and Football League clubs, and he was heavily involved at all levels. He also played a prominent role with the full internationals when Kevin Keegan called Les in during the time he was England manager.

Keith had found out about Mervyn coming in to replace Les, and I knew the situation could be awkward because Keith may have felt he would be the new coach, but I told him that I'd decided to bring someone in from the outside because the club was changing after getting promoted and I wanted someone new to come in. I also felt the role of assistant manager would be better suited to Keith. He'd really been doing the same sort of thing in an unofficial capacity while looking after the reserves and in terms of the coaching; he knew he would be involved with the first team anyway. Having got into the Premiership and with Les going and Mervyn coming in, I really did feel the focus was going to be on me more than ever before. It was going to be a very different ball game, and we didn't have too long to plan for it.

I feel a team that gains promotion through the play-offs is at a disadvantage because the season goes on longer, and the close-season is shorter. It gives you less time to bring players in and it also means you don't really know what sort of players you are going to be looking to sign simply because a manager will not know which division his club is going to be in until after the final. It was bad enough back then, but it must be even worse now because of the transfer window and the fact that any buying and selling has to be completed before the end of August, or you're left with having to wait until the following January before any more business can be completed.

After going on holiday early in June it was straight down to planning for the new season, and one of the first decisions to be made was exactly what was going to be done with the money we would get from being a promoted club. It was decided by Richard, the board and me that a third should go towards strengthening the team, a third should go into stadium improvement and a third should go into the bank as a safety net. It's a difficult time for a newly promoted club, because there are decisions to be made about how you are going to approach the season as a Premiership outfit. Some want to throw all their money into the team, while others, like Watford a few years ago, don't really spend anything. It's a gamble but all clubs who get promoted know just how difficult it's going to be to survive.

The win at Wembley had been tremendous, but the reality of it soon hit home that next day as we rode on the open-top bus, because less than 24 hours after beating Sunderland we were being quoted by the bookies as being favourites to be relegated from the Premiership. It's probably something every promoted team has to cope with, because when you get into the Premier League you start at the bottom of the pile. The teams who come up don't really have the financial clout to go and compete in the transfer market with the top sides, or even the sides from the middle of the table who are more established and have the structure in place to bid for certain types of players.

Usually teams who get promotion all tend to shop at the same store when it comes to trying to strengthen their squads. By that I mean that they will probably be looking at the better players from the division they've just left, or at players who are with clubs who have just been relegated from the Premiership. A promoted side might look abroad at players, but they will be restricted in that a lot of their targets might want too much money, or they won't particularly fancy playing for a side that have just been promoted and might be battling all season to stay in the Premiership.

When we got promotion in 1998 I knew I had to add to the squad that had taken us up, and I also knew I didn't have bundles of money to play with. I wanted a certain sort of player who could come in and fit into the set-up we had. I wasn't going to go down the foreign route, because not only would it have been too expensive, but the club didn't have the infrastructure or the scouting facilities for us to know very much about any of the players who might become available. I've never bought players on the strength of just watching a video of them in action. I always like to see them for myself in a match situation, and at that time I just didn't believe we could look at that type of transfer target.

I also felt I wanted players who understood what we were about as a club. Players in England would all have known about the way we beat Sunderland, and they would also probably be aware of the fact that we'd had to battle our way through from the dark days of not having our own ground. I have already said that I tended to sign players who are angry and hungry: they were desperate to be given a chance and had the sort of fire and passion I felt was needed. They had a point to prove and if they could prove it with Charlton that could only be good for the side. I recognized that we needed to get some Premiership experience into the squad, because the team that went up had precious little of it.

During the close-season I set about trying to sign players with those qualities for the start of the campaign, knowing we had very little time from the end of the match with Sunderland until we kicked off the new season. After a short break we managed to bring three players in during June in time for pre-season training.

Chris Powell had started his career with Palace but never quite made the breakthrough to regular first-team football with them. He moved on to Southend and began to develop a reputation as a very solid performer at left-back before getting a transfer to Derby. He'd played for them in the Premiership and had shown he could cope well enough with what the League had to offer. His style of play seemed right for the way I liked my teams to play and, as well as his defending, Chris had the ability to break forward with pace and to deliver good crosses into the middle. I'd liked him for a long time and once made an enquiry when he was at Southend and Peter Taylor was their manager, but the Essex club wanted too much money and we just couldn't afford the price. The Derby manager, Jim Smith, had decided he wanted to change things in his team and was prepared to let Chris go, but we had to break our own transfer record to get his signature, paying £825,000 for him.

I also thought that in order to compete and have a chance in the Premiership a team had to have the ability to score goals. We already had Clive, and Mark Bright had signed a new one-year contract, but at the age of 36 there was no way he was going to be playing in the first team week in, week out. Andy Hunt had proved himself as a goalscorer throughout his career and, having failed to sign a new contract with his club, West Bromwich Albion, he was available on a free transfer under the Bosman rule. He was a very good target man, an unselfish worker for the team and someone I knew I could rely on to do a job for the entire 90 minutes of a game. Once again it was a case of giving a player who was hungry the chance to show what he could do in a higher division, and the great thing from our point of view was that all he was costing us was his salary.

I had a bit of a doubt in my mind about the third big signing of that summer, purely because of Neil Redfearn's age. It was a bit of an extravagant signing in many ways because at the age of 33 I knew we weren't going to get anything like our money back if we ever wanted to sell him, but he'd just had a season in the Premiership with relegated Barnsley and managed to score 14 goals, 10 of them in the League, and we needed the kind of experience he brought with him. It was a chance to get a goalscoring midfielder into the squad, but it meant having to break our transfer record once again in order to do it by paying just over £1 million for him.

The pre-season went well and a week before the big kick-off I had a testimonial game against Hearts at The Valley awarded to me because I had completed ten years as a player and manager at the club. It was a boiling hot day and I think a lot of people were still on holiday, or just didn't fancy going to watch football. There was also the added problem of having one side of the ground out of action, because the West Stand was having its capacity increased and a new tier was being added. The end result was that the crowd figure for the day was just 7,211, which I have to admit I found a bit disappointing, particularly as we were just about to start playing our football in the Premiership for the first time. I had hoped originally that West Ham would provide the opposition, which I think would have brought another 3,000 or 4,000 fans. I thought a match had been sorted out but, although it may sound hard to believe, the Hammers manager Harry Redknapp and his assistant Frank Lampard forgot about the game. So by the time they were reminded of it the pair had already arranged their pre-season matches. The game with Hearts ended in a 1–1 draw, and it was a good workout for the team with the season's opener at Newcastle just around the corner.

We did well at St James's Park and showed that we weren't

going to be a soft touch. Our aim throughout the pre-season and in the talks we'd had with the players was to make sure we hit the ground running. We couldn't have asked for a more difficult game than the one at Newcastle, and it got even more difficult after what I thought was a bad decision by the referee, Dermot Gallagher, saw Richard Rufus sent off for supposedly catching Nikolaos Dabizas with his arm after only 25 minutes. It was similar to a lot of the decisions sometimes seen at the start of more recent seasons, when it seems as if some referees are on a mission to make some big decisions early on and then hope things settle down as the campaign progresses. Perhaps they should come into the season with a more laid-back attitude and then we wouldn't have so many games spoilt. That day at Newcastle saw a great team effort from us: we didn't buckle and came away with a 0–0 draw. The Geordie fans booed their team for not beating a newly promoted side with ten men. I think the game showed that we were going to make sure we had the right attitude going into the season, just as we'd planned in pre-season. Only 12 months earlier Barnsley had been promoted and they talked about making sure they were going to enjoy their year in the Premiership. We decided that wasn't for us and we wanted to emphasize to the players that when we went to big grounds like Newcastle it wasn't going to be just a day out.

A week later we had another special occasion at The Valley when we ran out against Southampton to play our first-ever home game in the Premiership. I don't think anyone would really have wanted to have played us on that day. Everyone was fired up and ready to go. It reminded me of the time we got back to The Valley and played Portsmouth. It seemed like there was only ever going to be one winner, but I certainly didn't expect the result to be so emphatic. We beat them 5–0 and, although it was only the second game of the season, the fact that we had scored five and not conceded any goals meant that we went to the top of the League for the first Premiership table of the season. It was great for everyone at the club and they even had T-shirts printed to commemorate what had happened. It was all a bit of fun and, despite the good start, I was under no illusions as to how hard it was going to be for us and what a long season lay ahead for everyone.

As if to emphasize the point our next game was against the champions Arsenal at Highbury. They didn't come much better than the Gunners but once again we showed real resilience and great character to dig in and come away with another goalless draw. So three games into the campaign we were unbeaten and hadn't conceded a goal, but it all changed dramatically in game number four when we went to Old Trafford and got beaten 4–1 by Manchester United. It was only the beginning of September, but already we had played away games at Newcastle, Arsenal and United. Welcome to the big time.

The thing I also remember about the United game was the fact that we stayed in a local hotel called Mottram Hall which, because of its great facilities, visiting teams often use when they play at Old Trafford. It also happened to be the place Jaap Stam was staying at, having completed a summer move from PSV Eindhoven. On the day of the game I was on my way to have some breakfast and passed Stam on the way. What struck me most was his physique, something which I believe has become a real feature of the Premiership over the years. The players are now real athletes, though I believe some are actually athletes first and footballers second, whereas ten or fifteen years ago it was probably the other way around.

As tough as it was I knew how much the players and everyone

connected with the club were enjoying playing in the Premiership. The whole experience was so different to what we had been
used to in the First Division. Going to grounds like St James's
Park, Highbury and Old Trafford was really what the players
probably loved most about the experience. They were playing
against the best in the country and the matches were watched
by sell-out crowds at some of the best stadiums around.

I think I was enjoying it all just as much as them, but it soon
became apparent that we were in a whole new ball game. One
of the biggest differences I noticed was the ability of other
teams to adapt and change their shape and formation. They
had the squads and players to let them do that. We started to
find quite often that if a team played a different shape to us and
they got one of their better players in a dangerous position,
invariably we were punished. It was simply because of the quality of player they had in their side and the fact that if they got
a chance they took it. Sometimes they didn't really have to
work for it, but if the ball fell kindly to a forward from the
opposition they usually scored, we didn't. It was the kind of
clinical play that you didn't really get in the First Division, where
you could quite often get away with things if an opposition
player was suddenly free with a chance to score. The standard
of play was better all-round. For example, in the Premiership,
you would get free-kicks on the edge of the box that went over
your wall and into the top corner of the net, something that
never seemed to happen in the First Division! We decided that
we would have to start matching up with teams, or in other
words adopt the same formation, in order to limit the sort of
chances they were getting.

On occasions throughout the season we found it really difficult to deal with, and because of it we got hurt several times

and came out on the wrong end of things. By the time October came around I'd decided I needed to try and bring someone in who would allow us to be a little bit more flexible if we had to be, and adapt during the course of matches if it was necessary. I went for defender Carl Tiler from Everton, who cost us £700,000. I knew that he could play centre of defence in a flat back four, but he was also able to play as one of the three centre-halves if I wanted to play five at the back.

We played a five-man defence in Tiler's first game for the club when we picked up our second win of the season with a 1–0 victory at Nottingham Forest. He actually got on the scoresheet two games later when we gave our home fans something to cheer about with a 4–2 win against West Ham. The match was on 24 October 1998, and that was as good as it got because unfortunately they didn't have too much to cheer for a very long time as we went on a terrible run of 13 League games and one FA Cup match without a win. The Premiership run also included eight consecutive defeats.

I've often thought about that run since and asked myself whether I should have done something negative tactically. Sir Bobby Robson told me some years later that if a team was having that sort of run he would play eight defenders, just to try and make sure that he stopped the rot and got something from a game. I never tried to be negative during all of it and I honestly thought the bad run was going to turn itself around. It's the worst sequence of games I've ever had and once again it highlighted the difference between the First Division and the Premiership. In the First Division you could lose two or three matches, but then the fixture list would throw up four or five teams who you had a very good chance of beating. In the Premiership that just wasn't the case, and that's why newly promoted sides can quite easily keep playing games and get into double figures without getting a win in any of them. They might get the odd draw, but those draws are not enough when it comes to the end of the season.

Unless you've been in that kind of terrible run as a manager it's difficult to understand just how it feels. With every week that went by I was trying to keep things together and stay level-headed, but the truth was my head seemed to be spinning for most of the time. I couldn't stop thinking about what was going on and the whole thing starts to take over your life. One minute you feel positive, have convinced yourself that things will get better and start to think more confidently about the situation, but it doesn't take long for the doubts and negative thoughts to creep in once more, as you question everything you are doing. Should you make changes to the team, do we change the way we play, are things going to turn around for us this week? They're the kind of thoughts that are going on in your mind 24 hours a day. We all know football is about results, but I've always maintained that the despair of losing is much greater than the euphoria of winning a match, and during the course of that run there was an awful lot of despair. It was an example of just how unforgiving the Premiership can be if you get into a bad run. With all due respect to the clubs, I knew that in the First Division over the previous years the fixtures would give you a chance by throwing up home games against the likes of Stockport, Crewe or Swindon, matches that you were well capable of winning. In the Premiership you could perhaps end up playing Manchester United, Chelsea, Newcastle and then Tottenham and Liverpool. Suddenly a team can find themselves going five games without a win.

The season proved to be a big learning experience for all of us, and I include myself in that. Perhaps I was a little bit too loyal to some players and maybe I should have left them out of the side at times instead of keeping them in the team. It was something I'd always done since taking over as manager. I had always given players a chance, even after they had bad games. I also I think there was also a reaction from some of the players in the squad who had helped us get promotion and then had not been able to hold down a regular first-team place. I'm sure some of them felt it was their big chance to play in the Premiership after all they had done for the club, and they weren't really getting a look-in. I could sympathize with them, because it was very similar to my own situation when I was a player under Lennie and we'd won promotion; because of injury I wasn't able to play and then, when I was fit, I couldn't get my place back after other people had come in and become first-team regulars.

Another thing I noticed that season was that we maybe suffered a little bit in matches because of the way we trained. The players at our club had always trained as hard as they played. That didn't seem to matter as much in the First Division, even though we actually had more games, but in the Premiership I think it sometimes left us a bit jaded and not as bright as we should have been.

As a manager one of the first things I always promised myself was that I would make sure no player in my squad would ever say that they didn't work hard enough as a team in preparation for a match. One of the worst things I used to hear when I was a player, particularly if the team was having a bad time, were other people saying all they ever did in training was play five-a-side or that they didn't do any tactical work. I made a vow no player of mine would ever be able to say that sort of thing about the type of sessions we laid on, and I think a big part of us being successful in the First Division was the way we trained and the fact that the players put so much into it. There was never any slacking and a lot of physical effort went into it, but in the Premiership that type of work can end up being counter-productive.

By the start of the New Year I'd added to the strikers by getting Swede Martin Pringle in on loan from Benfica with a view to signing him on a permanent basis, and in February I managed to add a genuine star name to the squad, when John Barnes signed until the end of the season.

John was at Newcastle at the time but when Kenny Dalglish left as manager early in the season soon after we had played Newcastle and Ruud Gullit took over, I think he found it harder to get into the team and we were alerted to the fact that he was available and wanted to go on loan to a club where he could play regular football. It was a tremendous chance for me to bring in someone who was not only a great player, but who also had real presence. I spoke to him on the phone and he was keen to come down and join us; the only trouble was I hadn't seen him play for a while and I needed to know about his fitness.

'Look, John, it's a bit awkward, but I've really got to see you play before I can make a decision,' I told him. 'Come down for a couple of days, play in a game and we'll take it from there.'

To his credit he didn't make any fuss and said he completely understood the situation. He was more than happy to train with us and play in the game. We arranged a special match against Peterborough behind closed doors at The Valley that we won 5–0 and signed him five days later. He hadn't played very much at Newcastle and it was important that he got some match fitness, so I asked him to play for the reserves just a couple of days after he put pen to paper. Mind you, I didn't really have the heart to tell him our reserve games were being played at

Welling. So the man who will always be remembered for his fantastic solo goal against Brazil, and who was recognized as one of the greatest left-sided players of his era, found himself heading for a non-League ground in the middle of winter to play in a Charlton reserve game against Cambridge United!

John had a great effect from the moment he walked through the door. Despite what he'd done in the game and all he'd achieved as a player, he was completely unaffected and fitted in easily. He also had the trappings of a successful player – it was probably the first time anyone had seen a car at the training ground that had video screens on the back of the headrest! He was 35 years old and although he may have lost some of his running ability, his football brain was first class and his skill was as good as ever.

On the day of the reserve game I told him to follow the minibus taking the kit over to Welling in the morning so that he would actually know where the ground was. I also warned him that when he turned up for the match in the afternoon he was going to find parking a bit of a problem, because of all the yellow lines around the ground. Keith and I made our way to the game and when we got there we saw John's 4 x 4 parked on the yellow lines. There wasn't really anywhere else close to the ground that he could have parked, and having to pay the price of a parking fine didn't seem to bother him too much. I think he just wanted to get out and play the match. He may have picked up a fine but at least the reserves managed to win the match 5–4.

From the day he signed for us our fortunes started to pick up a bit. He was paraded around the ground before a Monday night home match with Wimbledon and we ended up winning it 2–0. It put an end to the terrible sequence of results we'd had and on the following Saturday John made his debut against one of his old clubs, when he came on as a second-half substitute against Liverpool at The Valley and helped us record a memorable 1–0 win.

In the Premiership you've got to get into double figures when it comes to the number of wins you record in a season, and very rarely can a side hope to stay up and not get at least ten wins. In our next 11 matches we managed to pick up some draws, but recorded only one win. It meant that we weren't able to gather enough points to pull us away from the relegation zone, but as the season drew to a close we were still in there fighting and, with two matches to go, we went to Aston Villa for what turned out to be one of the most remarkable games of the year. We were both desperate for points. They wanted to get into Europe and we wanted to stay up

One of my other signings that season had been goalkeeper Simon Royce from Southend but, by the time the Villa game rolled around, I found myself with just one fit keeper in the squad, Andy Petterson. So we went to Villa Park with five outfield players as substitutes. Southampton were playing Wimbledon at Selhurst Park. We knew that if they beat the Dons we had to beat Villa in order to keep our hopes of staying up alive going into the last match of the season against Sheffield Wednesday at The Valley.

The Villa match seemed to have a real cup-tie atmosphere to it and we gave it everything. With just 11 minutes remaining we were winning 3–2 and looking as though we would be capable of hanging onto the lead. Alan Pardew had been doing some scouting for us that season and Keith had sent him to the Wimbledon match to keep an eye on proceedings and to let us know by mobile phone if anyone scored.

Everything seemed to be going well for us at Selhurst Park, because their match was goalless, but suddenly things changed in our own game. Julian Joachim equalized for Villa and then in the 80th minute Petterson was sent off for pulling down Joachim outside the penalty area. Not only were we down to ten men, we didn't have another recognized goalkeeper on the bench ready to take Andy's place. To top it all, at just about the same time as all of this was happening, Keith received a call from Pards to say that Southampton had taken the lead against Wimbledon.

The only real option we had was to send Steve Brown on as an emergency keeper and take John Robinson off. Brownie had put the gloves on before in his Charlton career and we knew he could do a job there. I later found out that the Villa match was the seventh time he's taken over in goal, and he actually set a club record in doing it, but I don't think any of that was going through his mind as we sent him on the pitch. As a player and as a character I knew I couldn't have a better person to have to rely on, but the circumstances that day were exceptional and we all knew how desperate the situation was.

The first thing he did was make a great save from a free-kick 20 yards out, and he also got his hands to the ball on a couple of other occasions to make sure the score stayed level. With Southampton in the lead and us drawing, I knew we had to go for it as the minutes ticked away. A draw was no good to us. We had to win to have any chance of keeping our hopes alive. With a minute of the game to go the match took another twist when Villa's Steve Watson was also sent off for pulling back Martin Pringle. It meant we had a free-kick 20 yards out and, before any of us on the bench had time to think about it, Danny Mills took over and smashed a shot into the net. There was no time for Villa to come back and we won the game 4–3. I later found out that just as Danny was about to take the kick Pards had phoned again to let us know Southampton had got a second, but in all the pandemonium Keith dropped the phone and was celebrating with the rest of us as the winner flew into the net.

After such an epic win and with a lot of press coverage going into the final match with Sheffield Wednesday, it was set up nicely for us to pull off the great escape act, but by half-time we already knew Southampton were beating Everton in their home match. We had gone into our game knowing that in order to survive we had to win and rely on Everton preventing Southampton from winning. The atmosphere around the ground dropped with the news that Saints had got another goal in the second half, and with 11 minutes remaining in our match at The Valley, Wednesday scored what proved to be the winner.

After just one season in the Premiership we had been relegated, but we'd got a taste of what it was like and we all knew we wanted to get back as quickly as possible.

16 **We are the Champions**

At most clubs the day after your final game will usually see the players assembled at the training ground for a bit of a get-together. A few things have to be discussed and dealt with, such as deciding on whether a particular player is going to be offered a new contract or not and releasing players on free transfers. I also liked to have a chat to the players who are going to be coming back for the start of the new season. John Barnes was one of the players I knew we wouldn't be seeing again. He'd only signed a short-term contract and his brief had been to try and help us stay up.

When John left on the Monday following the defeat by Sheffield Wednesday, he underlined the fact that he was a class act off the field as well as on it by making a point of standing up at the training ground and saying how much he had enjoyed his few months with us. He told the other players that he didn't think there was another squad around who worked as hard as they did, and there wasn't another club around who had gone through the sort of things we had. He finished by saying that he thought there was no reason at all why we couldn't go straight back up, and even though the season had just finished, I honestly think everyone in that room agreed with him. John had been superb during the time he was at Charlton and after saying his goodbyes to everyone individually and shaking all the players' hands, he was off.

Looking back on that season now I think it proved to be a turning point for the club. Obviously it wasn't nice getting relegated, but at the same time we had given it a real go in the Premiership and, had Wimbledon beaten Southampton instead of losing to them, things might have worked out differently for us. We had proved we could live with the big boys and Richard Murray certainly saw the whole thing as a beginning rather than an end. There was a real feeling that we could get straight back and that the next few years could see the club move to a new level.

Despite the relegation and what can so often happen to managers at other clubs in a similar situation, I honestly didn't think there was any justification for me being sacked and, to be fair, I don't think the thought ever entered Richard's head. Instead, he decided to offer me a new four-year contract. It might have seemed strange to some people outside the club, but it was entirely in keeping with the way Richard goes about things, and also with the plans he had for the club. I think he believed I deserved it, not only for getting the team up against the odds a year before, but also for almost keeping us in the Premiership as well. He knew I had always done what was right for Charlton in the past, even if it had meant having to sell players who were important to the team. He also knew that I always had Charlton's best interests at heart and I think he felt that the next four years could be the making or breaking of us as a club.

Having gone as far as we had it was important that Charlton kept on making progress. We may have just been relegated, but Richard saw a bigger picture and knew that we would be playing in the First Division with a much stronger squad than the one that had taken us to success in the play-offs. We also had the experience of a year's football in the Premiership, and that could only be good for us.

Years before I think our real ambition was to establish ourselves as a First Division team after all the turmoil the club had suffered but, having moved on since then and had the experience of the Premiership, things had changed. The approach was always going to be the same. Richard was never going to be the sort of chairman who spent money he didn't have. The club had grown and progressed because it had a solid base with people working for it who had a real commitment to Charlton Athletic. We had directors who were real fans and had put their own money in to make sure the progress continued. Getting back to the Premiership as soon as possible was going to be a key factor in that continued progress.

If we were going to bounce back at the first attempt I knew we had to have a squad of players in place that would be up there challenging from the time the first whistle was blown. One of the major ingredients of that squad was Mark Kinsella. He had been tremendous since signing from Colchester and had grown as a player just as Charlton had grown as a club. He was an inspiration as a captain and the players had real respect for him. Mark had proved that he could take the Premiership in his stride and he was also an established international for the Republic of Ireland. He was great to have around the place and there was no way we wanted to lose him, even though I knew there might be a problem.

When a club gets relegated from the Premiership, some of their better players inevitably become targets for other clubs. Usually those clubs have just been promoted and they are looking for players who have proved themselves at the top, but who might fall into the sort of wage bracket they can afford. I did it myself when I bought Neil Redfearn from Barnsley, but I was worried another club might come along and try to do the same thing with Kinsella.

We knew we had to act quickly to make sure that kind of scenario didn't occur and Mark was offered a new long-term contract. He was getting good money, though nothing like the salary some players in the Premiership were getting, and probably not as good as some of the Premiership clubs might have been able to offer him, but he also wanted to stay at Charlton. I think he recognized how good the club had been for him, and it had an effect on Mark's decision to sign a new deal. It was a really important signing for us and it enabled me to feel much more comfortable about planning for the new season. Mark signing was also another indication of the sort of loyalty there has been at the club over the years, and why there seem to have been been quite a few testimonials for players.

The good thing was that, unlike so many times in the past, we really didn't have to sell anyone. We could afford to keep the squad together and add to it rather than having to cash in on players, but after taking a call from Leeds manager David O'Leary one morning, we soon got into a situation of being made an offer we couldn't refuse.

David asked me if I would consider selling Danny Mills. I told him that I wasn't really keen to let anyone go and we didn't have to sell because we were in a decent financial position and wanted to build for the new season. Not long after that conversation I was with Richard driving through the West End of London. Richard's mobile phone rang and it was soon clear that the Leeds chairman, Peter Ridsdale, was on the other end of the line. I kept quiet and just listened in as Peter tried to discuss a bid for Mills. It was pretty obvious from what was said that our valuation and their figure were way apart, but soon after Leeds made an official bid for Mills. It started at something like £1.5 million and before too long it was £2.5 million.

It was a big fee particularly as little more than a year ago I'd paid only £400,000 for him from Norwich. When a big club comes in for a player he's not really bothered about the fees involved, unless he has something in his contract that says he's on a percentage of any transfer, but that never happens at Charlton. Almost invariably what does tend to happen is that the player has got wind of the whole thing. His agent probably already knows what sort of money the potential buying club is willing to pay his client and because of that the player becomes desperate to get away. Leeds were flying at the time they made their bid for Mills and, once we had accepted the inevitable, it was a case of making sure we did as well as we could financially from any deal.

We didn't have to sell Danny and we made it plain to all parties concerned that nothing was going to happen until we got the price we wanted. What started out as a £1.5 million bid very quickly escalated to a figure of £4,375,000. It was a huge fee, even though Danny was a good player and had done well for us. It was simply too good to turn down and it was a move Danny wanted to make. We were in the Charlton boardroom with Danny and his agent when we finally agreed to the deal. Once it had all been sorted out they left to travel up to Leeds and complete the transfer, and half an hour later Mark Kinsella turned up to sit down and sign his new contract. Danny had gone but I knew we had managed to secure the signature of a player who was going to be crucial if the club were to bounce back from the disappointment of relegation.

The fact that we had made the financial decision a year earlier to spend only a third of our promotion money on players left us in a very strong position. Perhaps if we had spent all of the £10 million and still got relegated we would have had to take some drastic action, and maybe Danny Mills would not have been the only player leaving. It meant that we never had to face the catastrophe some clubs have when they are relegated and have to sell to balance the books. In recent years clubs like West Ham, Sunderland and Leeds have gone down and had to sell their best players. That never happened to us. We were able to attack the First Division from a position of strength and that's not often the case.

The only new players to come in during the summer were goalkeeper Dean Kiely for £1 million from Bury and Greg Shields from Dunfermline for just over £400,000 to replace Mills. I also took John Salako on loan from Fulham and eventually signed him for £250,000.

We'd had problems in the goalkeeping department the season before and although Sasa had made such an impact when we won the play-offs he'd struggled a bit after that and I just felt we needed strengthening. Mervyn had taken a good look at Kiely and he had a lot of the sort of ingredients I like in a player. He was a good character who had played most of his career in the lower divisions but was very consistent. When I spoke to Neil Warnock, who was his manager at Bury, he told me he could count on one finger the number of times Kiely made a mistake during the course of a season. We knew Dean had a lot of ability and wanted to take the step-up in his career. All three players were really pleased to make the move to Charlton and saw it as a real opportunity.

There were a few people who left that summer as well. Brighty retired and started a new career in broadcasting. Bradley Allen went on a free transfer to Grimsby, having never really been able to get the sort of regular first-team run he wanted while he was with us. He was one of a few players we let go on free transfers, with Mark Bowen going to Wigan, Paul Mortimer moving to Bristol City and Andy Petterson being signed by Portsmouth. Neil Redfearn headed north once again after a season with us, when we sold him to Bradford for £250,000. They had just been promoted to the Premiership and, although he didn't know it at the time, Redfearn almost got a hat-trick. He'd already been relegated with Barnsley and ourselves, and at the end of that season just managed to avoid the drop with Bradford.

When I talked to the players through the pre-season period and we discussed the fact that we wouldn't be playing in the Premiership it was interesting to hear what they were going to miss most. It may surprise a lot of people to know that money was not at the top of their list. Quite obviously finances came into it, but they all said that the things they would miss most were the stadiums, the atmosphere and playing against the best players in the country.

I knew we would miss the Premiership and everything that surrounds it, but I also knew we had the nucleus of a really good team. Kiely in goal, Rufus at the back, people like Stevie Brown who could do a job in so many different positions. Andy Hunt up front, who had proved so dangerous in the First Division before, and then Robinson, Newton and Kinsella. Three players who showed they could do it in the Premiership and would be a real handful in the First Division. We also had Graham Stuart in midfield, who had been signed for £1 million towards the end of the previous season as we battled to try and stay in the Premiership.

Before the new season started we sat the players down and set them a few targets, using a flip chart to emphasize the points we were making. We asked them how many wins they needed to get promotion and how many games they thought they could afford to lose. We told them they needed to win 26 of their 46 League games and that they couldn't afford to lose any more than ten matches. We also set individual players some personal targets. We felt that players like Newton and Robinson were capable of contributing with their goals, and we told them what they should be aiming for.

We also knew what we were getting into because we'd only been out of the First Division for a season. We knew the routine and the fact that we'd have to play three games in a week at certain stages. We were prepared for the long trips to some games and that we wouldn't be playing in the best stadiums any more. We knew what we were in for, but we also knew that we had a team capable of bouncing straight back, mainly due to our strong financial position.

We started the season with two home games and won both of them, beating Barnsley 3–1 and Norwich 1–0, but then we went to Fulham and played a match which I think helped set the tone for the way we approached the rest of the season.

Craven Cottage is a nice ground right by the Thames, but I've always thought it was a bit strange the way you have to walk from the dressing rooms in one corner of the pitch right across to the dug-outs on the other side of the field, and on the way go past your own supporters who are to the left as you come out. On that particular day we didn't play at all well and were beaten 2–1. I wasn't happy about the way the team had performed: we looked lethargic and seemed to think we only had to turn up in order to get a result. When the final whistle went I decided to give them a bit of a 'blast', but instead of doing it in the privacy of the changing room I told them to stay on the pitch, mainly due to the fact that the dressing-room area is not the biggest and is a bit uncomfortable, but I wanted our fans to see it as well. So as the Fulham players trooped off the field I sat my team down in front of our own supporters who were still waiting to get out of the ground.

I wanted to let the players know how I felt, but I also thought it was important to let the fans know how I felt and emphasize to the supporters the fact that we were going to be giving the season a real go, with the aim of getting promotion at the end of it. The players stayed on the pitch and had an after-match team talk there and then. I went round to each one individually and told them what I thought of their performances in front of the fans, and I think they could tell from the body language that there was a rollicking going on. I think I needed to do it for myself, by getting my feelings off my chest, the players needed to be told the performance just wasn't good enough, and our supporters needed to see it.

There seemed to be a big response after that and I somehow felt I had the right formula to get out of the First Division. I knew you had to go to certain places and do certain things in the division in order to win matches. I think a lot of teams who are relegated with players in their side who have only really known the Premiership get a bit of a shock. We knew where we were going and knew the grounds. At that time I probably knew more about the First Division than I did the top flight, because we'd spent so many years in it.

I knew I had the right ingredients in the team to compete and win games. We had the ability as a side but for us to go up the attitude had to be spot on as well, and after that Fulham match I think it was.

Certain things may have changed for us. For example, we were able to take a flight to some games. The club were prepared to take the cost of something like that on the chin because it was seen as a worthwhile expense if we got the results we wanted.

We started to get results against the teams you needed to beat and draws against others. There were some defeats along the way, but in general I was feeling happy in early December when we went to Oakwell and got a draw against Barnsley and then took another point in our next match at QPR.

After the game against Barnsley their manager Dave Bassett, who I've got to know well over the years, told me that he'd been offered the Blackburn job following the departure of Brian Kidd. He had decided to stay because he felt a sense of loyalty towards Barnsley, who had given him a job when he was out of work, but he'd recommended me to the Blackburn board. Obviously I was flattered but at the same time I couldn't understand why Dave hadn't taken the job. Perhaps right through his career some of the loyalty he'd shown towards Wimbledon and Sheffield United had ultimately hindered his career. Dave has done fantastic work but whenever the really big jobs came up, his name was never really in the frame. He has said to me on several occasions that perhaps I'm the new Dave Bassett, because just like him I had stayed at a club for a long time. Nothing really came of his recommendation and Blackburn eventually appointed Graeme Souness.

What none of us could have known at the time was that the 0–0 result against Rangers at Loftus Road was to be the last time we failed to win in the League until early March. After beating Palace 2–1 at The Valley on Boxing Day we went on an incredible run that saw us win another 11 matches on the spin. We went from strength to strength at the top of the table and our form introduced a fear factor in other teams a bit like Reading during the 2005–06 Championship season.

It was a complete turnaround to the kind of form we'd shown in the Premiership the season before, when we had that terrible run. It was also so different mentally for me. A year earlier I experienced the despair and turmoil that a bad run can bring. This time the feelings were so different and the contrast was amazing. Any minor upset off the field the season before had seemed like a major problem; this time around nothing seemed to get in the way and anything that did go wrong was easily dealt with. When you're losing, small problems become big problems and there seems to be a cloud following you around. When you're winning it's as if the sun is shining on you all the time and the atmosphere at the training ground is so positive and bright. A good run is there to be enjoyed and we certainly enjoyed it that season.

We also had a good FA Cup run, beating Premiership Coventry along the way before losing 1–0 in the quarter-finals at Bolton. Although the Charlton fans always craved a good Cup run during my time at the club, and we really should have got something from the game at Bolton, I knew there was a more important encounter coming up. Two weeks after that Cup defeat we went to the Reebok Stadium again for a First Division match and this time beat them 2–0 thanks to goals from Martin Pringle and Andy Hunt. I came away from that game thinking we'd won the right match. The League was always our priority and getting three points was more important to me than getting through in the Cup because we wanted to get past that finishing line.

Realistically we all knew the run had to be halted by someone, but not many of us thought it would be in a home game against Swindon, a team who eventually finished bottom of the table. They beat us with the only goal of the game despite us battering them for most of the match but, even though we suffered a defeat, the great run meant we still had a 12-point lead over second-placed Ipswich.

There was no way any of us were going to start counting our chickens before they were hatched but, with only 11 games of the season remaining, it's safe to say we were all pretty confident that we could get the automatic promotion place we were aiming for. I had reinforced the squad during the course of the season, bringing in Andy Todd from Bolton and striker Matt Svensson from Palace, and we had a good group of players who had put an awful lot into the season during that great run of games. We owed it to ourselves and to our fans to make sure we did the job right and didn't make any slip-ups.

Andy Todd was a very good footballer who had played in the Premiership before with Bolton as a centre-back or holding midfield player. I'd heard that Bolton were willing to off-load Andy after he'd had a bust-up with their assistant manager Phil Brown. I also knew his dad, Colin, having played in the same Birmingham team with him. In fact, I'd actually met Colin and Andy on holiday during the summer and the three of us had a few conversations about the game and the fact that we had just been relegated. I certainly didn't think at the time that I'd be in a position to sign him a few months later, but when the opportunity arose I knew I would be bringing in a quality player. I'd tried to sign Svensson when he played for Portsmouth some years earlier, only for agents, the changing fee and other things to get in the way. I saw him as the sort of player who could help give us the push we needed as we aimed for promotion. I was happy to bring both of the players into the squad, and knew they would be good enough to stay with us if we got to the Premiership.

But as the season began to reach its climax we began to stutter a little bit. Automatic promotion was there for the taking, but instead of getting the wins we needed we kept on drawing games. We were at the top of the League and had recorded some good wins over Grimsby, Palace and QPR. It meant that we had a lead of 16 points over Ipswich and Barnsley, but then we drew at Port Vale and Forest. We broke a club record by reaching our highest points total in the league after the Forest game. The draw gave us 89 points, one more than we'd got a couple of seasons earlier when we came up via the play-offs, but we were still looking for the elusive win that could make all the difference and send us up with games to spare.

We had a great chance to seal everything when we played Steve Bruce's Huddersfield in a live TV game on a Friday at The Valley, but mucked things up yet again and finished as 1–0 losers. At least the results went for us that Saturday and we had another chance to make sure we went up when we played Portsmouth at home in our next match, another live Sky TV game on Good Friday.

I knew it was going to be a tough encounter for us because Tony Pulis had recently arrived as their manager and the new Portsmouth chairman, Milan Mandaric, had big plans for the club. I read somewhere that they wanted to 'do a Charlton', something that has often been said in recent years when smaller clubs talk about their ambitions, but we hadn't actually done anything at that stage because we still hadn't managed to cross the finishing line. We drew the game 1–1 just to prolong the agony for everyone. It was so frustrating because for quite some time people had been talking about us being the champions in waiting. We all wanted to win the League, though the main priority was just making sure we were promoted, whether it was in first or second place, but we were making it tough for ourselves.

The draw with Portsmouth meant we went 11 points clear of Manchester City, and Ipswich were also in the chasing pack. Both of them were playing the next day. Merv was going to QPR to watch their match with Ipswich, but I decided to go to see Tottenham against Wimbledon, who were heading towards relegation from the Premiership. It was the same old thing: they had a few players in their side with good Premiership experience who I thought might possibly do a job for us if they went down and we went up. They would also have fitted into our wage structure and transfer budget.

I took my son Michael with me and with Spurs winning the match we decided to leave early to try and avoid the traffic. We were driving along the M11 and heading for home when the voice of football commentator Jonathan Pearce came booming through the car speakers telling all Charlton supporters to get the champagne out because we'd just been promoted. I had made a conscious effort not to worry too much about what the other teams were doing that weekend and I wasn't waiting on the results, but as things turned out, although City had beaten Tranmere, Ipswich had lost at QPR and as a consequence we were up. Once Michael and I heard the news we both punched the air in excitement, and for a few seconds we were travelling at about 70 mph without me having any hands on the wheel!

The mobile soon started ringing as Merv, Keith, Richard and Peter Varney all became aware of what had gone on. After all the stuttering of recent weeks we had finally made it over that finishing line. It was a fantastic feeling and also a huge relief to all of us.

The next day the players were all in at Sparrows Lane because we were travelling up to play Blackburn on the Bank Holiday Monday. There was a great atmosphere at the training ground as we shook the players' hands and then reminded everyone that, although we had got promotion, it wasn't over yet. We aimed to finish the season as the champions and make sure we had a trophy to show for all the hard work and effort everyone had put in during the course of the season. We wanted to beat Blackburn but once again could do no more than draw; the good thing was Manchester City were held to a 2–2 draw at Fratton Park by Portsmouth and the result meant we had won the League.

It was a marvellous achievement but in a strange way I was disappointed that we'd become champions at someone else's ground. Our fans who had travelled to the game celebrated and the Blackburn fans applauded us as well, but I felt very much as I had done on the Wembley pitch after beating Sunderland. The job had been done and I felt a great deal of satisfaction, but I wasn't going to go leaping around. I wanted to reflect on it all, and I knew I would probably enjoy the whole thing more the next day when it had sunk in.

It was all set up for us to celebrate in style in front of our own fans by beating Ipswich at The Valley five days later. The only problem was Ipswich were desperate to keep the momentum going in their own game as they battled it out with Manchester City for the second automatic promotion spot and, like it or not, the edge had gone out of our game. We trained well and prepared properly for the match but on the day it seemed to be more about celebrating than getting the three points. We wanted to win but we had already done all of our hard work and the players had done what they set out to do by winning the League.

I remember Richard Rufus playing a ball up to Andy Hunt early in the game and the Ipswich defender Tony Mowbray came steaming in, headed the ball, headed Andy at the same time and got a whack on the side of his face for his troubles. Mowbray just got up and dusted himself off before getting stuck into another tackle. From that moment I knew we were in trouble because they were desperate for the points and we didn't have the same sort of hunger on the day, eventually losing the match 3–1.

I just felt we'd spoilt the party a bit but I don't honestly think our fans worried about the result too much. They were happy to be celebrating winning the League and the fact that we were back in the Premiership again. When you think that many of them would have been the same supporters who were with us at Selhurst, Upton Park and in the early days of getting back to The Valley, you couldn't really blame them for enjoying the moment and maybe pinching themselves at the same time. Two promotions in three seasons – we were back with the big boys once again and this time we had to make sure we stayed there.

I would have liked us to have beaten Ipswich in that last home game of the season and really put on a show for our own fans, but it wasn't to be. It was strange because after the game there were no huge celebrations – we all just got in our cars and went home in much the same way as we would have done after any other match at The Valley. The big difference was that we knew the job had been done and we had been promoted.

Just to round things off we managed to lose our last match when we were beaten 2–0 by West Bromwich at The Hawthorns. It meant they avoided relegation and the defeat put an end to another record for us when our run of 16 successive away matches without defeat came to a halt. So after that magnificent run we had which ended with the shock defeat by Swindon, we'd managed to finish the season by failing to win any of our last seven matches. It was disappointing, but looked at overall I have to say that I could understand it. We had put an awful lot into making sure we bounced back at the first attempt and the consistent level of performance the players had given was magnificent. We had a really good squad who were focused, and determined to get into the Premiership.

17 England Expects

Despite losing that last game I was at least able to start enjoying the fact that we'd got promotion. One of the things which always happens at the end of a season is the League Managers Association dinner. It's a time when we can all relax because the season is over and the pressure is off a bit. A couple of years earlier when we had been promoted after beating Sunderland at Wembley I'd been given the Division One award for Manager of the Year, although I actually got it before we played the final. It's always nice to get an award from the people who do the same job as you and know exactly what it is like. They recognize what you have been through and know better than anyone if you have done a good job. Having had the sort of season we had just gone through, and with that run of winning games we managed to put together, the LMA gave me the First Division award again, and I was just as pleased to receive it as I had been two years earlier. I gave my little speech and then sat down again at our table to wait for the big award of the night, the overall manager of the year.

Richard Keys from Sky TV was acting as master of ceremonies and he read out the list of candidates which included Sir Alex Ferguson and me. I fully expected Alex to get it as United had won the Premiership, but instead I suddenly heard my name being called out. Les Reed, who was on our table, nudged me and told me to go up and get the award, and as I made my way to the podium I remember feeling quite shocked but at the same time very pleased. It meant a lot to me and I suppose it just helped to underline what we'd achieved at Charlton that season had really made an impression on the people in the game. To bounce straight back from relegation is not an easy thing to do: I'd done it as a player with Birmingham, and now I'd done it as a manager with Charlton. I think the other managers realized how difficult it was. Winning the award when I was up against someone like Alex meant a great end to the season for me.

It was a really nice night for me and it just added to all the positive things that had happened at the club. We had been promoted as champions, we had money in the bank and the stadium was really beginning to come together. The trouble is it's never very long before one season ends and another begins. It's nice to reflect on the success you've had, but you soon start to think about the next season and what will have to be done during the summer. I knew I had a job on my hands and I knew we had to change in order to cope with the demands of the Premiership. I had players in the squad who were at the top of the tree when it came to the First Division, but might not be as effective in the Premiership.

There were areas in the side that needed strengthening and we decided as a club that we might have to push the boat out in the transfer market this time. In terms of the type of player we had I knew I needed to upgrade in certain areas. As I have already mentioned, the last time we got promotion the policy was to spend a third of any money we got on transfers, a third on the ground and then keep a third back as a safety net for what might happen during the course of the season. This time it was different. We decided to bring people in who could change a game for us, players who could make a difference. But it wasn't a case of spending loads of money and putting all of our eggs in one basket. We were in a good position financially and still had most of the money from the Danny Mills transfer. We also had the prospect of increased revenue because of playing in the Premiership once again, but we knew we had to spend any transfer money wisely.

There were also a couple of familiar faces who left in the summer of 2000. Anthony Barness went on a Bosman and joined Bolton, while Keith Jones, at the age of 34, moved on a free transfer to Reading. Keith had epitomized everything that had gone on at the club during his time with Charlton. He was never any trouble and always did a great job for me. The nice thing was the fact that he had got to play in the Premiership with us and, although he hadn't been a regular in the team that season, he always did a good job whenever he played. Perhaps my favourite memory of Keith during that Premiership season was the game we played against Middlesbrough at The Valley. We asked him to do a man-to-man marking job on Paul Gascoigne, and Jonesy carried out our orders to the letter. So much so, that when Gazza ran over to the Middlesbrough bench to change his boots, Keith ran over with him and stayed only a few inches away while Gascoigne tied the laces!

That summer we spent just under £10 million on four players: Claus Jensen from Bolton, Jonathan Johansson from Glasgow Rangers, Radostin Kishishev from Litewts Lovech and Karim Bagheri from Piroozi, who we felt we could take a bit of a gamble on. By November we had spent another £700,000 on defender Mark Fish from Bolton.

I didn't want to go down the same sort of route we had two years earlier. At that stage in the club's development we could almost afford to drop down into the First Division and then come back even stronger. This time I think we all knew that it was really important to stay up and then try and build on things. If we wanted to continue to grow we needed to keep the momentum going and make sure we competed in the top League. Each season there are only 20 teams who can do that, and having worked so hard to get there a second time in the space of three seasons, we wanted to stay.

It's never easy for a newly promoted club in the Premiership. I've already said that you are immediately installed as the favourites to go down, but it's more than just that. The whole aspect of running the club takes on a new direction. Everything becomes bigger and the amount of media attention given to a club, its chairman, manager and fans grows overnight. We'd had a taste of what it was like two years earlier and that was good preparation for what we could expect the second time around, but it's still a bit of a shock to the system for everyone involved.

Having experienced the sort of season we'd just had, our fans had got used to being happy most Saturdays because we were winning a lot of League matches, 27 in all. We only lost nine league games during the course of the whole season, but that all changes in the Premiership. Your supporters have to get used to the fact that an awful lot of their Saturdays will end with their team either losing or drawing games.

The big thing for any promoted club is to aim to get to the 40-point mark in the Premiership. That should guarantee you are safe, although there are exceptions – just ask West Ham who were relegated with 42 points a few years ago. If a newly promoted side can win 10 games, draw 10 games and then lose the remaining 18, they are almost certain to stay up and the job has been done, but losing virtually half of your matches and winning less than a third of them is a very different proposition to playing in the old First Division or Championship as it now is and romping to the title. Your fans, especially those who perhaps go to just the home games, may only see you win a handful of matches whereas in the previous season they will have been watching you win virtually every Saturday. It can take some time to come to terms with it all, but realistically the aim of any newly promoted team must be to survive in that first season.

When you look at what is facing you I think it's important to set realistic targets and not get carried away with the fact that you've just been promoted. Obviously the fans are looking forward to watching their team play against all the big sides and, as I've already mentioned, the whole atmosphere attached to the Premiership tends to lift everyone associated with the club. The reality for a promoted side soon kicks in when the fixture list comes out in June, and when a team tries to bring in some Premiership players to strengthen their squad.

As a manager you look at the division and know there are probably four different categories of team in the Premiership. There are the top sides like Chelsea, Manchester United, Arsenal and Liverpool. There are also other big clubs like Everton, Newcastle, Villa and Tottenham who are trying to get into that top bracket. Then there are the clubs who have established themselves in the top flight over the past few years like Middlesbrough, Fulham, Bolton, Blackburn and maybe these days Charlton. Finally there are the others who might be involved in a possible relegation battle, and almost certainly the newly promoted side will come into that last bracket.

When you look at the top four it's realistic to believe that you are unlikely to get anything from them. That's eight matches where your team could get beaten home and away, and none of the others are going to be easy either. You could quite easily lose three games on the spin and then find yourself playing against the likes of Arsenal and Chelsea. Suddenly you've lost five consecutive matches, something that would never have happened a year earlier. That formula of winning 10, drawing 10 and losing the rest is a really hard target for anyone going into the Premiership. A glance at the Premiership table when a season comes to a close will show that the relegated sides probably only win seven or eight of their matches.

That's why surviving is such a huge achievement: it means you can continue to grow and the money involved is huge, both in terms of what a club can expect to gain in revenue and what they will have to pay out to players. I've often said that I'd like to be a fly on the wall when a newly promoted manager has to sit down and try to negotiate a deal with an established Premiership player and his agent. The difference in salaries and the sums involved are mind-boggling.

Having had that year's experience I think we were better prepared as a club for what lay in store. We understood the routine of it all and how it was important to plot your way through a season. We were better off financially than we had been the first time around, but we were by no means able to compete with the big boys. When you know that clubs like Man United and Newcastle can pull in crowds of more than 75,000 or 50,000 every time they play a home game, and Charlton's capacity is just over a third of that, it becomes pretty obvious that in the Premiership size does count.

It was always Charlton's intention, and still is, to increase the capacity at The Valley, but it was put on hold for that first season back, because we realized that the only way things could be improved off the pitch was by having success on it, and as far as we were concerned in that summer of 2000 success meant finishing fourth from bottom.

In terms of our preparation that year things went well in the pre-season period, but there was one very tragic exception which left everyone at the club with a sense of disbelief and shock.

As part of our training we arranged to go on a short West Country tour and based ourselves at St Mellion Golf and Country Club, which had good facilities and a lovely golf course. The idea was that it would serve as the rest and relaxation part of a team-building and training exercise. We were also due to play three matches and, although it was a first-team squad trip, we decided to take along one of our promising young academy players, Pierre Bolangi, a left-back with a promising future. He originally came from the Congo and lived with relatives in Canning Town. I suppose that because he came from my neck of the woods I had a little bit of an affinity with him.

When I told him he was going with the squad I don't think Pierre could believe it. He had the greatest smile you have ever seen on a kid and he was beaming from ear to ear from the moment we set off until the day we arrived back at the training ground. Because we were all flush with money, having got our bonuses from the successful promotion season, the first-team squad had a whip-round for him, knowing that coping with some of the prices at St Mellion might be a bit beyond his wages as an academy player. He was a real joy to have around and everyone took an instant shine to him.

You couldn't help but like Pierre, he was full of enthusiasm and clearly grateful for the chance football had given him. He was with us to do a bit of fetching and carrying for the senior players, but also to join in the training sessions. Right from the start he earned the respect of the players because of his footballing ability and he became a real part of everything that went on. Players very quickly come to conclusions about new people when they are introduced to a group. Within the first five minutes they will have made up their minds whether he can play or not, whether he's going to struggle or not and whether he is going to be accepted or not. Pierre wasn't afraid to join in and give anything a go, and was even happy to stand up at dinner and blast out a song for everyone.

We all stayed in lodges with four or six players sharing, but it was a bit of a trek from the dining room to our accommodation. Some of the players decided to cut down the journey by hanging on to the golf buggies they had used on the course during the day in order to ferry themselves back to their room. The manager of the golf course got to hear about this; although he wasn't really upset and it was all in good fun, I thought it would be a good idea to walk to the lodges and have a word with them. The first person I saw driving a buggy was Pierre. He didn't know what to do and wasn't sure whether to stop, duck down behind the wheel or run for it. But through it all he gave me that great big grin of his, and I couldn't help smiling along with him. The players had sent him off on an errand and I think he was probably more afraid of letting them down than he was about the prospect of bumping into me.

He thanked everyone on that trip for letting him be there but the truth was, not only did he deserve to be included, he also helped to brighten the whole experience for everyone else with his personality and enthusiasm.

Not too long after that we went off to Denmark to play a first-team pre-season friendly against Lyngby, the team who had originally sold Claus Jensen to Bolton, and after flying back we were waiting to collect our baggage at Stansted Airport when I took a call on my mobile phone that left me absolutely stunned. Pierre Bolangi was dead. He had taken part in an exercise at an army-training base in Aldershot with the other academy kids and had drowned. It was a totally shocking piece of news and when I told the others in our party the sense of disbelief just grew.

Standing there in the airport I didn't know anything about the incident other than the fact that it had ended in tragedy with the death of Pierre, but it immediately reminded me of the time I'd been part of a Charlton party that trained with the Marines during our pre-season preparations when I was a player and Lennie was the manager. At the time it was fashionable for football clubs to take time off for a bit of a toughening-up session with the army. It was good fun and we got involved in things we would never normally do. At the same time I think the PE instructors with the Marines enjoyed the prospect of making sure they got a group of professional footballers fitter.

Some of the routines we did were quite difficult. We went on a group run one day wearing dungarees and trainers, and after about ten minutes we reached a small pond that we had to cross by hauling ourselves over it holding a rope which was only inches above the water. We all got soaked and then had to jog on after we reached the other side. It was quite tough but we found out that when the Marines do it they have to carry huge back-packs and a rifle. I also recalled literally being flushed through a huge water-filled concrete tunnel. You were pushed through by a Marine and then had to swim for one stroke before being dragged out at the other end by another Marine. Because Robert Lee was so petrified at the prospect he opened his eyes at the wrong time and had his contact lenses washed out by the dirty water. There were several more obstacles after that, including some rope climbing, before we finally finished the run.

We later found out that in poor Pierre's case he had struggled to swim across some water along with some of the other boys and had gone under. It was a terrible tragedy and, although they survived, some of the other young lads who were on that same training exercise understandably had to have counselling. I think we all had trouble coming to terms with what had happened and there was no way we could train on the day after we got the news. We all turned up at the training ground but we cancelled training because of the sombre atmosphere and actually gave everyone the next day off as well because it had hit everyone so hard. It was all so terribly sad and it was also something that should never have happened. Some time later an army fitness instructor was charged and convicted of manslaughter because of the incident.

It meant very little in the scheme of things but in my own mind I was glad that, just a short time before his death, young Pierre probably had one of the happiest weeks of his life on that West Country trip. In such a short period of time he managed to leave a lasting impression. When I think of him I remember that smile of his, and as a lasting memory the club have his picture hanging in the reception area of the training ground.

An incident like that puts everything into perspective. As we formed a circle on the pitch before our opening Premiership game at home to Manchester City, and stood for a minute's silence remembering Pierre, I honestly think it was all some of the players could do to keep themselves together and not break down. The atmosphere during the match itself was very positive and, similar to our home game with Southampton a couple of seasons earlier, there was only going to be one winner, as we beat City 4–0.

It was the perfect start but we then had a setback in a midweek game at Everton where we not only lost the match 3–0 but had Carl Tiler sent off for a double booking after an incident involving Mark Hughes. Although we lost the game I thought we played really well, especially as we only had ten men for more than an hour of the match .We drove back that night after the match and didn't arrive at our training ground until about four in the following morning.

A few days later we had a real ding-dong of a match at Highbury against Arsenal, scoring three goals but letting in five; at 3–3 we had some great opportunities to go into the lead only for Arsenal to go on and grab two more goals themselves. Arsenal had scored their fifth with just a minute of the game remaining when we were chasing the game.

What I'd noticed was that we were not only chasing the game at that time, we were also exhausted and I knew we had to plan some of our away trips differently. To play on a Wednesday night at Goodison against Everton with only ten men for most of the game, and then arrive home at four in the morning little more than 48 hours before going to Highbury, was not ideal preparation in the Premiership. We'd flown to some of the games in the previous season if it was a really long trip to somewhere like the north-east, but for the rest of the time we'd used a team bus. I decided that things had to change and we would fly to any game that would have involved a lengthy road journey. It may cost more to fly, but it meant we would be able to get back sooner after a match, and allow us to prepare for the next game with a better rest period in between.

The Arsenal match was a bit of a learning experience for us because not only did we put in a good performance, we never really knew whether it might have been even better had we felt fresher going into the game. We then drew at home with South-ampton and got another draw in our next game when our match at Pride Park against Derby ended 2–2, but unfortunately I will always remember the day for other reasons and the shock I received.

After the game I was standing by our coach outside the main reception area when I saw Martin Simons and, win lose or draw, you could always rely on him to lift your spirits. If you'd lost or drawn a game he'd tell you not to worry and pick out all the good bits from the team's performance, and if we'd won he was ready to make sure you celebrated and to tell you what a great performance it was. On this particular occasion Martin looked a mess. I'd never seen him like that – he just looked shell-shocked and drained.

'I've got some bad news,' he told me.

I knew Richard Murray wasn't at the match when I took my seat in the directors' box because he usually sat next to Keith and me during a game; I thought it was a bit strange that he was missing, but there was no way I would ever have guessed the reason for his absence. Martin told me that Richard's wife, Jane, was in a coma. Apparently she had been at home having breakfast and had been stung by a wasp. As a result of the sting she had suffered what is known as anaphylactic shock, causing damage to the brain. The news was incredible.

Only a matter of weeks before I had seen Jane at a barbecue that Martin used to regularly hold at his house each summer.

She was really happy that day, and things were going so well for her and Richard. His businesses were a success, the club had just been promoted and everyone was having a great time. That was to be the last time I was to see her. The brain damage caused by that freak accident saw her remain in a coma for almost three years before she passed away in July 2003. Jane was a lovely woman and when she was happy, so was Richard. She became such a part of things at the club and had a great personality.

I can recall going over to see Richard at his house one year, just after the season had ended. We were sitting in his garden going through all the usual stuff with regard to contracts for players and possible transfer targets during the summer, but he'd also asked me over to talk about a new deal for me and we were haggling over the details. Jane was pottering around sorting out her plants and overheard the conversation Richard and I were having.

'Richard, why don't you just give him what he wants?' she suddenly said, and then wandered off to get a bottle of champagne from the fridge so that we could all have a drink.

It was typical of her and also of the relationship she shared with Richard. She was a massive part of his life and I still find it difficult to understand how he managed to cope so well in the years that followed the incident. Richard spent most of his hours at Jane's bedside and explored every avenue open to him in an effort to give her the best medical attention there was. At the same time he was running his businesses and our club. His life had been dramatically changed in the space of a second or two, but he somehow managed to hold everything together. It was hard to know what to say to Richard. Jane was in hospital with no real chance of recovery and it was often difficult to get to grips with feeling so helpless.

On the pitch the team were beginning to adapt to the rigours of the Premiership as I'd hoped they would. Jonathan Johansson began to find the back of the net and we remained unbeaten in the League during September, a five-match run that included a win over Tottenham at The Valley and another at St James's Park against Newcastle. We also had a 2–2 home draw against Coventry at the end of the month, with Andy Hunt netting one of our goals. Incredibly it was to be the last first-team game he played for Charlton and at the end of the season he had to retire, having been diagnosed as suffering from post-viral fatigue syndrome.

When he came off the pitch against Coventry, Andy was completely shattered. Physically he had no energy and even putting a tracksuit top on as he sat on the bench proved to be a real effort for him. It was hard to comprehend what was happening to Andy but it seemed, right from the time he started pre-season, that although he was improving his fitness levels it was taking him much longer to recover. He was never really able to catch up with himself, because he had to keep pushing his body harder without it ever having properly recovered from the previous day's training. We later found out that he was sometimes so exhausted that he'd go straight home to bed after training and not wake up until the next morning. We had no alternative but to make sure he rested and did nothing in the hope that his condition got better, but it just never happened.

It was a terrible shame for Andy and a real blow to the squad. He did a great job during his time with the club and scored some vital goals for us, netting 24 times in the League during our promotion season, and at the time of the Coventry game he'd already scored four goals in eight games. It was difficult to know how we were going to replace him and he was another one in a line of vital Charlton players who have had their careers cut short because of illness or injury and who were forced to retire. When he did have to pack the game in Andy decided on a pretty drastic change of scene, setting up a business in Belize.

As soon as we realized that Andy might be out for some time I tried to sign John Hartson from Wimbledon. He had gone from Arsenal to West Ham, where along with Paul Kitson, he had scored the goals to ensure Premiership safety for the Hammers, but then left Upton Park for Wimbledon, in what seemed to many people on the outside to be a strange move. We agreed a fee for the Welsh international striker, but failed to sort out personal terms with him and the deal fell through.

The decent form continued and by the time November came around we were comfortably placed in 12th spot in the League, which might have surprised a lot of people who had predicted we would struggle. There was also a bit of speculation in the press about the possibility of me having some sort of role in the England set-up. It all really started with the abrupt departure of Kevin Keegan as England manager. There was the usual talk about who would replace him and the fact that he went without any real warning signs took everybody by surprise. At the time nobody was really thinking along the lines of appointing a foreign coach, and so people were looking for English managers who might have had the right credentials. I think I was mentioned by a couple of people because I was English and managing a team in the Premiership, but realistically I was never likely to be asked.

Obviously it's flattering when things like that happen, but there was no way I would have been ready to step into the job at that time. I've always maintained that getting virtually any post in football coaching and management is all about the timing. You have to be in the right place, doing the right thing when the opportunity arises. You also have to feel comfortable about your ability to do the job in the way you would want to do it. When Birmingham were interested in me taking over as manager at the time Gritty and I were in charge at Charlton, quite apart from anything else, there was no way I would have been ready to go there at that stage in my managerial career.

It was the same with all the England talk and, anyway, I was never likely to fit the sort of profile the FA was probably looking for. If you are going to take charge of the national team, then being English and having a good record in management are not the only criteria as I was to discover some years later. Eventually Sven-Goran Eriksson was appointed and, although it raised a few eyebrows with some people, I could understand the reasoning. If the FA felt he was the best man for the job at that time, then I think they had to go for him. He had managed in Europe at clubs that had won things, had experience of handling top international players, and at Lazio he had enjoyed tremendous success. He'd not been afraid to spend money while he was at the club and perhaps the Italians had over-spent in their effort to chase a dream, but if the FA looked at what was available to them in this country at the time and thought there wasn't an English manager with the right background, then appointing a foreign coach was a brave step and I didn't really have a problem with it, although I think a lot of other English managers did.

In between Keegan's departure and Eriksson taking over, I think Technical Director Howard Wilkinson, the former Charlton first-team coach now back at the FA, Les Reed, and chief executive Adam Crozier, who was becoming more powerful at the time, had some sort of discussion about the appointment of Sven-Goran Eriksson and how the FA should be better prepared in terms of having English candidates available should there be a vacancy in the future. There was an idea talked about of possibly exposing some of the younger English managers to the international scene. I think it would basically have been a kind of observing role, where perhaps people like myself would get a chance to see what it was like and what went into preparing an England team. Not just the training and coaching, but also to learn about the infrastructure and logistics involved behind the scenes. I was mentioned as one of the managers who might be included in such a scheme along with the likes of Peter Taylor and Steve McClaren.

I thought it was a good idea but nothing really came of it. I know Richard Murray wasn't really keen on me getting involved in anything like that and I could understand his point of view. He thought I had a big enough task on my hands with Charlton in the Premiership and he didn't want any distractions. Peter Reid had told me once that he'd found it virtually impossible when he tried to combine managing Sunderland with looking after the Under-21s. I've always found club management all-consuming and it must be very difficult trying to take overall control of an international team for a week and combine that with being in charge of your own team. I know Steve McClaren was involved as a coach with the senior squad and was also the manager of Middlesbrough, while Peter Taylor combined managing Hull with coaching the Under-21 team. But coping with doing both jobs must be extremely hard work. Howard Wilkinson did speak to me at a later date about perhaps helping out with the Under-21s but once again nothing more happened.

I really did feel it would have been a good opportunity if Sven-Goran Eriksson had encouraged three or four younger English managers to be part of the set-up when he took over. After all, if a young English coach or manager had ambitions of one day taking charge of the national side, where was he supposed to gain the necessary relevant experience? He certainly wasn't likely to get Champions League experience at club level, because if you look at those English clubs who regularly take part in the competition, they are managed by non-English managers. So the only real way to gain some kind of international experience is to take your own club into Europe in the UEFA Cup. That's why I thought the idea of just being in the background of the England set-up, observing what went on, seeing the problems at first hand and getting a genuine understanding of what the job entails, would be such a good idea. Being manager of England is not just about picking a team and letting them play. There are so many other things in terms of organization and logistics that go along with it. The planning that goes on for a World Cup tournament must be immense and to get a taste of what was involved in that has to be important: things like hotels, training facilities, scouting, fitness and preparation. I think having three or four managers around the scene would have helped to prepare possible future candidates, and in the natural scheme of things one or two may have decided for one reason or another that it wasn't right for them, but at least they would have had some exposure to the international set-up. As things have turned out the FA did already have their man in place when it eventually came to replacing Sven, because Steve McClaren went on to become well established as part of the England scene before his eventual appointment as head coach in May 2006.

In early December we took part in one of the best games of

the season, when we came back from being 3–1 down in our home match with Manchester United, to eventually draw 3–3. It was a fantastic occasion and anyone who was there that day will always remember it. When John Robinson equalized with five minutes to go, you would have thought we'd won the FA Cup as The Valley erupted with noise from our fans. I think it really brought home to us exactly what the Premiership meant to a club like Charlton, and days like that make everything worthwhile.

There was also another game in December that I will always remember, but for all the wrong reasons, and that match certainly didn't make me feel as though it was all worthwhile. On Boxing Day we made the short trip to Upton Park for a derby match with West Ham. We were doing well in the League and had just beaten Everton 1–0 in a home game. The team were confident and everyone was looking forward to the match, but instead of carrying on the good form we got hammered by the Hammers and lost 5–0. The first-half performance was terrible and we were already three goals down when we went in at the break. I made a comment afterwards that I hadn't seen a Charlton side play like it before, or even train like it. It was a midday kick-off and there were a few others in London that day that saw the home side running out easy winners. It made me wonder whether there had been some kind of psychological advantage to kicking-off early in front of their home fans. We really were bad and the second half was only marginally better.

I knew things had to change and I had to do something drastic for the away match with Manchester City four days later. In many ways that game turned out to be a real turning point for our season and also the start of Scott Parker's career as a major player for us in the Premiership.

Scotty was one of five changes I made for the trip north and I let the players know exactly what I expected from them against City. The attitude and application had to be completely different to what had gone on against West Ham and, to be fair to the team, they did exactly what was asked of them and we came away with a thoroughly deserved 4–1 win. Parker looked particularly sharp and his play in midfield really added something to our game. I was pleased for Scott because he had been at the club since he was a kid and everyone knew he had bags of potential. Although he'd played in the first team before I had felt he wasn't quite ready to take the step-up on a regular basis, and Scotty had begun to get impatient. Earlier in the season I'd agreed to let him go on loan to Norwich and I think the experience did him good. He came back to the club more determined than ever to get into the first team and when he played against City his attitude was superb. After that match I knew we had a proper player on our hands who could be a real influence in the team, and having been on the outside looking in, he wanted to make the most of his opportunity when it came along.

The West Ham game also had an effect on another player, because after that result Chris Powell found himself out of the side. I've never been afraid to drop the so-called 'bigger' names in any of my teams and dropping Chris was probably just the sort of kick up the backside that he needed. He didn't play another full match in the first team until the end of January, against his old club Derby, when he came back determined that it wasn't going to happen to him again, and we won the game 2–1.

We followed that up with a goalless draw at Tottenham in a match that was watched by Sven-Goran Eriksson. I doubt that Chris thought much about the fact that the new England boss was in the stands but, soon after that game, when Eriksson named his first squad since taking over, Powell's name was the surprise inclusion. Even Chris didn't quite believe it at first, but I couldn't have been happier for him. He's not only a good player he's also a very nice guy and at the age of 31 he got the kind of reward and recognition that he deserved.

It didn't stop at just being called up because, when the team for the friendly against Spain at Villa Park was named, Chris found himself in the side at left-back. It was a tremendous honour for him and also for the club, showing just how far we'd come. Chris was the first Charlton player to figure in an England team since Mike Bailey played against Wales in 1964. I phoned Chris before the game and told him to take the whole thing in his stride. The way he had played for Charlton had been good enough to catch Eriksson's eye and get him in the England team; all he had to do was make sure he played his usual game. He did well against Spain and showed that he wasn't just a one-game wonder when he was picked again by the England manager and went on to play five times for the national team, only just missing out on the World Cup squad for the 2002 finals.

It showed that you could play for a smaller club like Charlton and still play for your country. It was great for the club and certainly lifted our profile nationally. It also showed that Sven-Goran Eriksson was going to pick people based on performances. I think a lot of people were perhaps surprised that Chrissy was picked to play for England, but I wasn't. Eriksson had a fresh approach to the job at the time and Chris was in great form for us. I said at the time that if you'd landed from outer-space, been made England manager and picked players from the Premiership purely on their performances, then there was no reason for Chris Powell not to be included in an England team.

I have already said that 40 points was the magic figure we were aiming for when we were promoted and incredibly we managed to reach that mark in the game that followed our draw with Tottenham, when we beat Newcastle 2–0 at The Valley on 11 February. It was a great achievement and it meant we could start planning for the next season knowing we were virtually guaranteed Premiership football. It was also a nice day for me on a personal level because I was given a gold watch by the club to mark the fact that I had taken charge of Charlton for 500 games, and it was presented by Bobby Robson and Richard before the game.

As I talked to Bobby on the pitch, I mentioned to him that the next landmark was probably reaching 1,000 games, and we tried to remember the managers who had achieved that feat. It clearly got him thinking about how many games he'd taken charge of and he was convinced he must have been up near the 1,000 mark. He kept throwing different names of managers at the Sky TV people who were filming the event, asking them how many games they'd clocked up and became more convinced that his tally was near the magic 1,000. But Bobby had failed to realize that we were talking about English club management and he'd had several years in his great career where he had been in charge of England and then managed abroad, which meant his total wasn't quite as high as he'd thought. It was a little incident, but it showed the passion he has for the game and how much football means to him.

I don't think anyone at the club, including myself, would have believed before the season started that we were going to be safe by the time we got to February, but it was no fluke. We performed well as a team and as a unit. The side had done all we had asked of them and then a bit more. The players who had come in had integrated well and upgraded the overall standard of the squad, and even when things went wrong, we seemed to recover from them. If we had one or two bad results, like the Boxing Day game against West Ham, we bounced back, and when we lost the services of Andy Hunt because of injury and I couldn't get John Hartson, we were able to bring South African Shaun Bartlett in on loan from FC Zurich and he chipped in with some important goals.

Probably the only real disappointment was the way we went out of the cup competitions. We were beaten by Stoke in the Worthington Cup, which was bad enough and we didn't exactly cover ourselves in glory when it came to the FA Cup. We were paired with non-league Dagenham and Redbridge in the third round. A week before the game we'd had that good win at Manchester City and just five days before the match we'd beaten Arsenal 1–0 at The Valley. Virtually the same side that had beaten the Gunners went out and played against Dagenham and Redbridge. We didn't prepare any differently for the Dagenham game; in fact, we had them looked at four times and also watched a tape of one of their games. The players were as prepared for the match as they had been for the Arsenal game, but the non-League side took us all the way and only a goal four minutes from time kept us in the competition as the game finished 1–1 at The Valley.

A giant-killing act was on the cards for the replay, but we managed to win it with a goal in the first minute of extra-time after being given a real scare. Over the two games Dagenham and Redbridge totally outplayed us. It's hard for a football fan to understand how things like that can happen, but they do. We were a hungry Premiership side who had to fight for everything we got, and certainly didn't turn up at games to give the opposition an easy ride. It was one of those things that can so often happen in the Cup.

After squeezing through following the replay, we went and blew things at home against Tottenham in the FA Cup. With 50 minutes of the game gone we were 2–0 ahead, but then let Spurs back in it and ended up going out 4–2. The Tottenham result was disappointing but we all knew that the season was about making sure we survived in the Premiership and in the end we did that with a bit to spare. There was even talk towards the end of the campaign about us possibly sneaking into Europe because we were going so well. That didn't happen but we still surpassed all expectations by finishing in ninth place.

Our last game of the season was a home fixture against Liverpool who arrived at The Valley having completed a fantastic treble, winning the FA, Worthington and UEFA Cups, but they were desperate to make sure they secured a Champions League place for the following season by beating us and did it with a 4–0 win. It was a very flattering score-line because the game should have been out of their reach by half-time and we could have been three goals up, but we didn't take our chances and paid a heavy price, and once they scored there was only going to be one winner. It was disappointing to once again finish on a bit of a low at the end of a season in which we had performed so well, but there was still a mood of celebration about the place. The roof of the covered end had gone to make way for the development of a new stand that would see three sides of the ground connected in a wrap-round design. It was difficult to come to terms with what had happened to the stadium in the space of just over eight years since the club had returned. Everything had moved so fast and along with the success on the pitch and the improvements off it, the expectation levels were beginning to rise as well. We were still little old Charlton to many people, but we would have a ground that would soon hold more than 26,000 and, because of what we had just done, those fans would once again be watching Premiership football.

I was delighted and proud of what had happened during my time as manager, but in the days and weeks that followed that game against Liverpool my loyalty and commitment to the club were to face a real test.

18 **In Demand**

Not too long after the game against Newcastle Richard came to see me and said that he thought it would be a good idea if we started talking about a new contract.

He said how happy everyone was with what had happened, and I think the fact that we had already reached the magic 40-point mark with 11 matches to go probably also meant that he could start planning ahead with a bit more certainty. We batted the whole thing backwards and forwards for a few weeks and finally came up with a new deal which I verbally agreed. I was happy at the club and I was a Premiership manager.

I looked around the Premiership and felt I was at the right club. If I looked at the big clubs I certainly couldn't see anything happening at them. Arsene Wenger was at Arsenal, Alex Ferguson at Manchester United, Claudio Ranieri was at Chelsea, Gerard Houllier had just had a triple-cup-winning season at Liverpool, Glenn Hoddle had just been appointed as manager of Tottenham and Harry Redknapp was apparently just about to sign a new four-year contract with West Ham, but about a week after agreeing the deal the papers were full of stories claiming that I would be leaving Charlton. The reason for all the speculation was quite simple: Harry Redknapp had been sacked by West Ham.

Throughout my time as manager of Charlton there had been occasional stories linking me with this club or that one. Of course it was flattering for me, and it obviously meant I must be doing something right if my name was in the frame whenever there was a managerial vacancy. The truth was that the only definite attempts to get me to leave The Valley had come from Birmingham and QPR. Richard knew that there might be speculation concerning me if a job came up, but he is the sort of person who deals in fact and not gossip. If a team made an official approach he would let me know, and if I wanted to go and the club who were interested in me was willing to pay the right amount in compensation, he would shake my hand and not stand in my way. I think Richard probably felt confident that I wanted to stay and be part of moving Charlton onto a new level. We had a great relationship and had been through the bad times as well as the good times that had come along in recent years. He knew I was a loyal person by nature, but I think he also realized that loyalty would really be put to the test if West Ham wanted me as their manager.

It would be stupid to claim that West Ham mean nothing to me. As a seven-year-old I remember cheering as I watched the TV and saw them beat Preston in the 1964 FA Cup Final and then the European Cup Winners Cup the next year. In 1966 I was cheering again as Bobby Moore, Geoff Hurst and Martin Peters helped England to their famous victory over West Germany, and danced around the house with the rest of the family. We were all Hammers fans and as far as we were concerned, West Ham had just won the World Cup. As a kid I could probably have joined any club in the country when it came to signing schoolboy forms, but I chose West Ham because they were my team. I came from Canning Town, and used to stand on the famous North Bank at Upton Park as a youngster. I have great memories of seeing Geoff Hurst score six goals as West Ham beat Sunderland 8–0 in 1968, even if he did punch one in with his hand, and I was also there the day the great Manchester United side came to Upton Park in 1965 and won the League. Even at that time I had a bit of a personal link with the team, because the Charles brothers, John and Clive, who played for the club, lived just 50 yards away from me, and the West Ham striker Clyde Best also lodged at their house for a time. A couple of other players, Kevin Locke and John McDowell, coached at my school. It was as if the whole thing was mapped out for me, and I eventually joined the club as an apprentice.

I had already been coached on Tuesday and Thursday evenings by Frank Lampard senior and when I joined West Ham there seemed to be plenty of people I knew, but I got the shock of my life after only a month with the club when I was named as a substitute for the game against Everton in August 1974. I remember going on the pitch for the pre-match warm-up and one of our footballs strayed into the Everton half. Joe Royle kicked it back to me and I remember thinking how big he looked and couldn't believe that if I got on I'd be playing against him. It was clearly a case of men against boys as far as I was concerned, and before the game Ron Greenwood told me that if I did go on he'd stick me between Billy Bonds and Trevor Brooking; all I had to do was play it simple. I never did get on but it was the start of my West Ham career and until Paul Allen came along I was the youngest name to be stuck on one of their first-team sheets.

I progressed from the youth team through to the first team, but never really fulfilled my potential. It's still a regret I have to this day. I was in the same England youth team as Glenn Hoddle,

Bryan Robson, Ray Wilkins and Peter Barnes and probably on a par with them, but it all went a little bit sour for me; as a 21-year-old I was a bit headstrong and took advantage of the new freedom of contract rule to move on to Birmingham. There was no point in me hanging around and not getting a game at Upton Park. I wanted to play first-team football, and if it wasn't going to be with the team I'd always supported it had to be with another club. But I also knew I would always have an affinity with West Ham and I really enjoyed being in charge of Charlton with Gritty when we had our spell playing at Upton Park because the place held such fond memories for me.

I would be lying if I said that the thought of one day being their manager had never crossed my mind, but that never made me any less loyal to Charlton. When Harry went it was almost 17 years after I had first arrived at a run-down Valley and had that sandwich with Lennie Lawrence after he'd signed me from Villa. That's an awfully long time and, with the exception of that relatively brief spell at Brighton, I had been a Charlton man ever since.

The speculation that I was going to replace Harry seemed to begin from the moment the news broke about him going. In the build-up to the Liverpool game I was constantly being asked about whether I'd be interested in going to West Ham and I was even asked about it by our own club's match-day announcer on the pitch after we'd completed a lap of honour following our last game of the season against Houllier's side. He asked me if I was going to leave Charlton and go to West Ham. I have to admit I was a bit taken aback by it, but I was more concerned with the fact that once again we'd ended our season by losing in front of our own supporters.

I went away with the Charlton vets team for a few days to

play a game in Spain, leaving all the speculation behind me, but it hadn't died down by the time I got back. It was then I discovered my postman was a West Ham fan and so was my milkman. They both wanted to know whether I was going to be leaving Charlton and going to Upton Park, as did a check-out assistant at one of our local stores. Carol was out shopping one day and when she handed over her credit card the guy took one look at the name and asked if she was my wife.

'Is he going to come to West Ham?' was his next question, and then kept her there for about ten minutes trying to get more information while the line of people standing behind her continued to grow. I got similar treatment from taxi drivers, but after a while it looked as though West Ham were going to go for Steve McClaren. I decided that instead of getting caught up in all the speculation I would get on with a holiday in Italy that Carol and I had planned. We were due to go for a week and the plan was that when I came back I would sign the contract with Charlton which was having the finishing touches put to it, but it was while I was out there that things took a new twist when a third party told me in no uncertain terms that if I wanted the West Ham manager's job it was mine. Suddenly I had an awful lot to think about and any plans of having a relaxing holiday went out of the window. Even with the offer of a new improved contract from Charlton on the table, I knew I could earn more from moving to Upton Park, but I also knew my decision was going to be about more than just money.

There was an emotional pull coming from both Charlton and West Ham. I was happy and content at Charlton. They had become my club and I felt we had both been through a lot together. Against all the odds we were now in the Premiership and had just finished ninth in the League after getting promotion.

The club was moving in the right direction and we'd all put so much work into what had gone on. West Ham might have been my club as a boy and I suppose in many ways I will always be a supporter, but I just didn't feel as comfortable about the prospect as I knew I should do if I really did want the job. When I came back from Italy the decision I had to make was whether to encourage the third-party stuff or not. In the end I decided I wanted to stay at Charlton. I believe that life is all about timing, and as far as I was concerned, once again I felt it wasn't the right time for me to move on.

I felt a move to West Ham at that particular time just wouldn't be right for me. With no disrespect to them, I got the impression it would be more of a rebuilding job that was needed there, and having worked so hard to get Charlton to the position they were in, I didn't want to walk away from it all. I had been through the scenario of having to sell my best players to balance the books. As things stood at West Ham, Frank Lampard junior was on his way to Chelsea, Rio Ferdinand had already gone to Leeds, and from the outside it looked as though the reason they had to do that was to balance the books. Perhaps they were living beyond their means and it was known at the time that West Ham had the sixth biggest wage bill in the Premiership. Nevertheless it was a very tempting situation for me, but I also enjoyed a certain lifestyle with Charlton. Living in Essex I was surrounded by West Ham supporters and my kids went to school with Hammers fans. That's fine when you are the manager of Charlton, but not so good if you are the West Ham manager and can never really escape from the job. But perhaps the bottom line was that I felt a sense of loyalty towards Charlton and all the people involved with the club.

I'd arranged to meet Richard in a West End hotel when I got

back from holiday, and the meeting was very similar to the one I'd had at his house a few years earlier when the prospect of managing Queens Park Rangers had come up. When I walked into the room I don't really think he knew what my decision was going to be, but I told Richard I wouldn't be going anywhere and signed the four-year contract we'd verbally agreed on before the whole West Ham situation arose.

A lot of people at the time said to me that I should have gone. They believed that it would have been a good career move and thought West Ham were a bigger club than Charlton. They pointed to the fact that I'd been at Charlton for a long time, perhaps too long, and I needed to show other people that I could go and manage another club. I could understand what they were saying and why they were saying it, but having made the decision I was comfortable with it.

It was the third real opportunity I'd had to take over as manager at another club but, like the Birmingham and QPR situations before, I decided to stay. West Ham went on to appoint Glenn Roeder as their manager, finishing seventh in his first season, and nobody could have been happier for them than me.

I think I've been lucky in most of my career as a player and as a manager because pretty much all of the major decisions have been mine. I've decided when it was right to move on when I was playing, and as a manager I made the choice to stay at Charlton on the three occasions when there was a definite possibility of me being able to move on to another club. Each time I knew that if things didn't work out I had nobody else to blame except myself, but I honestly believe that I made the right decisions over the years, and if there's one thing that has probably been the overriding factor in making those decisions it was loyalty. I know the club had faith in me when they gave Gritty and me the job and then again when Richard put me in sole charge, but I think I repaid that faith shown in me.

Having sorted out a new contract with Richard and signed the deal it was important that we didn't stand still as a club and a big part of that was making sure we continued to improve the strength and quality of the squad. We had spent a lot of money bringing in new players the previous season and knew we were going to have to do the same again. The fact that we'd sur-passed expectations by finishing ninth certainly didn't mean it was going to be any easier for us, and there was no way we could afford to stand still.

The first thing we'd managed to do that summer was sign Bartlett on a permanent basis. He had done a very good job since joining on loan and gave us a presence in attack which gave me options when picking the side and changing things if I needed to, but I still felt we were short on a bit of quality in cer-tain areas. A year earlier we had broken the record for a trans-fer paid by the club when Claus Jensen joined us from Bolton, and in July 2001 we broke it again by paying out £4,750,000 to Wimbledon for Jason Euell; we also spent just over £4 million getting Luke Young from Tottenham. Both of them had good Premiership experience and could play in more than one posi-tion for me. There was another summer signing that was a bit special for Keith, when his son Gavin joined us on loan from QPR as cover for Mark Kinsella, who picked up an injury before the first game of the season.

We didn't exactly have the best of starts when Everton came to The Valley and beat us 2–1. Things improved in the next game when we managed to put an important three points on the board with a 1–0 win at Ipswich, but the win came at a cost. Richard Rufus went into a full-blooded tackle with Marcus

Stewart and damaged his knee. It was an injury that was to keep him out of action for seven months, and it was a taste of things to come for me.

Ironically, Richard had just agreed a new four-year contract with the club and was due to sign it before the Ipswich match, but on the Thursday before the game when I asked if it had all been done he seemed a bit vague about the whole thing, so I insisted he go to The Valley and sign it that day. The reason was quite simple: it protected him in case of injury. I'd been in the situation too many times before and knew how worrying it can be for a player if he gets a bad injury and isn't sure about his future. We'd been haggling with Richard for a long time over a new deal for him and he finally agreed the details on the Tuesday before the Ipswich match. But on that Thursday when he told me he still hadn't signed I couldn't help thinking about Matt Holmes. I'd mentioned the possibility of a new contract with him but nothing actually got signed before he was injured at Wolves.

'Don't just leave it Richard,' I told him. 'I want that contract signed before Saturday, because if you get injured I don't want to be in a position where things can change.'

Little did either of us realize just what was around the corner, and the injury he picked up was a big blow, not only to Richard but also to the team, because Rufus played such a massive part in the side.

We started to pick up all sorts of injuries during the next few weeks. Every team and every manager has to deal with injuries during the course of a season, but we seemed to get a real glut of them at various times, and for a squad of our size it made it difficult to cope. Not being able to pick a player because of injury or suspension is bad enough, but when you lose one of the best members of your squad because he's had a bust-up with a team-mate in training it's even harder to take. That's exactly the situation I had to deal with on the eve of our away midweek match with Villa towards the end of October.

Like any other team we always placed a lot of emphasis on set-plays, whether it's taking them or trying to defend against corners and free-kicks. After the main training session was over we went through our set-plays for the Villa game. The ones we would be taking if we got the chance, and also the ones we thought we might have to defend against. Whenever we did this Mervyn organized them and on this particular occasion I helped out by taking free-kicks which we asked the team to defend.

In our very first season in the Premiership after winning the play-offs, we never used to put anyone on the line when we defended a free-kick with a wall inside our own penalty area, but after coming up for the second time we decided to change that. The rule was that if there was a free-kick that meant we were lined up with a wall in our own penalty area; one player was designated to cover one of the posts and the other was down to keeper Dean Kiely. With this in mind I began taking free-kicks, moving the position of the ball all the time to see how the players reacted and to make sure they lined up in the way we wanted them to.

At one point I took a very quick free-kick before they had lined the wall up properly and Deano scrambled across and saved it but Andy Todd, who should have been the man looking after one of the posts, never went on the line. I told every one that they had to be alert to quickly taken kicks and then moved the ball again and took another. I think there were a few words exchanged between Toddy and Deano, but it didn't seem to be anything out of the ordinary and at the end of the session Dean went off to put some ice on a finger injury while the rest of the players stayed out and stretched off. When the players went into the changing rooms, Mervyn, Keith and I collected all the gear as we usually did, picking up the balls, bibs and cones that had been used during that morning's work. It all seemed normal and ordinary, but when we got to the main building, everything changed.

Someone came running out and told me that Toddy had hit Deano. We went in and saw Dean sitting there with a bloody nose, while Andy was shut in a room at the back to make sure the situation calmed down.

The main area at Sparrows Lane is for the players and we don't think its right to have people wandering around, so when Dean's agent turned up that day he waited outside while Deano went to get some ice. Apparently, as Deano went inside he walked passed Toddy in the hallway and Andy hit him. There was no row or anything like that, no shouting match – it just happened as a progression of what had been said during the set-piece routines.

The first thing I had to do was get Toddy into my office and ask him exactly what had happened and why. He said he was really sorry about it all and that he'd just lost his head. Andy claimed that some words had been exchanged during the free-kick routines and that he had snapped, but what really disappointed me was that all of that had happened 20 minutes before Toddy actually whacked Kiely.

So just when I'd thought we'd prepared the team in the best way we could for the next day's game, I had a goalkeeper with a possible broken nose and blood all over his face, a defender who was shut in a room cooling down at the back of the training ground, and we were about to go off and play Villa. Terrific!

I had to make a decision there and then. I knew there was no way Toddy could travel and at that point I wasn't sure whether Dean would even be fit enough to play, but we had to get the squad on the team bus and set off for the journey to the Midlands. We patched Kiely up and he went off to hospital and had some X-rays done, and then I told Andy that after what had happened I had to leave him behind.

Toddy went home and we went off to Villa. Deano later declared himself fit to play in the game the next day, but there was suddenly a bad atmosphere in the squad. People like Mark Fish and Claus Jensen both knew Andy from their Bolton days, and they were friends of his; then there were some of the players who were probably friends with Dean; and finally there were players who were friendly with both of them and didn't quite know how to react to what had gone on. We lost the game at Villa 1–0 and it was a bad night for everyone; the incident was something we could have done without, but I also realized it would have repercussions.

I knew I couldn't just sit back and do nothing about what had gone on and I decided that not only would he have to be fined and suspended, but I would also have to let Toddy go. It was a real shame, because as a player I never had any problem with him, but this wasn't just a minor flare-up and it was up to me to take some action. I told Andy and I also told his father Colin. Todd senior wasn't happy at all with me and let me know it, but I told him that I felt I'd really been left with no alternative.

We told Andy that he could go on loan to another club if he wanted to and Palace were interested in taking him, but we couldn't work a deal out with them over the amount they were willing to pay during the course of any loan. In the end it was Grimsby manager Paul Groves who came in and signed him.

We did a deal allowing Grimsby to pay only a percentage of Todd's wages during the loan period, but also insisted that if they managed to avoid relegation from the First Division, they paid his salary in full. Palace hadn't wanted to pay Andy's full salary either, but because there was no danger of them being relegated, we'd asked for a bigger percentage and I think they got a bit upset when they found out about the Grimsby deal. Andy managed to almost single-handedly keep Grimsby up that season and it was because of his performances for them that Blackburn came in with a bid which was to reach £1 million and we let him go to Ewood Park. So that one training-ground incident not only left a bit of a bad atmosphere for a while, it also cost me a centre-half, and with Rufus out as well it was something we could ill afford.

If we needed a bit of a lift following the Villa game we certainly got it in spectacular fashion 11 days later with a match that was very special to every Charlton fan.

After the defeat at Villa we suffered another setback when Liverpool beat us at The Valley, and there couldn't have been too many people believing we were going to get much out of a visit to Highbury on 4 November. Just to give us added confidence going into a game against one of the top sides in the country, I was told that the last time a Charlton side had won there was October 1956, more than a year before I was even born! It's not the sort of statistic you really want to hear, but the performance against Arsenal that day not only tore up the form book, it also helped to write a new chapter in the history of Charlton Athletic.

Nobody who was there that day will forget what happened. It was the day Charlton showed that they could not only compete with the big boys, but also that they were capable of beating them on their own turf. On a fantastic Sunday afternoon for the club and our fans, we beat Arsenal 4–2 and in the process Claus Jensen scored one of the goals of the season.

We were actually 4–1 up at one stage in the game, and I don't honestly think anyone inside the ground that day could believe what was happening, whether they supported Arsenal or Charlton. We could have been four down in ten minutes because Arsenal played like Arsenal could, and we couldn't get anywhere near them. They took the lead through Thierry Henry but then the game swung in our favour as first Steve Brown equalized and then the Arsenal keeper Richard Wright gave away an own goal and we went in 2–1 up at the break. Jensen's goal was our third and it was brilliantly taken. He floated the ball from a really tight angle into the far corner of the net and from the moment he picked it up on the right side of their box he knew exactly what he was going to do with it. It was the sort of class you need in the Premiership if you are going to compete. When we got our first taste of the League a few years earlier, teams were doing that sort of thing to us throughout the season, and quite often it was the difference between winning and losing. That was why I thought it so important to get players like Jensen into the club when we got promoted for a second time. Jason Euell rounded off our scoring that day with a fourth before Henry got a second for Arsenal with a penalty.

Before the game, as a way of making a point about the need to score goals, I'd actually reminded my midfield players that goalkeeper Peter Schmeichel had scored more goals than them. I needed the team to start scoring from midfield and Claus broke his duck in the best possible way. I was more than happy to be able to present Claus with the Goal of the Month trophy a few weeks later for his effort against Arsenal. The win wasn't just a little piece of history for the club, it also helped to boost everyone's confidence, and coming so soon after the Andy Todd incident it was just the sort of result to help everyone forget and move on.

Our performances against other London clubs in derby games was to become a real feature of our season, and we followed the Highbury win with a pulsating encounter against West Ham at The Valley which ended in a 4–4 draw. Typically, a couple of ex-Charlton players came back to haunt us. Paul Kitson, who was with us on loan almost two years earlier, scored a hat-trick, and former apprentice Jermain Defoe got the other goal.

By the time we played Newcastle at The Valley in our next home game we were really suffering because of injuries and I found myself with just 14 fit players to choose from with a game against Chelsea at Stamford Bridge looming large just four days later. I spoke to Richard Murray after the Newcastle match and said that I needed to get a couple of players in. I was particularly keen to get someone in at the back, but I think we surprised a few people when we revealed that Porto captain Jorge Costa was coming to the club.

Our scouting network, like so many other things at Charlton since I first took charge with Gritty, had improved out of all recognition. Gone were the days when we hardly had enough scouts to cover the country. Like other Premiership clubs Charlton now have a sophisticated operation that not only covers the UK, but also Europe and the rest of the world. It is such an important part of any club's organization and in Jeff Vetere I think we had one of the best people in his field. His official title at the club was overseas scouting co-ordinator, and it was his job to have his finger on the pulse with regard to any possible players who may be a target. It helps that he speaks five languages and whenever I went abroad to look at a player, his name had invariably been filtered down through Jeff. He usually made all the arrangements for a trip and quite often came with me to watch matches and look at players on the Continent.

It was through Jeff that we found out that Costa could be available. There was no need for me to have tapes of Jorge and go and see him play a few times as I would normally do if we were going to possibly sign a foreign player. I'd seen Costa play well for Portugal in the Euro 2000 championships, and there was no doubt that he was a quality defender of proven international class. I think there was a feeling among a lot of agents at the time that Charlton were never really likely to sign foreign players. That wasn't the case, but if I was going to sign a foreign player I liked the idea of going for someone who was already familiar with British football. So when we signed people like Jensen, Johansson and Fish they had already had experience of our football and knew who we were. The big problem I thought we might have was to convince Jorge that Charlton was the place he should play his football in the lead-up to the 2002 World Cup finals in South Korea and Japan.

The big trump card we had was the fact that Costa had fallen out of favour at Porto, who had said that he wouldn't play for them after an incident during one of their games. The story we were told was that Jorge had been substituted in a match and threw his captain's armband to another player as he left the field, but it fell on the floor and the Porto chairman took it as an insult to the club. As a consequence Costa found himself out in the cold with the prospect of not being able to play first-team football again. If that happened there was no way he was going to be able to hold down his place in the national side and so we offered him a way out which he grabbed with both hands.

He arrived on a Sunday night at The Valley where Richard and I were attending a function, and neither of us were prepared for the greeting we got when we went to the front entrance to welcome Jorge to English football. Our eyes were blinded by flashlights because he'd been followed by reporters and TV crews from Portugal, who had got wind of the fact that he was about to sign for Charlton. Although we thought it was a secret the news had obviously got out.

We whisked him off to a local hotel with his agent who spoke very good English, but I don't think Jorge took in anything that was said because he was in a bit of a confused state. He knew he had to leave Porto, but coming to London was a bit hard for him to take; however, he agreed to sign for us and was pitched into the squad for the Chelsea game three days later. Jorge came on as a late substitute for Mark Fish and was part of a team that caused another upset by winning 1–0 with an 89th-minute goal from Kevin Lisbie. Three days later he started the home game against Tottenham and we maintained our excellent form in derby matches by winning 3–1. So Jorge had only been with us a matter of days, but was involved in two games and helped us pick up six points. He hadn't even had time to go back to Portugal to tidy things up before heading to London. When he went home for a few days after the Tottenham win, he must have been thinking the Premiership was a bit of a doddle, but it wasn't too long before he was getting a taste of reality and what life for a smaller club in England's top League was like. As well as Costa I also brought Chris Bart-Williams in on loan from Nottingham Forest to give us a bit more depth in midfield, and we managed to steady things well enough over the next few months, once again reaching the 40 points mark earlier than most people would have anticipated.

We did it in the return fixture with Spurs when Chris Powell scored the only goal of the game against the team he supported as a kid, and we all celebrated at the end of the match, knowing just what it meant to have won a game that gave us 41 points. That match also signalled the return to the team of Richard Rufus, and you would hardly have believed he'd been away. As usual Richard flew into tackles as if his life depended on it. The fact that he'd only just recovered from a potentially career-threatening injury that had kept him out of the side for seven months meant nothing to Rufus. He only knew one way to play and that was what made him so valuable to the side.

It was our first ever double over Tottenham and, incredibly, extended our unbeaten run in London derby Premiership matches to 12. Just for good measure, we'd managed to do the double over Chelsea in a home game a couple of weeks earlier, and having banked the all-important points tally I wanted us to go on and finish the season with a bit of a flourish. Unfortunately it was not to be, and instead we found ourselves hitting a really bad run of results.

Of the eight games we had left in the League we failed to win any of them and ended the season taking just three draws from the matches as we lost the rest. It wasn't a particularly nice feeling to limp home across the line once more. To make matters worse we were still looking for a point in our last home game of the season against Sunderland to make absolutely sure that we stayed clear of any relegation problems. We got it in a 2–2 draw which enabled us to go to Old Trafford a couple of weeks later in a more relaxed mood for our final match of the season.

As well as getting the point we needed, the match against Sunderland at The Valley was memorable for another reason. It marked the retirement of Clive Mendonca from the game. Clive had struggled with injuries for some time and hadn't played a game in the Premiership for a couple of seasons. In the year we won the First Division championship he'd played 19 matches and scored nine goals, just the sort of average you would expect from a great striker like him. He wasn't just a very good footballer, he was really dedicated to the game as well.

I can remember in our first season in the Premiership after his goals at Wembley had got us promoted, Clive was carrying a bit of an injury and we were due to play at Selhurst Park against Wimbledon on Boxing Day. We trained on Christmas morning but we didn't want Clive doing too much in case he hurt himself. He was always a great trainer and would put 100 per cent into everything he did. He hated being held back if we told him to take things easy for one reason or another and so that afternoon he decided to do a little extra training of his own. The man who had rightly become a legend with the Charlton fans could be found kicking a ball around in his back garden like a kid with his new Christmas present, and in doing so he put himself out of the Wimbledon game by injuring himself! From the moment he signed for us he had become a popular figure at the club with players and fans alike. He was honest, genuine and an excellent striker. I offered to keep him at the club and give him a coaching role, but I think he decided to return to the north where all of his family were. It was fitting that the tribute should come against his beloved Sunderland, the team he supported, and both sides clapped him onto the field that afternoon as Richard Murray and Martin Simons made a presentation to him.

We rounded off the season with a 0–0 draw at Old Trafford against Manchester United and finished 14th. It was a more than respectable position for us, but perhaps we'd raised expectation levels too high once more by the way we over-achieved the previous year with that ninth-place finish. The match was Jorge Costa's last for the club. He did a really good job for us and was a very popular figure with the players and fans, but it was always a short-term arrangement and there was never any chance of him signing on a longer contract. We flew back from Manchester to Heathrow airport and Jorge went on from there to Portugal. Before he left I presented him with a Charlton shirt that all the players had signed. I think he appreciated the gesture and I know he enjoyed his time with us. He went on to play in the World Cup and then re-established himself back at Porto. In 2004, with Jose Mourinho as their manager, Jorge was part of the Porto team that won the Champions League, and I was really pleased for him.

The night of the final I was on holiday in Portugal's Algarve having a meal with Carol and two friends of ours, John and Sally Hayes – John is a mad Charlton supporter and one of the club's sponsors. We were watching the football on a TV in the restaurant, but found out that none of the waiters were that bothered because they were Benfica supporters and actually wanted Porto to lose. When we got back to our hotel the four of us decided to have a nightcap, which turned into two or three. The combination of seeing Jorge win the match with Porto coupled with a few drinks prompted John and I to teach the waiters behind the bar a new song. We gave them a blast of the verse Charlton supporters made up when Jorge came to the club, and sang whenever he played in the team. By the end of the evening every time we approached the bar the two waiters would whistle the tune and smile at us. The song had also surfaced again the year after Jorge left us and returned to The Valley when we played Porto in a testimonial game for John Robinson. I could see how pleased he was to hear our supporters singing it and know that they remembered him. We kept in contact with him and despite all his ability and what he's achieved as a player, Jorge is a really humble man. Maybe because of that Charlton was just the right club for him when he decided to briefly play in England and I think we both benefited from the experience.

The Sunderland game had also seen the official opening of the North Stand, taking our capacity to more than 26,000. It was a fabulous achievement for the club, and Richard Murray was rightly proud as he stood on the pitch that day and looked around the ground. His influence on Charlton and on my own career in the 11 years since he arrived on the scene could not be underestimated, and I think the two of us had developed quite a special relationship during that time.

19 Big Brother

I don't suppose it can be easy for a very successful businessman to come home and tell his wife that he's about to take over a virtually bankrupt football club, and that he's going to throw money at it without expecting to get any return, but that's pretty much what Richard Murray must have done when he decided to get involved with Charlton.

When he came on board with Martin Simons shortly before Gritty and I were appointed nobody could have known at the time just how important the two of them would be to the club. Ironically, the move to Selhurst Park might have alienated a lot of Charlton supporters, but one man who bought a season ticket and watched all the home games was Richard Murray. Although he had gone to The Valley to watch some matches it was really when the club began to ground share that Richard started to watch Charlton on a more regular basis. Selhurst was a pretty easy drive for him from his home in Surrey, and he took the opportunity to watch top-flight football during the years Lennie struggled to make sure the club stayed in the old First Division. Richard and Martin and their wives, Jane and Leigh, knew each other socially, as skiing friends, and when they both got involved I think the idea was that they would put money in and get 5 per cent of the club each.

Charlton basically needed money for wages, and at the time the club was effectively owned on an equal footing jointly by Roger Alwen and Mike Norris. When Mike had financial problems and had his assets possessed by a bank, it was Richard who negotiated with the bank to get the shares back and sort out a lot of the financial problems, which included getting the contractors back on site at The Valley for the club's eventual return in 1992.

I think by that time both Richard and Martin were well and truly hooked and in their different ways have played a massive part in helping the club get to where they are today. The fact that the two men are very different characters has helped in the way they have gone about things. Over the years Richard has been the one who has got involved in the more day-to-day running of the club and its business, including all the transfers and contracts, while Martin is probably seen more as the public face of Charlton. The supporters know he's just as much of a Charlton nut as any of them and they can relate to him easily. Both men and the rest of the board are first and foremost Charlton supporters and all of them have put money into the club.

Richard's commitment to the cause was pretty clear from the very early days and the more he became involved the more his influence spread through The Valley. As well as putting a lot of his own money into the club I think he has also been instrumental in persuading others to do the same and become part of the board in the process. During the time he has been in charge over £25 million has been put into the club in equity. In simple terms people have put money in but haven't taken anything out. It's a situation that may amaze a lot of people but it is also typical of the way the club is run and why Charlton have continued to progress on and off the pitch.

I think Richard decided very early on in his relationship with Charlton that it was something he was going to be involved in on a long-term basis. He didn't see it as a five-minute wonder that would just be a nice little hobby compared with his other business interests. He worked at it and had a pretty clear vision of the way he wanted the club to work when he took over as chairman.

Once he had decided the only way forward was to have one manager and not two, it was Richard who convinced the rest of the board that it would be the right thing to appoint me. I don't think anyone else was pushing for a change, but Richard wasn't happy with the situation and made a brave decision which could have backfired on him. I think he knew, just as I did, that Steve was probably more of a favourite with the fans because of his long association with the club. For whatever reason Richard decided he wanted me to go it alone and if I had cocked the whole thing up there would have been a lot of people happy to see us trying to wipe the egg off our faces.

Happily things worked out for both of us in that first season and I can honestly say that our relationship went from strength to strength.

I don't think Richard would have ever got involved in Charlton if he didn't genuinely feel he could make a success of it. In those early days it was important that both of us took a long-term view of what we were trying to achieve. He made it clear that he would back me when it came to what I was trying to do on the field, but at the same time he wasn't about to start promising me money to spend that wasn't there. The plan was that he would look after the club and make sure a solid infrastructure was put in place, and I had to try and build a team that would continue to grow and make progress. If we're both honest, I don't think either of us could have predicted how well things would work out when I agreed to take charge on my own in 1995.

The plan to begin with was to make sure we were a decent and well-established First Division team playing in front of 12,000 or 14,000 people at The Valley, but because of what happened in the years that followed the whole picture changed dramatically.

The relationship between a chairman and his manager is a key factor in any club, and Charlton are no different. I never forgot that I was an employee, but in many ways Richard was more like a big-brother figure to me rather than a club chairman. We were by no means bosom buddies and we didn't tend to socialize very much, but it was a very easy and relaxed relationship. In the early days I think Richard would admit that the business of football was all a bit new to him, and I think he liked to pick my brains a bit when it came to players and tactics. These days he certainly knows his football, but he was never the sort of chairman who was forever asking me why I'd picked a particular team, or why I wanted to buy a certain player. He always backed my judgement on players and tactics, which I'm sure couldn't always have been easy when the club now has almost as many people on the board as I had in my first-team squad.

He sometimes phoned up on a Friday evening to see what the team was for the next day but was happy to let me get on with the football side of things. Quite often getting a call on a Friday would be the first time we had spoken all week, and yet I've heard from other managers that some of their chairmen are constantly on the phone, wanting to know exactly what they are doing and checking on pretty much every move they make. We hardly ever saw Richard at the training ground. He came in at the beginning of a season to sort the players' bonuses out, and he might occasionally sneak in for a bit of physiotherapy, if he'd injured himself playing tennis or having a run because he likes to keep fit, but that's about it. A good indication of his style and the way he is happy to stay in the background came the day Charlton signed a player a few years ago.

'This may be the last time you see me,' Richard told him, and although the player thought he was joking, I knew he was being deadly serious. Richard is not the sort of person who courts the limelight or publicity. He is quite happy to keep a low profile and enjoy the success he has made of the club.

Although he is one of only 20 Premiership chairmen I think a lot of people would struggle to name him, and certainly wouldn't know what he looked like, but I think that's the way he likes it. In the early days he used to leave before the end of a game so that he could avoid the traffic. He wasn't interested in making a meal of things and doing the whole socializing bit. I got the publicity and the plaudits when we did well because I was the manager, but everyone at the club knew it was about teamwork off the pitch as well, and nobody deserves more praise for the way things have gone than Richard.

He was always tremendously loyal, not only to me, but also to anyone who works for him. It's no coincidence that throughout his business interests you will find people working in his companies who have been with him for a very long time, and Charlton is no different in that respect. I think it is because of the loyalty he shows others that makes them very loyal towards him, and he also lets people get on and do their jobs without any fuss. He might set targets but they are never unrealistic targets and in all our time together I can't ever remember having a row with him. I think the only time he really got a bit upset with me was over the Mendonca transfer, when he was slightly exasperated and had been trying to do the deal without being able to get hold of me on the phone.

When he first gave me the job there was never any question of him putting added pressure on me, even though in many ways we were both going to live or die by the decision. As well as his loyalty he's also 100 per cent honest and I think he saw that in me as well. Whenever I went after a player I always treated the club's money as if it was my own. I think that's the way it should be. If the money was there for me to use he never hesitated in letting me spend it, but if it wasn't there he told me, and that meant I always knew exactly where I stood.

We had the sort of relationship which was able to take a knock and I think that comes down to the loyalty thing. If you have a strong relationship you're able to take a knock and then move on. As a person he's not flashy or extravagant. He's understated but very determined and successful. Richard recognizes and identifies qualities in other people and is more than happy to let them have their head. That doesn't just apply to me, but to anyone working at the club, and I suspect it's the same in his other businesses as well.

I think the strength of Charlton has been its continuity on all levels. Richard may be understated in the way he approaches running things, but he's very clever at motivating people and getting the best out of them, which is why they stay around and are so loyal. I don't believe Charlton could have been as successful as a club if the right sort of leadership wasn't there at the top. Richard has to take a lot of credit for that and on a personal basis I always felt happy and relaxed about the sort of relationship we had. He helped to create a good working environment for me to function in and knew I enjoyed being part of what the club achieved. I'm not saying that ours was a unique chairman–manager relationship because I don't know about other clubs, but I can't believe I could have had a better person to deal with during the time I was in charge.

I'll always be grateful to him for giving me the opportunity to manage a club on my own and for showing faith in my ability to do the job, but I'm realistic enough to know that the main reason for me being in charge for so long was the fact that we were successful on the field. It's more than 15 years since I was first appointed with Gritty and in that time most clubs would have had about six or eight different managers. I think that probably made things easier for Richard as he tried to build and improve Charlton.

Without blowing my own trumpet, I honestly feel I did a decent job during the time I was in charge at The Valley, and having such a good relationship with my chairman helped me do that job.

20 Teamwork

If my relationship with the chairman and the board helped me do my job during my time as manager, then the coaching team I had around me was equally important.

From the very first day as a manager you quickly realize how important it is to get things right off the field in order for the players to perform on the pitch. I have already said that I never wanted any player of mine to moan about the fact that all they ever did in training was play five-a-side matches. I always felt that as a player I under-achieved and because of that I was determined not to let the same thing happen when I became a manager. When Gritty and I took over in 1991 we leaned heavily on each other and established those ground rules which definitely helped us to form a structure we could work within. Obviously, the scale of everything connected with the club was different then and the staffing levels were a fraction of what they are these days.

Although we didn't have a stadium of our own at the time we always had the training ground and that became our base. We used to turn up there each day and see the same faces. There only used to be a handful of people around the place: a couple of physiotherapists, the groundsman, press steward John Yarnton and his wife Barbara, who used to make the sandwiches for everyone, and the odd person from the club who would pop in for one reason or another. In the early days I actually used to take about five different loads of kit home each week, which Carol would clean, and Arnie Warren gave me an allowance for all the washing powder!

Needless to say it's not like that anymore and although a lot of the familiar faces from those early days are still around, the club has grown and operates on a different level now. In the first few years when Gritty and I were in charge we had a Christmas party for everyone at the club, which we held in a local pub because there weren't that many of us – that's certainly not the case now. The pub simply wouldn't be big enough to accommodate everyone. The first team alone has an awful lot of people to help it function. There's a medical department, physiotherapists, a couple of masseurs and a performance manager, as well as kit managers. It's all a far cry from that first day when I turned up for training after signing from Villa as a player.

The club has grown and moved on and I suppose that as a manager I must have changed as well, but in terms of my own working environment and the way I liked to operate I think it was always quite similar. Having started off as a joint manager with Steve, I was well aware of how important it was to have someone with you who thought along the same lines, but also brought something else to the table, so I was lucky to have Les Reed come in to the club and do the job he did after Richard put me in sole charge.

The appointment worked out well for me and for him, but I thought long and hard about the type of person I wanted and it was really no surprise to me that our working relationship was so good during the time he was at Charlton. Having known him for so long I was well aware of the sort of character he was and the qualities he had as a person and as a coach. Along with Keith Peacock, Les did a lot to raise the standard of our play during those three years and I learnt a great deal from him. There was no doubt he really enjoyed being involved in club football and rightly got great satisfaction from the fact that he left us having helped Charlton into the Premier League.

When Les went and I brought in Mervyn to replace him, it was important for me to know I was getting someone with a different mix of qualities once again. We weren't old mates but had known each other for a long period of time, and I felt that his career as a player, coach and manager gave him the sort of experience I was looking for. Happily it worked out well, as did Keith's position as assistant manager. Although, as I've said, it was a role he'd already been filling in many ways, I think it was important to put an official title on it.

I think Keith, Mervyn and I formed a really good team during our time together. It's nice for the players to hear more than one voice in training and we shared a lot of the coaching throughout the week. It's a system that worked well for us and I felt very comfortable with the two of them. I'm not one of those people who doesn't like to delegate, and it was good for me to know they were more than capable of getting on with things without me being around.

Any appointment can be a gamble, but when I asked Mervyn to come in as first-team coach I was pretty certain I knew what I was getting. His experience, personality and coaching ability was just what we needed at the time, and although his first season with us ended with relegation from the Premiership after that play-off promotion, I was even more convinced that he was the right man for the job. He not only fitted in well with

Keith and me, he also got the respect of the players, which is always a good sign. Like Les, he is a different personality to me and his methods are not the same, but that is exactly what you need on the training pitch. Players love to have variety in their coaching sessions: it keeps the training fresh and it keeps them on their toes in the way they respond to what is being asked of them.

It was great for me to have someone like Keith around from the moment I became a manager. I know a lot of people thought he was going to get the job when Steve and I were appointed. He was a real Charlton man and had gone off and got very good managerial experience in both this country and in the States. To Keith's credit, once Roger Alwen and Mike Norris had made the decision to give the job to us there was never a hint of resentment and he couldn't have been more helpful.

That help continued when Gritty left and I know that both Les and Mervyn enjoyed working with Keith. He's got tremendous respect and great contacts within the game, and his upbeat personality had a very positive effect around the place. He took a lot of the burden away from me and dealt with things that could become very time consuming from my point of view. He was a great buffer between me and the players and also between me and agents. He was good at organizing and would deal with our scouts and also other clubs when it came to things like possible transfers and loans. Keith was able to sift through a lot of what was aimed at me and would then push through the kind of stuff he felt I ought to be dealing with.

I sought his advice on a lot of matters and the same was true with Mervyn. If I was watching training or if I was looking at a match we were playing in, I would talk to both of them to run through any points I had. I liked to know whether I was seeing things in the right way, or perhaps not picking up on certain points they had noted. During a match I tended to flit between the directors' box in the first half and the touchline in the second. Keith was usually with me when I sat upstairs, and Mervyn stayed on the touchline. Before I said anything to the players at half-time or the end of the game, I would have a minute with the two of them so that I could talk to the players about the most important things to come out of the match. I also talked to them about team selection and I liked to listen to their views and opinions before making my final decisions. The three of us spent a lot of time mulling things over and I think the players would sometimes be amazed at how much discussion had gone into making a particular decision. As much thought went into naming a substitute as it did when deciding who was going to be in the starting line-up.

Once the season begins the routine is relentless because after you have got over a game the focus is on getting ready for the next one, and in the Premiership the build-up and attention given to any match is immense. It is an incredibly tough League to play in and it can be very cruel as well. Although I enjoy being a manager I've always felt there is no way I could ever do the job successfully if I went about it trying to be a one-man band. Of course I always tried at Charlton to make sure we had a good team on the pitch, but I knew it was equally important for me to have a good one off it as well in order to do the job properly.

We'd surpassed expectations in our first season back in the Premiership by finishing ninth, and perhaps hitting the golden 40-point mark so early in our second season was even more of an achievement in many ways, but as we prepared for a new campaign neither Keith, Mervyn nor me had any illusions about the size of the task facing us in the summer of 2002. Every season in the top flight means a club can grow in terms of its finance and infrastructure. As a manager you can also start to think about signing better-quality players and strengthening the squad you have, but if your team is not one of the big established sides then keeping your head above the murky relegation water is still the number-one priority.

I knew the squad needed strengthening but, as for any other manager, getting the right players into your club at the right time is never easy. Soon after the season had ended with the draw at Old Trafford I bought defender Gary Rowett from Leicester for £2.7 million, and keeper Paul Rachubka from Manchester United for £200,000, but I wasn't able to bring in any more new faces until August when free agents Jesper Blomqvist and Robbie Mustoe joined for the start of the new season.

When I'd looked at the fixture list and saw our first four home games I knew they would be tough but, at the same time, I never really thought we'd end up without a point from our encounters with Chelsea, Tottenham, Arsenal and Manchester United. It's the sort of thing that can easily happen in the Premiership if you're not careful, and exactly the reason some clubs find themselves stranded at the bottom of the League with only a few games gone. The good thing from our point of view was that although we couldn't win at home we did manage to beat Bolton and West Ham on our travels and picked up a useful point at Southampton. One game we didn't win was the match at Aston Villa; they beat us 2–0 and had a very familiar face in their starting line-up that night – Mark Kinsella.

After the heavy defeat by West Ham on Boxing Day in our first season back in the Premiership, I had made changes and got a result in our next game when we went up to Manchester and beat City. We'd done some running in training before the Christ-mas period that year when the players had to snake through a trail, twisting and turning as they went; it became evident that Mark was struggling with a knee problem and although he played in the West Ham defeat, he clearly wasn't right. Mark was one of the changes that day against City and Scott Parker came into the side. In many ways it was the start of Scott show-ing that he was ready to play a major role in the side.

Although Mark got over that injury it was pretty clear that Scotty had come of age and, like Bowyer before him, he'd become too good a player to leave out of the side. By the time the season started in the summer of 2002 I knew in my own mind that Parker and Jensen were probably going to form the core of our midfield. When the Villa manager, Graham Taylor, made an enquiry for Mark that August I felt I had to let Kins know. If I was going to play Parker and Jensen he was going to be down the pecking order at our club, and I had to explain to him that perhaps it was time for him to go and play in a side where he was probably going to be first choice. It was an opportunity for him to move, and at the age of 30 get a longer contract. In the end I think he reluctantly realized that it was the right thing to do for himself at that time in his career and he moved to Villa for a £1 million fee. I took a lot of criticism from the local press and media for selling Mark, but at the same time I felt I couldn't hold Parker back.

It was the end of an era as far as Charlton was concerned because we'd said goodbye to one of the most influential players I think there has ever been in the club's history. I also believe he was probably my best buy as manager of the club. As a player he went from Colchester to being involved with the Republic of Ireland in the World Cup, and in his six years with us he probably put in 12 years' work. He dragged us along and we dragged him along, he trained like he played and led by example.

Perhaps one of the biggest compliments I can pay him is to say that as my captain he reminded me very much of the way Billy Bonds went about things. He was quiet around the place but everyone respected him and knew what he did for the team in matches. If a training session was a bit lacklustre, he would pick it up. He was always totally focused and I think his performances helped us progress from being an average First Division club to one that was capable of getting promotion. His work-rate was tremendous, he was a great passer, was excellent at getting in last-ditch tackles and could really strike a ball well. After having him around as part of our team for so long it was a bit strange to see him in a Villa shirt that night and the result only added to the fact that we hadn't made a great start to the season.

By the time we played Middlesbrough at The Valley in front of the Sky TV cameras on a Sunday afternoon in mid-October we had seven points from our first nine matches, and were bottom of the table. We desperately needed a win and we got one when Jason Euell scored what proved to be the only goal of the game after just five minutes.

The victory was a relief for everyone but it couldn't hide the fact that we were in trouble and needed to start putting some points on the board to stop all the talk of doom and gloom that was beginning to start, with people predicting what a tough struggle it was going to be for us, and that maybe the Premiership had caught up with us.

I think that we were still a bit of a novelty act to a lot of football fans. They liked us and admired what we'd done as a club, but I think they saw us as living on borrowed time. Some people seemed to think that there was no way we could sustain the success and growth we'd enjoyed. They thought the signs had been there the season before. We might have finished ninth after winning promotion, but then we ended up 14th in our second season and perhaps some thought the third season would be the one that caught up with us.

Although I always believed it was going to be a tough season, I also knew that we'd improved the squad and that the experience of being in the Premiership for two consecutive seasons could only help when it came to producing what is needed to compete in English football's top division. The win over Middlesbrough not only brought a much-needed three points, it also put an end to a run which had seen us fail to win at home since March. There wasn't an immediate improvement in results following the game, because we lost three of our next four matches, but then we embarked on a mid-season run that saw us steady the ship and turn things around.

By the time February rolled around not only were we sixth in the Premiership, but I'd also been given the manager of the month award and the team had managed to win 13 games, giving us a very healthy 45-point haul. Once again we'd broken through the 40-point mark in the Premiership with plenty of games to go, and once again we had the sort of disappointing end to the season that has become an all-too-familiar part of Charlton teams in recent years. The 3–0 home win against Villa on 22 February proved to be unlucky 13 in many ways, because in the remaining ten matches of the season we managed just one more victory and one draw. Only four points from a possible 30, and yet we were home and dry as a club and could look forward to yet another season in the Premiership.

After that Villa game Graham Taylor remarked that although Charlton hadn't actually won anything in the last 10 years in terms of the big trophies on offer, we were definitely the most successful club during that period. What he meant was that we'd come out of all the adversity we'd suffered and were now a club who were competing in the Premiership. I think most people in football knew what he meant, and perhaps it takes someone who's been in the game for a long time to recognize just what it takes to be in the sort of position we'd managed to reach.

Our last game of the season was a home defeat by Fulham and even at that late stage and with the poor run we'd had, there was still a chance that we could have ended the season in tenth place. Fulham won the match with a penalty from Louis Saha in the 33rd minute after he'd been brought down by Dean Kiely. Deano got his marching orders as a result of the incident, but in the 66th minute Jason Euell had the chance to put us level from the spot when he was brought down by Alain Goma. Had he scored and the match finished as a draw, we would have ended the season in tenth place and the club would have picked up an extra £1,006,000 in merit money. It's an indication of just how high the financial stakes are in the Premiership, and how one missed opportunity can mean so much to a club.

The match also marked the end of a link to those early days when Gritty and I were in charge and we were playing our home games at Upton Park. More than ten years earlier John Robinson had come to the club on the eve of Robert Lee's departure to Newcastle, and the £75,000 we were ordered to pay for him at that transfer tribunal in 1992 turned out to be an absolute bargain. Just like Mark Kinsella, Robbo became a real favourite with the Charlton fans and played such a significant part in what the club achieved during his time with us. At the start of the season he had been granted that deserved testimonial against Porto, and although he was never a regular in his last season with us, he still made a contribution, playing ten League games. He was granted a free transfer in recognition of what he'd done for the club and the loyalty he'd shown, and was given a tremendous ovation by the supporters before the kick-off. He deserved the applause and the fact that he had stayed at Charlton for so long was another example of the sort of loyalty that has played a major part in the progress we've made.

To end the season with a poor run was disappointing and, although we improved on our placing from the previous year by finishing 12th, it left me wondering what might have been if only we had just managed to maintain some decent form in that last quarter of the season. But I also knew what a massive achievement it was for the club to be safe by the end of February – it was another indication of just how far we had come.

In December there had been another reminder, when we celebrated the tenth anniversary of being back at The Valley by beating Liverpool 2–0. We had more than 26,000 fans in the ground that day, and when I looked around the stadium and thought about the opposition we had just beaten, I almost had to pinch myself to make sure it was all true. From the portakabins, wet paint and euphoria surrounding the memories of the win against Portsmouth a decade earlier to playing against and beating a team who had finished the previous season as runners-up in the Premiership was quite an achievement. But as happy as we all were after the win against Liverpool, there is also a much sadder memory, because it was also the day that Steve Gritt's daughter, Hayley, died after a long illness.

Gritty, along with all the other people who played in that

match against Portsmouth, will always hold a special place in the history of Charlton, but not one of us involved in that game would ever have imagined the way the club would progress in the years that followed. That progress needed to be maintained, just as I felt it had been in all of my previous seasons as manager. But I was more aware than ever that in order for that to happen you need to keep improving the quality of your team.

I knew I already had a good solid squad who were gaining experience with each season they spent in the top flight, but I also knew that in the Premiership special players can mean the difference between winning a game, or ending up with nothing. When I got the chance to sign just such a player, I knew I couldn't afford to miss out on the opportunity

21 Ripped Apart

At the start of each of our previous three years in the Premiership we had always talked about making sure we stayed up. That was the priority and if we were successful, then we all knew we'd had a good season, but by the time our fourth consecutive campaign in the top flight rolled around, the club's ambition had changed and we started thinking about a new goal.

We still knew that we had to get those 40 points and make sure we remained a Premiership club, but we also started to ask ourselves whether it was possible to make the top 10. Although we had managed to do that in our first season after winning promotion, it hadn't been repeated in the two years that followed, and in reality it had always been a case of us punching above our weight. When you looked at a club of our size and resources, most people would have thought we were more likely to be relegated than establish ourselves as a top half of the table Premiership club. But if you can keep on improving the quality and experience of your squad, there's no reason why you shouldn't think about making that next step.

If we were going to do that I knew I needed new players. We'd already bought defender Hermann Hreidarsson from Ipswich towards the end of the previous season and in the summer of 2003 we went back to the Portman Road club to sign midfielder Matt Holland. I also wanted to try and add a different type of player to the squad, someone who would lift us and frighten other teams. I wanted to try and get one of those special players who can make a difference and turn a defeat or a draw into a victory.

Whenever we'd played against West Ham and Paolo Di Canio had been in their team, I'd got an uneasy feeling when the ball went to him and I wanted someone like that in my side. If the Italian forward got the ball I always felt he was capable of causing us problems and hurting us. He was hard to handle and unpredictable, just the sort of player I felt we were lacking.

West Ham had just been relegated from the Premiership despite getting 42 points and I made a few inquiries to see if there might be a chance of signing him, knowing that I had to overcome a couple of obstacles if I had any hope of pulling off the deal. The first problem was going to be his wages. I knew that there was no way we could afford to pay him what he'd been getting at West Ham, and the other problem was actually managing to make contact with him.

I'd heard that as soon as a season was over Paolo liked to head straight back to Italy and wasn't seen again until the start of pre-season training. When the PFA issued their annual list of players who were free transfers, I saw that Di Canio lived in Loughton, which was only a few miles away from my own home. Although we knew we would have to talk to his agent if a deal was going to be sorted out, I wanted to make personal contact with the player, so I drove to his house. I knew Paolo probably wasn't there but I thought he might have someone who kept an eye on the property. When I got to the house it looked deserted and it was pretty obvious nobody was in, so I climbed over the gates, ran to the front door and scribbled a message on a piece of paper which I stuffed through his letter box. It simply said, 'Paolo please call me I want to talk to you. Alan Curbishley.'

When we eventually talked to his agent he told us to make a financial offer and he'd put it to Di Canio, but there was no way I was going to fax an offer without knowing if Paolo would actually get to see it. I knew that it also might be a case of us not making the best financial offer, but being able to make the best football offer and one that would appeal to him. I said I wanted to meet the player and talk to him, which is what finally happened. Paolo flew in from Italy on a Saturday and Richard and I went along to his house the following day determined to sign Di Canio and I made sure I took a video along with me to help in the negotiations.

About a year earlier the club had made the video to help try and persuade people to sign up to long-term season tickets which were being sold for the North Stand. It was only a short piece of film but it contained all the significant moments in the club's history, including the more recent struggles as Charlton battled to get back to The Valley. I wanted Di Canio to see the video, firstly to let him see how hard we'd worked to get to where we were, and also to show him we weren't the richest club in the world, which I thought might help when it came to talking about the sort of money we could offer him.

The first thing I noticed when we arrived and he opened the front door in T-shirt and shorts, was that he looked like a real athlete. I knew he hadn't done very much training, but he still looked extremely fit, and at the age of 35 he was in great condition. As soon as the introductions were over I said I wanted him to see the video I'd brought with me, and as we all sat down and watched it on his big plasma TV screen, I could see him looking on in amazement. He suddenly got a real idea of what we were about and I think it caught his imagination, especially the history of the club and the time they won the FA Cup Final in 1947. He even asked to keep the tape and I could see he was beginning to get really keen on the idea of a move to us. I don't think he liked the idea of leaving England on a bit of a losing note, having just been relegated with West Ham, and he had a few confrontations with Glenn Roeder. Paolo had been out of the side because of injury but got himself fit for the run-in when Trevor Brooking took temporary charge towards the end of the season, and although they went on a good run West Ham couldn't avoid the drop. I knew the relegation had upset Di Canio because he'd had such fantastic times there and knew he'd left them on a real low.

I went into the kitchen with him and he made me a cappuccino while Richard stayed in another room negotiating with his agent. Suddenly the agent called out for Paolo to join them and I started to believe that maybe a deal had been struck, but when he came back into the kitchen I could see from his face that all was not well.

'Boss, boss, boss,' he said shaking his head. 'I know what Charlton have done, I know where you have come from and I realize you don't have lots of money, but boss, boss, boss, you must have more money than that. I can't accept the sort of offer your chairman has just made me!'

I asked him to make me another coffee and had a five minute chat with Richard. Happily I could see Richard really wanted to get the transfer done and after some more negotiations he came out of the room and announced that we had a deal. It was agreed that Di Canio, who'd missed most of pre-season training because he was recovering from an injury, would go back to Italy and then return to have his medical before signing.

As usual with a new player I picked him up and drove him to the surgeon for his medical. I do that because I like to be there in case there are any problems and it's also a chance to talk to a player over a reasonable period of time, allowing us to get to know each other a little better. I knew he had a bit of an injury but he got past the medical and signed for us on a one year deal.

In the Premiership we'd had a few problems at home trying to break teams down and I felt that having signed Di Canio we now had someone at the club who could help us do that and unlock defences. I knew we had someone who could make a difference even if he only came on for 30 minutes in some games I believed he would be a good substitute. I didn't think I was getting a player who would be in the team every week, but I did feel I was getting one who had different ideas and could do different things when called on.

August proved to be quite a busy month for us, because apart from Di Canio we also signed another striker, Carlton Cole, on loan from Chelsea, and midfielder Stephen Hughes who was a free agent after leaving Watford. As soon as Paolo arrived he lifted the place and I think the other players could see he was taking the whole thing seriously and wasn't just with us to take the money and go along for the ride. He showed real profes- sionalism from the start and I think he warmed to us straight away. He liked our training, liked the attitude everyone showed and liked the fact that we were organized. I think it was some- thing he responded to because he was such a good professional.

Whenever we played a five-a-side match they were competitive and I think he enjoyed that. He also took on board exactly what we were about as a club, which I think was important to him and to us. The day he signed he went into our club shop and bought about 15 shirts with his name on the back to take back to Italy and give to his friends. He was always very good about doing things like making personal appearances on behalf of the club and was perfect for us. There was a mutual respect because we realized what he'd done as a player and he realized what we'd done as a club. It seemed to work from day one and the fans loved him.

He got a great welcome at The Valley before our first game of the season against Manchester City, even though he wasn't quite fit enough to play in the match. It turned out to be the sort of occasion where we could have done with a bit of his magic, because we ended the afternoon losing 3–0, making it a pretty disappointing anniversary for me because I was celebrating my 600th game as Charlton manager.

Paolo did get involved in our next outing when he came on as a late substitute and we ran out convincing 4–0 winners at Wolves. He gradually got himself fit and was desperate to play in the team. We had a pretty indifferent start to the season, but it really seemed to get a kick-start during one week towards the end of September. We came through a thrilling home Carling Cup match with Luton to win 8–7 on penalties after the game had swung backwards and forwards, to finish 4–4 after extra-time, and we followed that five days later with a 3–2 home win against Liverpool in the Premiership with Kevin Lisbie scoring a hat-trick.

By this time Di Canio had become a real part of things; although he hadn't started that many games, he was involved with the squad and always ready to contribute. When he did play he showed the kind of commitment and unselfishness we needed. He played really well on a wet Monday night at Blackburn and it was from his corner that Hermann scored the only goal of the match, although I'm not too sure Di Canio liked the journey there. We flew to the game, but Paolo hated flying. I'd heard stories about him having a plane stopped on the runway when he travelled to a match with West Ham because he was so scared, and he'd then made his own way to the game in his car. I'd also heard that he never really played in away games which were further than the Midlands, apparently because of various injuries, and I'm sure it had nothing to do with having to fly! Scott Parker and Stephen Hughes also hated having to fly, and the three of them used to sit at the back of the plane screaming whenever we hit the slightest bit of turbulence. I think they must have been holding hands for mutual support, because they were all rooted to their seats and couldn't wait for a flight to end. The match that followed the win at Blackburn showed just what a class performer Paolo was and why I wished I'd had him in my side when he was three or four years younger.

We played Arsenal and the match finished 1–1 with Di Canio getting our goal from the penalty spot. But it was the way he took it that stood out in the mind and really endeared him to our fans. Instead of trying to blast the ball or place it in the corner of the goal as most players do, he opted to chip it over Jens Lehmann as the keeper dived to his left. Having the audacity to do that was something we just hadn't seen before from a Charlton player and perhaps never will again. People still come up and talk to me about the penalty because it was so special. It wasn't showmanship or arrogance, it was just someone with the ability to turn a game, because he had the skill to do it.

The team gave me the perfect present in November when

they beat Fulham 3–1 at The Valley on my birthday in a game that saw us reach the giddy heights of fourth in the Premiership. It was the club's best start for 50 years and it was also an important win for another reason, because we weren't going to play again for another couple of weeks due to an international break.

Scott Parker had continued to show what a great player he was and the arrival of Di Canio seemed to act as a bit of inspiration for him. I could see Scotty taking note of what Paolo did in training and the way he went about things. The way he trained, what he ate and drank and how he conducted himself generally. I think Parker responded to it, and I think Di Canio could recognize what a class act Scott was. So too could Sven-Goran Eriksson, because he called Parker up and he became another Charton player to win full international honours.

As far as I was concerned it was no more than Scott deserved. He'd matured into a tremendous player, just as I always thought he would do and was starting to reap the rewards after chomping at the bit to get into the side. Scotty had come through the ranks and as soon as we saw him there was no doubt we had an exceptional talent on our hands. When he was just 12 or 13 years old, Gritty and I used to have him training with the first team. He would come in during school holidays and certainly didn't look out of place playing alongside seasoned professionals. He was always itching to get into the first team even as a teenager, and was forever coming to see me saying he was better than a lot of other players at different clubs who were his age, but playing first team football.

'But Scott,' I told him, 'those players who are 16, 17 or 18 might not be around when they're 21 years old. When you get in our side you'll stay and I'm not going to do that until you're strong enough both mentally and physically to cope.'

After letting him go on loan to Norwich for a month late in 2000 he came back more desperate than ever to play in the first team. He got his chance because of that 5–0 Boxing Day defeat at West Ham and never really looked back after that. After his full international appearance against Denmark Scott continued his brilliant form for us, and after scoring two superb goals at Southampton in a game we should never have lost 3–2, he put in another great performance a few weeks later on Boxing Day as we beat Chelsea 4–2 in front of a delighted Valley crowd. It was a tremendous result for us and I know a lot of people still rate it as the best game they've seen at The Valley since the club came back in 1992. It was also another example of just what a terrific player Scott was. It was probably also the match that finally prompted a move for Parker and at the same time ripped our season apart.

By the time we played Wolves at The Valley early in January I honestly thought we had a chance of causing a real upset in the Premiership that season. We were fourth in the table and I had a team where at least eight of the players were picking themselves each week, simply because their form was so good. We had something about us and at the heart of the team was Scott Parker. He seemed to have clicked into a different gear when Di Canio arrived and we were getting the benefit. He was everywhere on the pitch and could break down moves and then set us off on an attack in the space of a second. Quite often he'd play like two men with all the work he put in and some sides just didn't know how to cope with him. He was particularly good when he sat in the middle and broke things up, but loved to come forward whenever he could.

When we played Wolves we got ourselves 1–0 ahead and I

asked Scotty to sit in midfield and hold his position. I wanted him to be our defensive anchor but he was romping forward and I was screaming at him to hold his position and stick to what I'd told him to do. He just did his own thing and produced a great bit of play that helped set up one of Jason Euell's two goals as we won the game 2–0. When he came off the pitch I grabbed Parker and he just started laughing, even though I was having a go at him.

'I don't think I'm going to ask you to do that any more,' I told him. 'You're so dangerous when you run with the ball, perhaps I should let you get forward a bit more.'

What I didn't realize at the time was that Scotty was probably trying to score a goal and leave on a high in what would be his last game for the club.

After the match I went into the dressing room to have a word with the players and then quickly did my press conference so that I could get back in time to have a drink and chat with the Wolves manager David Jones, who is a good friend of mine. But when I got back to my little room which was just next to the team's dressing room, David wasn't there. Instead, Mervyn and Keith were there with Richard Murray.

'Alan, I've got to tell you something,' said Richard, and I could see from the look on his face that I wasn't going to be too happy with the news he was about to give me.

He explained that he'd been contacted the night before by Chelsea and they wanted to buy Parker. Apparently Scott also knew about their interest and had gone into the room before I arrived to find out from Richard exactly where he stood, because he already knew of Chelsea's interest in him.

My mind went back to the summer of 2002 when Richard had called me from the Landmark Hotel in London where he'd been in a scheduled close-season Premiership meeting. He'd been talking to Trevor Birch, who at the time was Chelsea's chief executive, and it was clear the West London club fancied Scott.

'You better get over here Alan and listen to what they have to say,' Richard insisted.

This was all pre-Roman Abramovich and Ken Bates was still the Chelsea chairman, but they were still not afraid of spending a few bob when it came to buying players and were clearly becoming a force in the English game. When I started to hear details of their offer I thought they were having a bit of a laugh with us. They wanted to pay around £5 million and spread the payments over a five-year period. I couldn't believe it.

'Are you sure?' I asked Trevor. 'You're offering me only £5 million for my best player and the money isn't even going to be up front!'

I told Richard that as far as I was concerned, if he accepted the offer, I was off. I just wasn't going to have it and in the end I think Trevor Birch was left in no uncertain terms that the transfer wasn't going to happen. I could see why they would want Scotty, because not only was he a good player, he was also instrumental in helping us beat them on quite a few occasions, and their manager, Claudio Ranieri, must have known that the common factor in those defeats for his side was Scott Parker. I knew after we'd beaten them in that Boxing Day game that they might get serious again about signing Parker, but I never thought their interest would be as immediate.

On the Monday after the Wolves game Scott came to see me, but I think he was a bit surprised by what I said to him.

'You're not going,' I told him. 'I've got a club to run and I'm not letting you go.'

Chelsea had made their offer during the January transfer

window which is right in the middle of the season. It's a terrible time to lose any player because you're into your season and the disruption can be immense. Scott was my best player and I didn't want to lose him, but it was the timing which was so upsetting. I'm realistic enough to know that the bigger clubs can always come and get your players if they want to, but at least you have a better chance of coping with it if you're not in the middle of a season.

The other thing which upset me was that I felt they'd insulted us with the offer they made, which was similar to the kind of figure Trevor Birch had talked about, but not spread over the sort of long five-year time-frame that had been mentioned before. It seemed to me that Chelsea had a bit of a change in policy when it came to trying to do a deal with us. Whereas they didn't seem too fussed about the money they were splashing out when Roman Abramovich first took over and they not only paid the asking price but paid it all up front, that seemed to change with us. It was as though they wanted to be a bit tougher and stronger when it came to negotiating future transfers, perhaps they felt they had been taken advantage of in the past, but why pick on us? I knew from that moment that it wasn't going to be the best of times because of what was likely to follow.

When Scott came to see me I think he thought the whole thing was cut and dried. He believed he had a gentleman's agreement with Richard, but he certainly didn't have one with me and I told him so.

'But you said I could go to a top three club,' he insisted.

'No Scott,' I told him. 'I said that when you do leave here, they are the clubs you should go to.'

I recalled the conversation I'd had with him some time ago.

It was before Abramovich took control of Chelsea and they had moved themselves into the top three. I'd actually listed the clubs.

'Manchester United, Arsenal and Liverpool,' I said. 'If you leave here you've got to leave for those clubs.'

I never once said he could leave, I was giving him an example of the clubs he should be aiming to join if he ever left us. He reminded me of the time we'd walked off together after a match at Old Trafford. Paul Scholes got away with an outrageous tackle on Parker, but Scotty had just got up and carried on. The same sort of thing happened in a match with Liverpool, when Steven Gerrard sorted him out and Parker just dusted himself off and played on. As we walked off at Old Trafford I pulled him over.

'If you carry on like this, these are the sort of places you're going to end up,' I claimed. 'You're top three, but you've got to come to these places and let them know who you are, and that's why you've been sorted out today.'

It was meant as a bit of praise and also as a motivating tool to show him what he could achieve in the game, but as far as Scott was concerned, that type of thing translated into me saying he could go as soon as someone like Chelsea made a bid.

As the week wore on Scott became more and more distraught because of the situation he found himself in. We were having daily meetings and there were also numerous phone-calls. He kept repeating himself.

'The chairman said I could go, you said I could go to a top three side, Chelsea are a top three side.' He said it over and over again. He told me that at Charlton we were never going to win the Premiership and probably never going to get into the Champions League. We may not even win a cup. He wanted the chance to be involved in all of those things and he wanted to be in the England team. As far as he was concerned I was denying him the chance to do all of that.

'I'm sorry Scott but I'm not going to sanction it,' I insisted. 'I think what's going on is out of order. For a start you're worth a lot more money than they're offering, and it seems obvious that the reason the whole thing is out in the open is to put more pressure on everyone.'

He insisted that Richard had told him he could go, but I pointed out that if that was the case he should have got his agent to get it in writing, or had it put in his contract. I could see the whole thing was really beginning to get to him and it was also having a draining effect on me. I actually phoned Scott's agent after the first couple of days after the story broke and told him he should get over and see his client, because I knew Scotty was in turmoil and it was almost as if he was grieving having had someone torn away from him.

There was no way I could include him in the team for our match at Everton, because his head was all over the place. We had a 1–0 win up there to maintain our good form and the fourth place we'd earned in the league, but it was Chelsea, the team just one place in front of us, who were causing all the problems for me.

As soon as Monday came around I had Scott in to see me again saying that he couldn't understand my attitude, telling me what he'd done for the club. I never once denied he had always given everything to the cause when he pulled on a Charlton shirt, but he was completely unable to get his head around what I'd actually said to him in the past. He kept on insisting that I had said he could go and as far as he was concerned I was now backtracking on that. He even said he might do a story in the papers letting everyone know.

'If you go into the papers and say that, I'll sue you,' I warned him. 'I know exactly what I said and it's not what you're claiming.'

That set him off on another blast at me and the situation was getting worse by the day. There was no way I would ever have wanted to deny him a career opportunity, but I was doing my job. Morally I had a problem with it because I knew he could probably treble his wages by moving to Chelsea, but I felt as if I had been left to deal with it all and I knew it had to be resolved. It wasn't a good situation to have around the training ground. I didn't want to see Scott in the state he was in, and I didn't want all of his good work for the club to be forgotten. Richard was out of the country leaving Peter Varney and me to deal with matters. I knew Scotty was probably going to go, but I had to do my best for the club, and I think I did because we ended up with a deal worth more than £10 million. It was a real struggle for Peter and me, and we were joined near the end by Richard. Eventually the three of us got the deal done and we had to admit defeat, as we let Parker go to Stamford Bridge. In situations like that the bigger club is always going to get their man if they are prepared to pay the price, and from the smaller club's point of view it's important that they get the right money.

On the day Scott left we were training for our home game with Bolton and I had a chat with Matt Holland and Paolo.

'He had to go,' said Di Canio. 'We all love Scotty, but he had to go.'

They both realized the realities of life in the world of football and I think they both summed up the way everyone felt about Scott.

Once the transfer had gone through I spoke to the media and felt I had to defend our position as a club. During all the press talk Martin Simons had given the impression that we weren't going to sell Scott for the £10 million figure that was being bandied around, but we had done and obviously the press wanted to know why. I did say that Scott had let me know in more ways than ten that he wanted to go, and in the end we had to do it. In hindsight I suppose that comment was a bit unfair on him, but the whole thing had become so protracted and I'd had enough of it. I suppose the situation might have been different if Chelsea had offered the £10 million straight away, but it just crept up and I was caught in the middle of it all.

To be fair to Scott, once he'd got the move, he handled himself brilliantly in the press. I'd had a go at him and he felt a bit sore about that, but he swallowed it all and got on with his life. A week after the transfer I sent him a note just thanking him for what he'd done when he was with us, and telling him that he had it in his locker to go on and do whatever he wanted in the game. I also reminded him that he needed to keep playing the way he had for us in order to get the rewards, and I wished him all the best for the future.

We actually played Chelsea at Stamford Bridge soon after he signed for them but he wasn't going to play against us, and instead watched his new team defeat his old side 1–0. I bumped into him on the day and it kind of broke the ice between us, and a month later I saw him again when I was having a cup of tea with John Hayes after playing golf at The London Club and Scott walked in with John Terry. He came over and we spoke, but I think he still felt a bit awkward, because although he was talking to both of us, he kept looking at John Hayes and not me.

It was a shame that the transfer dragged on the way it did and it was also a shame that it happened when it did. It left me with no real time to get anyone in, although winger Jerome Thomas did join us in a £100,000 transfer from Arsenal. It reminded me a bit of the Robert Lee transfer. We'd been top and Newcastle had been second, Chelsea were third and we were fourth. Kevin Keegan took my best player and damaged me, Chelsea took our best player and damaged us. Having been at Charlton as a manager for nearly 13 years I just thought I'd earned the right to finish as high in the league as we possibly could. Having Scott in my side was a crucial part of the equation, but he'd been ripped away from us.

Fourth position was the highest we reached that season and after Parker left our form fluctuated a bit, but the good thing was that we stayed in the top half and never dropped lower than ninth. I think we could have finished in the top four and been the surprise package, just as Everton were to prove to be a season later. When we went to Anfield for our match with Liverpool there was still talk of possible European football and the historic 1–0 win we got up there only underlined the fact that we were in with a chance. Shaun Bartlett got the winner in the second half and it was our first win there in more than 50 years. On a personal note it was also pretty satisfying for me because it was the first time I'd ever won at Anfield as a player or manager. The victory against Liverpool was our seventh away win of the season in the Premiership and there was no doubt that form played a big part in making sure we stayed among the leading clubs.

Having had such a good campaign, in true Charlton fashion, we didn't exactly make things easy for ourselves as we came to the last match of the season with Southampton at The Valley. We knew that if we won the game we could finish as high as seventh and that if we lost we could end the season as low as 12th.

To finish seventh was going to mean our highest ever placing in the Premiership and Paolo had started to realize he could be a part of a special piece of history for the club. Nobody was more determined to make sure we beat Southampton that day and it was his little flick that helped set up Jason Euell's opening goal after 36 minutes. We won the match 2–1 with another goal from Carlton Cole in the second half, before David Prutton pulled one back for them. By that time Paolo was off the pitch having hurt his ribs, and when we got back into the dressing room after the game he was gone. His ribs were hurting him so much that he'd gone to hospital for X-rays and then flew to Milan the next day.

I felt I had to contact Di Canio, not just to see him again and thank him for what he'd done, but also because we had to decide whether we were going to offer him another contract. We finally got in touch with him and I flew out to Italy with Jeff Vetere. When we got to Milan a beaming Paolo was outside signing autographs as he waited to pick us up in his blue Ferrari. We went for a meal with him choosing the food and wine and he was great company as we started to discuss my plans for the new season. I told Paolo that I wanted him to come back to the club and sign a new contract with us, but at the same time I wanted him to know that I was going to try to sign new players, and if he did come back he might not play as much as he had before. I flew home and left it to Richard to talk with Di Canio's agent about a new contract.

We agreed a deal and he came back to do the pre-season with us. As part of our preparations we played a friendly game at Luton which he played in. I could see something wasn't quite right with him and I said as much to reserve team coach Glynn Snodin on the day. It was as if his heart wasn't really in what he was doing, but it wasn't until the following Monday morning that I found out exactly why that was.

'Boss, I've got a big problem,' were his first words to me as he sat in my office at the training ground. Paolo told me that Lazio wanted him to sign for them and as he told me the story he spoke really quickly, as if he was pleased to finally get the whole thing off his chest. Lazio was his first love in football and even though they were offering him a greatly reduced contract to the one he had with us, it was clear there was no way we could keep him. I spoke to Richard and told him what the situation was, and like me, he thought it was best that Paolo went back to Italy. I think Di Canio was disappointed to be leaving us, and perhaps he wouldn't have done it for any club other than Lazio. He may have only been with us for one season but he'd left us with something. He wanted to help get us our best ever Premiership position, and he'd been part of the team that achieved that.

He was never really a problem for me even though a lot of people said that he might be. I never asked anyone about him before he signed for us and the main reason for that was because I didn't want to be turned off the idea. Normally I would ask all sorts of people in the game about a player I was going to sign, but I didn't want to go down that route with him. He was a true professional and if he had his little moans and grizzles when he was left out of the team, that was understandable. I think he was a bit upset with the way he was perceived in this country by a lot of football fans, but he was never any trouble. I remember him coming in one day and he looked very down. I asked him what was wrong and he produced a newspaper article.

'Look at this,' he said pointing at it. 'They have put me in a 'bad boys 11.' I don't drink, I don't smoke, I don't go to nightclubs or get involved in fights. All I did was push a referee and they say I'm a bad boy, but I'm not a bad boy!'

I could understand what he meant, having seen the way he worked and dedicated himself to the game. It was obvious he loved football. He was passionate about what he did and perhaps that was the side of him that led to the famous push on referee Paul Alcock when Di Canio was playing for Sheffield Wednesday in 1998, earning him a bit of a reputation, but that was never in evidence with us.

He became part of the club within a very short period of time and I know he enjoyed his stay. Towards the end of his season with us I organized a short break to Spain. At first Paolo wasn't keen on going but he knew he wasn't going to be given a choice, and I soon found out that the main reason he didn't want to go was because he thought it was going to be just a boozy few days away from home. He said that if that was the case he'd sit in his room as he'd done on previous trips, but I told him that he had to come with us and it was important that we all did it as a squad because although there'd be a bit of rest and relaxation, it wasn't going to revolve around drinking, and we'd be training and acting in a professional manner while we were out there. In the end he decided to come and I think he thoroughly enjoyed the whole thing. He even ended up singing with the owner of an Italian restaurant on our last night there when we all went out for a meal as a squad. It was another example of how well he fitted in during his time with us and if he was a bit of a big fish in a smaller pool, I think that suited him and it certainly suited us. He always trained well and was dedicated to his profession, sometimes a little too much so. We had to stop him doing extra work in the gym he had at his house, but that was just the way he was made and it was also probably why he was able to play at the top for so long. When he came to us I said that if Alex Ferguson had been thinking of signing him a year or so earlier, that was good enough for me, and it summed up how I felt. He had that touch of quality that I think we were lacking before he arrived and it was important that we maintained that calibre of player at the club.

Having finished the season so well, I was still left with the fact that I'd lost both Parker and Di Canio. To add to the problems I had that summer, both Gary Rowett and Richard Rufus officially retired and Claus Jensen decided he wanted to leave and sign for Fulham. It was not an ideal situation, but it was all part of what my job was about. I was paid to manage what I'd got.

22 Managing What You've Got

It was very early on in my managerial career that I first heard the phrase, 'You've got to manage what you've got.' The words came from Alex Ferguson and when I heard them I thought they summed up perfectly just what the job I do is about.

As manager of Manchester United Alex has to do certain things to try and achieve certain goals each season, and as manager of Charlton I had to do the same. Exactly just what was expected of us in terms of success and failure may be different, because it's all relative. But your job as a manager is to manage, using whatever resources are at your disposal. It's the same for any manager at any club; we all have to operate in different circumstances, but we're all doing the same job. Whether you're in charge of a club in League Two or in the Premiership, the job is still all-consuming. There are pressures at all levels of the game and if you fail there is often no way back.

People talk about the 'managerial merry-go-round', as if we are all swapping places on a regular basis, and if you get the sack at one club, then another soon comes along to offer you a job. But the reality of the profession is very different. In the first ten years after the Premiership started there were 458 managerial changes, throughout the 92 clubs in the top flight and in the

Football League. In 2005 only 31 of the original 92 managers were still managing in the Leagues, and another 30 were involved in professional football in another capacity. It goes to show just how high the casualty rate is, and also how important it is for a new manager to make a success of his first job.

I was happy to be one of those 31 still managing; in fact only Alex, Dario Gradi at Crewe and me were still with the same clubs we were in charge of when the Premiership started in 1992. Between the three of us we had put in 55 years with our respective clubs, but that sort of thing is likely to be unheard of in the future, because there seems to be less and less time given to managers to develop a club and a team. Everybody wants success and they want it quickly. The philosophy of so many club chairmen seems to be that if they don't get promotion or win trophies within a few years, the solution is to sack the manager and get a new one.

It's incredible to think that had Alex not been given time after being appointed as Manchester United manager in 1986 he might not be there now, and they might have missed out on all the success they've had since they won their first trophy under him by beating Palace in the FA Cup Final 16 years ago. Dario Gradi's brief at Crewe has been different to Alex's at United. He's had promotions and relegations and at the same time has developed young talent, which the club have then been able to sell to help keep them going. But within the confines of what he's had to operate with nobody would deny he has been successful and done a good job for the club, and his chairman and board of directors obviously feel the same way because he's been there for 23 years.

I might have been at Charlton for less time than Dario and Alex have been at their clubs, but during my 15 years the changes we experienced were immense. It was an incredible time for everyone connected with the club and a continual learning curve for me. I always wanted to be a manager and when I got the opportunity with Steve Gritt I was determined that I was going to do the job to the best of my ability.

Managing is something I felt comfortable with from the very first day and the fact that Gritty and I were both players as well at the time wasn't a problem. Unlike a lot of other people, I actually think it's easier in many ways to still be playing when you first manage, because you are more involved with the players and can influence things on the pitch. The players can also see you are able to get about the pitch and can physically demonstrate what you want from them. Steve and I both knew that we had to do well in the job otherwise we could find ourselves out of work, and I think that first season did a lot to steady things for us and for the club.

Like any other job the more you do it the more experienced you become, but no matter how long you are a football manager there are always new and different situations for you to have to deal with, not all of them concerned purely with football. As the manager of a club the general welfare of the players is ultimately down to you. It's not all about winning and losing matches; there are other problems that come your way as well, and no matter how experienced you become some of them take you by surprise.

I once had a young player come to me petrified that he might have AIDS. He had a brother who was in prison at the time and he had apparently claimed that he had AIDS. The complication in the story came from the fact that the player had slept with his brother's girlfriend, and he had convinced himself that he must have contracted the disease. We actually took him to be tested and were able to get the results very quickly, which happily for the young kid were negative.

On another occasion we had a player who was arrested on suspicion of being involved in an armed robbery. The police turned up at the training ground one day to tell me that he was in custody and being questioned. It later transpired that he had been given a lift by some of his mates, and when the police stopped the car they were all travelling in, they found a gun in the boot which had been used in a robbery. I'm glad to say that after more enquiries it became clear the player was an innocent party in the whole thing and no charges were ever brought, but it was still a bit of a shock to the system to be told that one of your players might be caught up in something like that.

The general day-to-day workload of any manager is heavy, and it's not just about training and picking a team for a match. I've always felt you need to put in the mileage when it comes to looking at the opposition and potential transfer targets. If you want to do the job properly there are no short cuts. That was true when I first got the job and it was certainly true throughout my time at Charlton. If you want to make a career in management I think you have to start as you mean to go on.

When a manager gets his first appointment the thought which is probably uppermost in his mind is that he has to stay in that job and not get the sack. If he's a success and does well then either he stays with the club or perhaps a bigger and better opportunity comes along which he might go for, but if he fails these days, then the statistic I've already mentioned probably means he'll struggle to get another job as a manager.

Just like players, managers want to operate at the highest level of the game and that means the Premiership. But as a young manager if you're going to get there, it's most likely that you will have to do it by getting promotion and taking a club up. There are very few British managers without previous experience of the division who get a Premiership job by being elevated into one.

Of the current crop only David Moyes at Everton, Mark Hughes at Blackburn, Stuart Pearce at Manchester City, Gareth Southgate at Middlesbrough and Fulham's Chris Coleman fall into that category. As a young manager operating in the Football League the route to the top division is very difficult, but once you are there it becomes obvious very quickly that the job changes.

Of course the basics are the same and any manager will have his own way of tackling the job, but what changes most are all the things that surround operating in the Premiership. The quality of player, the stadiums, the crowds, the media attention, and, last but not least, the money are all so different. There is no doubt at all that the rewards are there for a manager as well as a player in the Premiership, and I accept that I got well paid for what I did at Charlton in the Premiership. I had pressures but then so do many people in other jobs and they may not be as well paid, but one of the biggest differences for a football manager is the fact that everything he does is so public. Games in the Premiership are analysed and shown on TV for days, while the papers are always full of football stories on their back pages and sometimes on the front as well. If a plumber makes a mistake installing some central heating he may get in trouble with the people he's working for, but that's about as far as it goes. If a team loses or gets into a bad run the manager is under the microscope on TV, on radio and in the papers, with all sorts of things being said and written about him. It's all out in the open and very public.

This can sometimes have an effect on your family. I've already mentioned how my wife Carol had that 20 questions session at a check-out counter when there were rumours about me joining West Ham, and some years ago my son Michael came home and told me how the dad of one of the kids at his school had said I had better watch out because I might be getting the sack. I think the team were going through a bad patch at the time and there might have been the usual speculation when that sort of thing happens, but it just showed how different it was for Michael compared to someone else at his school whose parent might be having some trouble at work.

Nobody forces any of us to go into management: we do it because we want to and because football is such a big part of what we are about. Whether it is more enjoyable now than it was a few years ago, I'm not so sure. I think one of the things that seems to have disappeared for me in recent years is the social side of being a manager. Even if I go back only five or six years, it seemed as though managers would hang around longer after a game and have a drink and chat about football. These days in the Premiership a team will often be flying back after a game at our place and they leave so early that I probably only see their manager for a few minutes before they have to go. I also think one of the big changes has been what managers actually talk about to each other now. There was a time when all a group of managers would be talking about was football and bits of skill they'd seen from different players. These days the one topic that seems to dominate is money: the size of transfer fees, the money players are asking for and the different finances involved in the game, especially the size of the agents' fees. Managers 20 years ago didn't get the rewards there are today, but I have a feeling it was probably more fun.

As I've said, Alex's words to me all those years ago certainly seemed to sum up exactly what you had to do as a manager, and he is a prime example of someone who has done just that throughout his career. You don't get success just because you are with a big club, and the reason Manchester United are in the position they are today is down to the way he took the job on and managed what he had. People often ask me about the managers I admire in the game, both past and present, and Alex has to be right up there. I admire managers who have taken on the job with a club and moved it on, so that it's totally different to when they arrived at a club.

Brian Clough is obviously a classic example of someone who took a club from nowhere and made them into European champions during his time at Nottingham Forest. What he did was phenomenal and I can't see that it's ever going to be repeated. The only sad part of his time there was that they were relegated right at the end of his reign, and it would have been nice for him if he could have left the club on a high, just as Martin O'Neill did during his time at Leicester.

Another manager I admire is George Graham for what he did at Arsenal. Not only did he win cups and championships, he also brought so many players through from youth level to the first team including people like Tony Adams, Paul Merson and Ray Parlour. He built a club, got the youth set-up going and won things.

When I look at Alex and all his achievements at United I also think a lot of people forget just what an amazing job he did at Aberdeen. Not only did he break the monopoly of Celtic and Rangers, he also got the club into Europe and won the Cup Winners' Cup with them. In many ways, doing that was probably on a par with what Cloughie achieved. Everyone knows about his winning record at United, but he's done some other things that may have gone unnoticed. Old Trafford has improved immeasurably as a stadium during his time due to the success he's achieved on the pitch, and he has introduced an abundance of home-grown talent into the game. He's produced and brought through international players like Beckham, Giggs, Scholes and the Neville brothers, any of whom would have cost an absolute fortune in any transfer market. If he were to leave tomorrow the club, as big as it always was, would be in greater shape than when he took over and for me that's the sign of a good manager.

Arsene Wenger is another manager who has done a great job since he joined Arsenal ten years ago. He has won trophies and maintained a really high standard in the Premiership during that time. He has introduced young players, albeit mainly foreign, into the Arsenal first team and what his side have done on the pitch has helped to generate money to enable the club to move on.

Without wishing to blow my own trumpet, I think there are some similarities between Alex, Arsene Wenger and me. We've all been at clubs for a long time, we've all built or re-built stadiums, we all took our clubs to different levels on the field in terms of performance and off the field in terms of gates. We also brought young players through. Although the two of them operated on a different financial level to me, neither spent money they couldn't afford to spend. Of course they have won major trophies, but Charlton are currently enjoying their eighth season in the Premiership during the past ten years, and in that time they've had two promotions. It's all relative but, as Alex said, you 'manage what you've got'.

The same is true for Jose Mourinho, and when he went to

Chelsea he had to sit down and decide just how he was going to attack the job and manage them. It seems to me that one of the major things he did was to improve their organization as a team and make them more disciplined as a unit. The emphasis was much more on teamwork and the players responded to that. He went into a club where, within reason, he knew he could probably buy anyone he wanted, but it's what you do with that kind of buying power that is important. They have been very organized the last two seasons and have won quite a few games 1–0, some when they haven't played too well. It strikes me that the team goes into a week knowing what is expected and how they have to play. Perhaps when Claudio Ranieri was there he liked to change things around a bit from game to game and they didn't do too badly under him, but Mourinho has come in and improved them as a team. He's given the players a format that they are comfortable with and produced a team that has given Manchester United and Arsenal something to think about. I've got a lot of time for him and his record at Porto was second to none in the way he took a relatively small club and won the Champions League with them.

The one thing I would say is that perhaps he needs to count to ten sometimes before saying something. I know the press love him because he's come in and decided to be big and brave, giving the media lots to write and talk about, but I think in some ways that has detracted from what the team achieved with back-to-back Premiership titles. If he allowed his side to do the talking I think Chelsea might get more recognition for what they do on the pitch.

Like Arsene Wenger and Rafael Benitez at Liverpool, Jose Mourinho has come to England and won things. You sometimes hear people going on about the number of foreign players and managers in our game, and although it's true that there are a lot of players from abroad, mainly in the Premiership, there aren't that many managers. It's just that the ones who are here tend to have the top jobs.

There isn't one English manager currently in the Premiership who has managed a team in the Champions League, and unless one gets into the top four with the club they work for it's difficult to see how that will change. The trend seems to be that the big clubs will continue to look abroad when they have a vacancy, and because the Champions League is such a big part of what the top clubs are about, it appears they want a manager with experience of the competition.

England certainly isn't an exception in having foreign managers – it happens all over the world – but perhaps where we are a bit different is in the way we don't tend to have English managers going to teams in Europe. There have been notable exceptions such as Bobby Robson and Terry Venables, who both had success abroad, but we don't tend to export our managers in quite the same way. On a personal level I don't know if I would ever fancy managing abroad. I enjoy our brand of football and love the Premiership, even if the workload can be heavy at times and you operate so publicly.

Sven-Goran Eriksson got it in the neck earlier last season after losing the World Cup qualifier against Northern Ireland in Belfast. There were calls for his head and he got an awful lot of stick because of the way the team performed, but in terms of the squad he had at his disposal Sven must have known that he had players to compare with the best in the world. I honestly believe that for some time he had perhaps as many as eight players who would probably get into most other sides in the world. They are of the right age group and none are really inexperienced when it comes to international football. Players like Ferdinand, Terry, Cole, Gerrard, Lampard, Owen and Rooney, not to mention Beckham. The problem that night in Belfast seemed to be what shape and system England played.

When I've watched major tournaments, it seems to be the teams with some fluidity that tend to be successful. I'm talking about sides with good defenders and full-backs who can get forward, midfield players who can create and score goals, as well as midfielders who win important tackles. Forwards who not only know how to score, but are direct and purposeful so that they put the opposition defenders on the back foot. I happen to think we've got those sort of players in this country, but I think the big problem at times has been fitting them into a shape they are comfortable with. I'm convinced you play a system that is best for the players you have. Once you identify your best 11, you fit the system around them. You may want to play 4–4–2, 4–5–1 or 4–3–3. Whatever system it is that you employ, you have to have players comfortable in certain areas of the pitch, and they need to be used to the role they have so that not too much thinking time is used up in a match situation. They should do things almost instinctively.

I've always believed that a big part of being a professional in a position of responsibility is the ability to take control of a situation, particularly when the pressure is on, and make a decision. That applies to any profession and it certainly applies to football management.

When he first came into the job Sven was quite lucky to have inherited such a good group of players. He had the nucleus of a very good side with young talent that was going to mature at just the right time for him. Having seen what has happened in the past few years with the England team, it seemed to me that the World Cup finals in Germany would be the perfect stage for them to perform and push on from the last couple of tournaments, with a great chance to get in the last four because the quality of the players in the squad would give us a chance to do just that.

As I have already mentioned, I was never negative about a foreign manager being in charge of the England team. If the FA felt there was no one in place at the time who could have stepped in and that Eriksson was the best man for the job, they had to go for him. When it was decided that Sven would be leaving after the World Cup none of the English candidates had managed a team in the Champions League and if you were looking at an English manager who had managed at the highest level and won things, then you had to go back to Sir Bobby Robson.

It's not the fault of the FA, because they can't tell clubs who they should employ so that they can get the right sort of experience.

In football management one moment you can be flavour of the month and then a couple of results down the line that can all change. Over the years I've been asked loads of 'what if?' questions when there's been speculation about different jobs. In the fall-out from that result against Northern Ireland I was mentioned, along with a few other English managers, as a possible future candidate for the job. I'd be lying if I said it wasn't flattering, because at the very least it meant that I must have been doing something right. The talk soon blew over, but what I didn't realize at the time was that just a few months later the English manager's job would become such a heated topic of conversation when Sven's future departure was announced. I found myself in the frame again, only this time all the talk had a lot more substance to it.

23 **A Bent Deal**

It suddenly seemed the job of managing had got a lot harder as I prepared for the start of the season in 2004. I wasn't feeling sorry for myself, but it was a fact that within a very few months I had lost some of my biggest players. We may have just finished seventh in the Premiership, but I wouldn't have been human had I not thought of what might have been if Parker had not gone to Chelsea when he did, and it wasn't just the loss of Scott that I had to contend with. Although they hadn't played any real part in the previous season there had been a hope that Richard Rufus and Gary Rowett might recover from their injuries, but as time went on it became increasingly clear that wouldn't happen. Rufus hadn't played since April 2003, and Rowett only took part in the first game of the season against Manchester City before being out for the rest of the campaign. In the end both of them had to officially retire in the summer of 2004, so not only had I lost my best player in Parker, I'd also lost Rufus who was my best defender and Rowett, along with striker Carlton Cole who had completed a season-long loan from Chelsea.

Pre-season is always an important time in terms of preparation for what is to come and making sure the players are fit and in no doubt about the way you want them to play when the real action starts in August. It's also a time when you want to have your squad in place, with any transfer business already done. The reality is that quite often by the time you start training at the beginning of July there are still transfer targets out there that you haven't managed to get for one reason or another; it can be frustrating but it's also a fact of life. As soon as a season ends most managers will have a list of players they want to try and buy. You know the gaps you want to fill in your squad, either because the team needs strengthening in certain areas or because players have left and need replacing. I knew for certain when I drew up my own wish list that summer those same players would also be targets for another half dozen clubs in the Premiership.

Charlton couldn't go out and shop at the same store as Chelsea, Manchester United, Arsenal, Liverpool and Newcastle. Those clubs were in a league of their own in terms of buying power and attractiveness, offering any potential target Champions League football, or at least the very real prospect of it. But I did want to upgrade the squad we had and continue to try and bring in the sort of players we might not have done in the past. The previous summer we'd got Paolo Di Canio, who was a different type of player for us. Some people had warned me against it and said he could be trouble and it wouldn't work, but that wasn't the case. Paolo enjoyed his season with us and we enjoyed having him at the club. The move worked because he did give us something different and he appreciated what we were all about as a club and took the whole thing on board as I'd hoped he would.

After Parker went all the talk was about how much money I had to spend, and that I had the biggest transfer budget of any

Charlton manager ever, but there haven't been too many of us in recent years and transfer fees have moved on a bit since Lennie left in 1991. Having a lot of money may sound good, but the reality of trying to spend wisely in trying to bring in the people you want can be very different. The mechanics of a transfer have always been the same. A manager wants a player, checks to see if he is available and if a fee and personal terms can be agreed the player joins your club, as long as there are no medical problems.

That in essence is what happens, but the way transfers are conducted these days is very different to when I first became a manager. The haggling in a pub over a few quid when Alan Pardew signed for us is light years away from even the most basic transfer now. Back then you hardly ever heard of agents, but I can't imagine there is a deal concluded now without an agent being involved. I'm not the sort of manager who says there is no place for agents in the game. It's a fact of life that they are part and parcel of the fabric of football now, and like any other profession there are good ones and there are bad ones.

They have become one of the big forces in any transfer deal and are just as influential as the buying or selling club. Ten years ago you could go into a room with a player having already negotiated a fee with his club knowing the only real stumbling block to a possible deal would be wages or a medical problem. Agents just didn't really come into the equation, but that has changed in recent years, and they can now be a stumbling block in negotiations because of the money they may want to conclude a deal. Clubs are paying a lot more money out in general these days when it comes to transfers, and some of the stories I've heard about are frightening. I don't think there's any doubt that a lot of people in football resent the amount of money agents get. In so many transfer deals these days you pay the selling club, pay the player and pay the agent. For a time I think there were clubs up and down the country questioning what they were paying agents, but I think the whole system has improved because of the transparency which now goes along with transfer deals where people can see what agents have been paid.

In past years that wasn't always the case and with the way things were set up it was quite conceivable that some agents could get paid by the buying club, the selling club and the player! There have been cases where a foreign club has called in an agent to help sell a player. They may have said they wanted £2 million for the player and if the agent sells him to a club, he would get a percentage of that fee. But there was nothing to stop the agent asking clubs for £3 million for the player, paying the buying club what they wanted, and then taking the rest of the money himself. It was stories like that which have helped prompt some of the new practices and that can only be for the good.

There's no doubt that in some cases agents probably earn too much money, but you can't do without them. Managers have all got close ties to certain agents and over the last ten years I've been asked to sign with all sorts of agents who want to represent me. I was at a League Managers Association meeting once and asked whether it was right for managers to have an agent. At the time I was probably the only one in the room who didn't have an agent, although I've since employed the First Artists agency to act for me on purely commercial matters such as writing this book. I can see the problems which come for a manager who is closely affiliated to a particular agent, because he may end up buying most of his players through him. But all the managers I know who have agents themselves still have working relationships with the other agents. Maintaining those relationships with agents is vitally important for a manager and a club. They have their ear to the ground, they talk to other chairmen and chief executives to find out who is available and they are part of the football world. If you don't have that relationship you're not going to hear first-hand what players are available and you're not going to be in the loop.

I think that perhaps Charlton have been at a disadvantage at times because the club made a bit of a stand against some of the money asked for, but that's not always the case elsewhere and some clubs' bills for agency fees are phenomenal. In some ways it's gone from wondering what a potential selling club will be asking for a player, to wondering what the player's agent will be asking for. I know of some deals which have broken down, unbeknown to the player, because his agent has asked for too much money. Some clubs take the view that it's sometimes worth paying over the top just to make sure they secure the signature of a player. An agent may quote a figure to a club which would be his fee if his client moves, and I know of instances where they've been given more just to make sure the deal gets done and there's no competition. One chief executive was known as 'Father Christmas' because whenever agents went in to see him and do a deal, they always came out smiling with what they'd been offered.

I'm not for one minute saying agents are not needed in the game, because it's very difficult for players to negotiate contracts on their own, but at the same time I've always thought that the best agent for a player is the Professional Footballers' Association. They know exactly what the pay scales are, because they have access to them as the union looks after players, and I don't think their fees are comparable at all to the commercial agents. There are some agents out there who you only hear from when there's a contract discussion or a possible transfer involving one of their clients. They don't phone up to see how their player is getting on and they don't even go to watch him in a match. They don't follow up on any personal problems a player might have, and generally keep their distance. Then there are the other sort of agents who regularly visit their clients and are involved in things like their welfare and other matters. You have to deal with all of them, whether they are good, bad or indifferent.

At Charlton if we thought an overall deal was too much, we'd back off and not do anything. The club missed out on players because they did not bow to the agent's demands, and to the pressure of it all. It's a scenario which I'm sure has happened all over the country and it means you lose out on a player. I think I've got the reputation as one of the straightest managers in the game and only once in all the discussions I've ever had with agents have I been asked if I wanted anything out of a deal. He basically told me what his fee would be and suggested that he could add a bit on top which would be for me. It's not something I would ever do or get involved in, and I'm happy knowing that not one agent can point a finger at me and say they ever gave me anything for a transfer deal.

Having the sort of transparency that exists now is good because before the system was potentially open to so much abuse. There's a hell of a lot of money involved in big transfers these days and consequently an agent's fee for being involved in a deal can be huge as well. Let's say a player is involved in a £10 million or £18 million transfer; you could be looking at an agency fee of something like £3 million or £4 million. There are staggering sums involved, and if you don't cringe at some of the big money being paid out in the game, you've lost touch with reality. But that's the situation we find ourselves in and we have to get on with it. When it comes to the Premiership the figures are huge, and on a personal level the money I earned in recent years compared to the wages I was on when I first entered management was totally different. It's the same with the players. When Charlton came into the Premiership for the first time we knew we were in a different financial ball-game, and we had some players on around £250,000 a year, which was a big hit for us. In recent years you'd be looking at paying players something like three or four times that.

So whenever I tried bringing players into the club I knew we were making a huge financial commitment and it was important that I got it right. There can never be any guarantee that a transfer will work out, but it's not just a question of targeting someone and hoping it all goes well. I've always liked to do as much homework on them as I could before even getting close to making a bid. In the summer of 2004 I knew we had a hole in the squad because of the players we'd lost, and I wanted to try and sign people who would make a difference in much the same way Di Canio had, so we set out sights a bit higher. The trouble is, in doing that it tends to mean you have a more difficult time because there is more competition from other clubs for the player you want and he has more options open to him.

I felt it was a shame that Carlton Cole decided to go to Villa on loan and not stay with Charlton, because I thought we were the right club for him and he would have done well with us. I needed a striker and we decided to chase Southampton's James Beattie. They had their valuation of the player and we thought it was too high. There was a lot of talk about quite a few clubs being interested in him, but as the weeks went by it became clear that wasn't the case. We hung in there for quite some time, but weren't prepared to pay the asking price. In hindsight, perhaps we should have just made the decision not to go ahead with it as soon as we heard what Southampton wanted, but the idea of possibly signing him seemed to drag on for a long time before the deal died.

As part of our pre-season we went on a ten-day trip to China and left a couple of our internationals behind because they'd had a shorter summer having played for their countries. One of them was Jensen, and it was while I was halfway across the world that I discovered via a phone call from Richard that Claus was off to Fulham. He had a year left on his contract and didn't want to sign a new deal. He had nothing against the club or me; it was simply a case of him feeling it was the right time for him to move and he left in a deal that was worth more than £1.5 million. Richard asked me who I wanted as a replacement and I immediately told him to go after Tim Cahill at Millwall. As I've said, I had a good track record with Richard when it came to getting the players we wanted. We worked well as a team and each covered certain areas during the course of a transfer which usually ended in us getting our man, but because I was in China there was no way I was going to get the chance to meet the player. Richard agreed terms with Millwall, and then had to meet the player and his agent to try and thrash out a deal.

That summer I think we ended up learning a valuable lesson. When you've got a player you really want and you're in a room and are negotiating with him, you just can't afford to let him leave. By that I mean you have to make sure you nail down a deal, otherwise it leaves the door open for another club to step in, and that's exactly what happened with Cahill. Everton, who were always interested in him anyway, came in and bought the player. I'm not saying it would have been different if I had been there to talk to Cahill, but because I was so far away at the time I was left wondering what might have been.

I've already mentioned what a big part Jeff Vetere played in helping us get Jorge Costa on loan, and he came up trumps again with the news that French Under-21 international Mathieu Flamini was available as a free transfer from Marseille. I'd already seen him play for the Under-21s and his club, so I knew that at 20 years old he was a really good prospect. We got him over to England and had a meeting one Sunday in one of the West Stand boxes at The Valley.

Flamini and his agent travelled over and met with Peter Varney and me, but this time it was Richard who was missing from the equation because he was on holiday. We thought there was a northern club in this country interested in signing Flamini, and wanted to get the deal done but after we made our best offer he decided to leave without anything being concluded. Once again we'd let a player leave the room and not too long after that we paid the price, because although we kept in contact with him and his agent, Arsenal suddenly seemed to appear from nowhere and snapped him up. I actually thought at the time that he would stand a chance of playing more football with us than with Arsenal, but he has ended up featuring in a lot of games for them and showing the quality I knew he had. So once again we found ourselves being unsuccessful in trying to sign a player. I had managed to bolster the squad by getting defender Talal El Karkouri, keeper Stephan Andersen and midfielder Bryan Hughes, but I knew I still lacked people in key areas and time was running out.

Our transfer luck began to change a few weeks before the season was due to start when we bought winger Dennis Rommedahl from PSV Eindhoven, and as the big kick-off approached it emerged that Liverpool and England midfielder Danny Murphy might be available. We agreed a fee for him but so did Tottenham, and we knew we would be in competition with them for his signature. Having failed with Cahill and Flamini I was determined that we wouldn't miss out again. Both Richard and I knew that once we got Danny in a room we had to convince him to sign for us. This time the double act was back in action and we settled into our usual routine. We both met the player, Richard met the agent, and then I talked to Danny. We both had another session with them, and then Richard spoke to the two of them again. We knew he wanted to talk to Tottenham to see what they could offer him, but I think both Richard and I were confident that we had convinced Danny that Charlton was the right club for him, and in the end he chose us.

With just days to go before the season started, I finally managed to bring a striker into the club when Francis Jeffers signed from Arsenal, but the summer had been a real struggle on the transfer front, and it occurred to me that perhaps it was easier when you don't have any money to spend because the targets are more straightforward. When you start to get into the situation where you are trying to sign players of a higher calibre you sometimes also get into a bit of an auction. Our whole player acquisition that summer was a problem, because although we did get people in, they arrived late, did little of the pre-season with us and had trouble settling in. We also had the China trip which, although successful, proved time consuming and meant I was not in the country at a vital time.

The 2004–05 season turned out to be the most draining season I had ever experienced during my time with the club.

After ten years in sole charge of the team and another four as the joint manager, I could not remember ever feeling that way before. I couldn't wait for the season to come to an end and throughout the campaign I felt as though I wasn't just managing a football team, I was also engaged in a fire-fighting exercise.

As a squad we had lost key players like Scott Parker, Richard Rufus, Gary Rowett, Claus Jensen and Paolo Di Canio. We failed to get some of our transfer targets during the summer leading up to the start of the season, had a disjointed pre-season that included a draining trip to China, and when we did sign some quality players they found it difficult to bed themselves in.

As a consequence we never really got things together in the League and by the end of October I felt we could be in serious trouble if I didn't do something to remedy the situation. After playing ten games in the Premiership we had picked up 12 points and were in eleventh place in the table. It wasn't a bad position at that stage in the season, but I still couldn't help having an uneasy feeling about how the team was playing and the fact that as a squad we didn't seem to be functioning in the way I had hoped. In the space of a week we had two terrible results which really highlighted the problems there had been since the opening game of the season. On a Wednesday night at The Valley we lost a third-round Carling Cup match 2–1 to Palace, who virtually fielded their reserve side, and we followed that up by losing at home by the same score to Middlesbrough in the Premiership three days later.

As a manager I knew I had to take some action. A week after that result we went to White Hart Lane to play Tottenham and I made a decision that seemed to infuriate a lot of our supporters and also upset some of my players, but I believe it possibly saved us from being sucked into a relegation struggle for the rest of the season. I also know that I will always be able to look back on that decision and say that I did the right thing.

For the game against Spurs I decided to switch to a 4–5–1 formation. I needed to make us tougher to beat as a team and give us a base with which to start picking up some points. The switch in formation had an immediate effect and we came away from North London with a 3–2 victory. From the time of that win until we played Spurs again at The Valley in March we picked up 31 points. It was a total that kept us in the top half of the table and ensured Premiership football for another season, allowing Charlton Athletic to continue its growth as a club.

But even during the successful period between the Tottenham games, I could never really feel comfortable with the way things were going. I had signed striker Francis Jeffers from Arsenal during the summer and he came to us not only wanting to play, but expecting to play as well. The trouble was, after changing things around in the game at Tottenham, Francis found himself out of the side. That became a problem. Jason Euell was another player who was unable to get a regular first-team place, and that became another problem.

Players like to play, but as a manager you can only really make 11 of them happy each week, and they are the people who are being selected for the team. Although we were picking up points and getting some important results, the overall performance of the team on many occasions wasn't as convincing as it should have been. When you've got the situation as a manager where your team on the pitch can't put the team off the pitch in its place, you have a problem.

You will always have players in a squad who think they

should be in the first team, and they will come to see you and voice their opinions. It's something I can understand and all part of being a manager, but it's also something that can become draining over a long period of time.

It wasn't that we had an unhappy squad but, because we never really established a winning pattern and often had to grind results out without the kind of excitement and flair we would all have liked, it certainly won't go down as one of the happiest seasons of my 15 years in charge.

In recent years we had managed to make sure of our place in the Premiership by reaching the magic 40-point mark well before the season ended. As I've already said, those 40 points usually ensure safety from relegation and allow a club to start planning for the future, knowing they are going to be playing top-flight football once again. By the time we beat Tottenham 2–0 at The Valley on 16 March 2005 we had amassed 43 points and knew we could look forward to our sixth uninterrupted season in the Premiership, but I also realized we had another nine games to go.

I desperately wanted us to finish higher than our seventh position the previous year, and at that stage there was every reason to believe we were capable of doing just that, and thus get into Europe, but in the final weeks of the season we followed an all-too-familiar pattern and failed to win another match. It was the inevitability of it that really began to get to me, because so often in recent years we had allowed the same sort of thing to happen. Instead of finishing with a flourish we had allowed our season to fall away and left a bad taste in the mouths of our supporters. Of the nine games we had left after the Tottenham result, we managed just three draws, and lost the other six matches.

It was a terrible record and as the poor run continued during those final weeks, a lot of people began to question whether I had perhaps been at the club for too long. Had I got fed up with it all and gone stale? Were the players not responding to me any more? Had I lost my touch after being in charge during the most successful period in the club's history? It wasn't exactly discontent from our fans but there were murmurs. A few voiced their opinions on radio phone-ins and even the media began to openly ask me if I was thinking of moving on. To be honest, I did start to ask the same sort of questions of myself.

When the Sky TV cameras caught up with me after the home game with Manchester United at the beginning of May, reporter Geoff Shreeves asked me about my future at the club and whether it might be the time to move on. My answer to the question left the whole matter open to speculation because I didn't say I would definitely be staying. I suppose I had been caught a bit by surprise and just tried to be as honest as I could.

I was probably at a bit of a low point. We had just been beaten 4–0 in front of our own fans and it was the manner of our per-formance in the last 30 minutes of the game that upset me so much. It wasn't what I expected from a Charlton team, and it wasn't something I was prepared to accept. I knew what had happened. The team had simply tried to make sure they didn't get beaten 8–0. But it all looked so helpless and it was a gutting experience for me. The match was shown live on TV, I could see our fans wandering out of The Valley with 20 minutes to go, and it looked as though United could score goals whenever they wanted to. In all the time I'd been at the club it was prob-ably the worst feeling I'd had; even getting relegated from the Premiership in 1999 didn't feel as bad. It was the acceptance of the situation that I couldn't take. I felt sorry for the fans but, if

I'm honest, I felt more sorry for myself and with two games to go I couldn't wait for the end of the season to come.

Driving home after the match I started to think about what had gone on and decided I was never going to have a Charlton side play like that again. I know teams can sometimes drift into giving performances like that, but I believed it shouldn't happen to us, not when you thought about where we had come from and the struggles we'd had along the way. I wondered whether we had people in the squad who thought they'd 'arrived', and perhaps had become blasé or too precious. The afternoon had been a shock to me and it wasn't something I would forget.

After that Sky TV interview I got a few calls from other managers that I respected. People like Graham Taylor, Steve Bruce and Sam Allardyce, all of them offering words of advice and encouragement. Graham in particular was very good, because I suppose he could see parallels between the two of us, having spent so long at Watford and done such a great job there. A lot of fans spoke to me as well in the days that followed and asked me not to leave the club. They needn't have worried, I had no intention of walking away, but when I sat down in the summer with chairman Richard Murray I knew something had to change.

To be the manager of a football club for 14 years is a very long time, particularly in this day and age. It was easy for people on the outside to put two and two together and then come up with five, suggesting that I'd been around for too long or that I needed to move away. Having been at Charlton for my entire managerial career I didn't feel I was going stale, but I did feel that for the sake of the club and for my own sake, I needed to take a slightly different approach and freshen things up. At the end of any season I always took time to sit down and analyse what had gone on during the previous months, the rights and wrongs, the successes and the failures. I tried to see what I could learn from the season, correct the mistakes and improve on my overall performance. Most of all I always wanted to continue to build on what we'd done as a club.

When I had time to reflect on the season I realized that over-all we hadn't done too badly. In fact, despite the way I felt at the end of it, the season had been a success. It was a season of re-building and re-grouping, and we'd managed to do it in the Premiership. The only really disappointing thing had been the tailing-off of our form in those last nine matches but we'd finished eleventh, which for a club of our size was another remarkable performance. The last few weeks of the campaign had been like pulling teeth, but I also knew we were the envy of many teams in the Premiership, and certainly any of the rele-gated sides would have willingly swapped their season for ours.

In many ways I suppose that for much of my time as manager of the club we over-achieved, and because of that the expecta-tion levels were raised. After finishing seventh in the previous season perhaps we were expected to go one better and get a European place or win a cup. I certainly would have loved us to do just that, but it never happened. It was not because the team hadn't tried hard enough and, although we had a poor run-in, there was no way the side deliberately switched off. Everybody wanted to finish as high in the League as possible and no professional footballer likes losing or being part of a bad run. We had just completed five consecutive seasons in the Premier-ship, and our average placing during that time worked out at tenth in the league, leaving us seventh behind Arsenal, Manchester United, Chelsea, Liverpool, Newcastle and Aston Villa, but ahead of teams like Tottenham, Middlesbrough and Blackburn. The conclusion I came to was that although the season had ended so badly, the bigger picture showed how well we had done.

For so many years Charlton have collected praise for the way the team perform on the pitch and for the progress the club has made off of it. Charlton are often held up as role models for promoted sides who hope to establish themselves in the Premiership, and the reason for that must be that the club are viewed as a success. I think during my time we set high standards for ourselves and maybe because of that the way things turned out in the 2004–05 season made me, and a lot of other people associated with the club, feel a little flat. I would have liked us to entertain more, especially in front of our own fans at The Valley, but quite a few of those supporters will remember the dark old days when I first took over with Steve Gritt in 1991 when we didn't even have a ground of our own to play on. For them, just being in the Premiership and seeing the team playing at The Valley again must almost seem unreal. Like me and quite a few people on the board, they have been through the mill when it comes to Charlton Athletic.

Every club believes they are special, but whenever I think about my time with Charlton, both as player and as manager, I get the feeling that I have been part of a unique experience. The end of the season may have come as a relief, but it also gave me the chance to draw a line under what had happened.

I knew I had to change things and bring some players in, but I also realized that would only be possible within the budget I had. Richard and the board had a share issue, which in reality meant they were once more ready to dig into their own pockets and stump up some more money. They raised around £4 million and I also had some money left from what had previously been taken in. As I started to look at possible transfer targets I knew

I had about £6 million to spend. You tend to have maybe three possible players for any one position you are looking at. If you don't get your first target, you go for the next player in that position and so on.

One of the players I'd hoped to sign 12 months earlier was Darren Bent at Ipswich, but they were very reluctant to let him go and wanted more money than we were prepared to offer. It left me feeling very disappointed by the whole thing and I think Darren would have liked to have come to us but it wasn't to be. It became pretty common knowledge at Portman Road that we liked the look of Darren, and he even got the nickname 'Bobby', as in Charlton, because of what had happened. Having lost out once I was determined to try again but the only problem was Ipswich were in the play-offs and I knew that if they were to eventually be promoted, my chance of signing him would disappear again.

At the same time I wanted to bring a defender in and I'd been impressed by Gonzalo Sorondo, the Uruguayan international who had just finished a season on loan at Palace from Inter Milan. I wanted to try and put a similar deal together but knew there might be a problem with his work permit. Another defender I liked the look of was Jonathan Spector, a young American who was with Manchester United. I'd actually asked Alex about him six months earlier but was told he was on his way to Blackburn for a loan spell. In the end it never materialized but I asked again in the summer and was told that a season-long loan might be on the cards. Alex said he'd speak to Spector and tell him about us and the fact that, at 19 years old, it would be good experience for him. I'd done my homework on Jonathan and knew he was good right across the back, and I'd got good reports on the reserve games he'd played for United. Another defender who was on my list and in the background was Anthony Gardner at Tottenham, and I was looking at Blackburn striker Jonathan Stead and Newcastle midfielder Darren Ambrose. It was a hectic time because like a lot of other managers I was trying to keep tabs on what was happening without being able to tie anything down. During the course of any day I probably also took about 20 calls from agents bombarding me with players and I'm sure that was the case for other managers as well.

Things started to click into place for me when Ipswich got knocked out of the play-offs by West Ham. Richard made contact with their chairman, David Sheepshanks, and a fee was agreed for Bent. We also made contact with Sorondo and his agent and got the impression that the player would be keen to come to us if something could be worked out with Inter and the work permit dealt with. I actually spent one day meeting Stead in the morning, Sorondo in the afternoon and Bent in the evening, but at least I felt we were going in the right direction.

Stead decided he wanted to move north rather than south and went to Sunderland, but happily the Darren Bent deal went through and it was done early in the summer. I was really pleased to get him and when we did meet I think he could see I wanted him at the club and that I knew all about him. Having watched Darren in matches so many times I could sit down with him and say what he was good at, what he was bad at and what he could bring to us. I always think it's important to build up a rapport with a player and that's why a few weeks later I flew up to Manchester on a Saturday afternoon to have a couple of hours conversation with Spector before flying back to London again. Jonathan was due to drive down the next day anyway, but I thought it was important to let him know that I cared and wanted him at our club. Two days later he signed the loan deal and I had two new players in my squad.

Things moved on again during the time I was on holiday when West Ham, who had been promoted to the Premiership having won the play-off final against Preston, made a bid for Paul Konchesky. He'd been a very good player for us and had come through the ranks to reach full international level with England, but he'd been unhappy at not being played regularly in his favoured position of left-back. I just couldn't guarantee him what he wanted. I could understand his frustration and he'd done a great job for me during his time with the club. It was agreed to let him go and Richard spoke to Tottenham about the possibility of getting Gardner. Nothing materialized on that front but pretty soon two more players came in. The first was Darren Ambrose from Newcastle, whom I'd asked about during the previous season, and the other was another midfielder Alexei Smertin on a one-year loan deal from Chelsea. We also managed to get Sorondo in after satisfying the necessary criteria for his work permit, although it went to appeal, and I had to go before a panel to help argue our case, which included video evidence and statements from the Uruguayan football association and the national manager.

So in a fairly short period of time I'd managed to bring five players into the club and improve the quality of the squad. It was a real contrast to the way we had gone about things 12 months earlier, and I hoped the new players would help to continue the club's growth as a Premiership outfit. It had been a long and hard journey to the top flight of English football and in the process we had become role models for other clubs.

24 Doing a Charlton

I can't quite remember the first time someone said, 'We want to do a Charlton,' but as soon as I heard it I knew exactly what they meant. The club seemed to have reached the stage where they were held up as a blueprint for any club hoping to establish themselves in the Premiership, and its success both on and off the field which has encouraged others to try and follow in Charlton's footsteps. It's a great compliment to know that other people in the game view the club in the way they do, and it is yet another example of just how far Charlton have come as a club. But without wishing to sound arrogant, and with all due respect to the people, I honestly don't think they can hope to do the same as Charlton because I believe the club is unique in the modern game.

To think that in my 15 years in charge as a manager we progressed from being a homeless club, with no money and a threadbare squad, to becoming an established member of English football's top League is quite incredible. If you look further back to the time I joined the club as a player the whole story becomes even more remarkable. To have left our own ground and then gone on to win promotion in the same season was amazing enough, but to have to share with another club for more than seven years and battle our way back to The Valley in the fashion we did, is something I don't believe will ever be repeated. Once we had our own ground again the ambition and drive to improve the club year after year, both on and off the pitch, was always there. It took an awful lot to get to where the club is today and the reasons for it can't be easily summed up. So what makes Charlton the club it is? There is no easy answer to the question and perhaps the only way I can hope to try and explain is by giving an insight into the way we thought, functioned and went about our business both on the field and off it during my time.

Any manager's job is to get the best out of his players and to get the best results possible for the club he manages. At Charlton I think there was always a realistic expectation about what we could and should achieve. I think the fans had a big part to play in that and so did the chairman and board of directors. I have already stated that Richard never set unrealistic levels of expectation and that helped me to do my job. He allowed me to get on and manage the team without putting undue pressure on me. There seemed to be a general understanding at Charlton that we all got on and did what we were paid for. You hear all sorts of stories about other managers, chairmen and boards of directors, but although the Charlton board is probably larger than most other clubs I certainly didn't get any hassle from them. I think there was a stage in the 2004–05 season when I'd missed four or five successive board meetings, but it wasn't a problem because they knew I was out at matches looking at players and other teams. That was more important and they let me get on and do my job, which essentially was to look after the playing side of things and make sure the team performed well on the pitch. I have always had fairly basic ground rules about the way I like to go about my work and it was important that the players were in tune with what I wanted to try and do.

When Darren Bent and the other new players began pre-season training with us after their summer moves I think they realized very quickly what we were about, just as past players had done when they joined Charlton. I like to think that when a player arrived for training at 9.30 each morning we would be working to improve the team and to improve them as individuals. They would know what I expected of them in terms of application, dedication and professionalism when it came to their training. I think any player who was ever at the club during my time will say that they all knew where they stood and all knew what was needed in training. If anybody fell below what we wanted, they stood out like a sore thumb, and it just wasn't tolerated. I've often said that we trained as hard as we played and if you were to speak to Paolo Di Canio I think he would confirm that. He was a bit surprised by some of our sessions because they were so fierce, but he soon responded and clearly enjoyed the training. I often told the players before a session, 'We're going to do this one for us,' and by that I meant me and the coaches, because we wanted to put across specific points to the squad. Later on we might lighten things up a bit and tell them a particular piece of training was for them so that they could go out and enjoy themselves.

Our whole working week during the season was geared towards our next match, and I've always believed in leaving no stone unturned when it comes to giving the players the right preparation and information they need to tackle the job of beating a team. Of course, the end result isn't always what you want and no matter how well your team performs, the reality is that you can't win every game. We might have had a poor end

to the 2004–05 season, but we had a great start to the following campaign. All managers and clubs have their own routines
and way of approaching matches, and I always asked my teams
to at least give me a chance. By that I mean that they had to
have done everything they possibly could to get the right result.
If they did that and failed, I could accept it, but what I could
never take was seeing my team fall below the standard that was
required. When it all works to plan and you get another vital
three points it makes everything worthwhile, and we had a
result just like that when we travelled to Middlesbrough at the
end of August 2005 for a live Sunday TV game.

We had already started the season well with a win at Sunderland on the opening day of the season and another at home
against Wigan, both newly promoted sides just getting to grips
with the Premiership, and a lot of people thought we might be
in for a struggle against Middlesbrough. The players were obviously confident after their good start, and when they turned up
for training on the Monday before the Sunday game Merv,
Keith and myself had already discussed what needed to be done
for our preparation before we faced Middlesbrough. It was a
week which was pretty typical of what went on throughout a
season and perhaps illustrates the way we liked to go about our
business on the training pitch.

Monday: We put on three 25-minute sessions. The first
involved Keith, Mervyn and me each taking a group to do
some specific work. I took Darren Bent and the two wide men
who would be in action at the weekend, Jerome Thomas and
Dennis Rommedahl, while Keith took the midfield and Merv
the defence. We all went off and worked on things we felt
would be needed in a match situation. Things like Dennis and
Jerome getting closer to Benty on the pitch and being very

direct, getting Thomas and Rommedahl to run off the ball when they were not in possession in the hope of being played in, and making sure their crosses landed in the right position. All three groups then got together for a five-a-side match which was played with the right kind of attitude. We didn't have games that ended 10–3, and the matches were always tight and competitive. Finally we split into our three groups again and the players worked on individual skills specific to their positions in the team. If we were doing a finishing session, the forwards would finish from positions they were likely to find themselves in during a match, and the midfielders would do their finishing from places on the pitch they were more likely to be occupying.

Tuesday: Training started with a general small-sided game to help get the players warmed up, and then we concentrated on phases of play, where we tried to reproduce what happens in a match situation in certain areas of the pitch and how we would cope with it. Everything was done at a tempo and with a purpose. We looked at attacking and defensive phases with the players basically rehearsing how they would play and cope with different scenarios.

Wednesday: More of a general day. Two groups started by playing a short, sharp session of keep-ball, and then we moved on to a small-sided game, finishing the day with fitness work involving sprints and weights. After training the players were taken to our Pro-Zone room which is where a stack of computers and video equipment helps monitor and produce information about exactly what players do on a pitch, the sort of runs they make, their work-rate, passing and moves that take place during a match. We showed them footage of some attacking play from previous games, highlighting what they were doing right and what they were doing wrong, whether we'd got enough people in the penalty box and in the right positions, and so on. We ended the day by showing a compilation of some very positive attacking situations they'd created in past matches.

Thursday: The players were given the day off.

Friday: Soon after the first-team squad arrived I told them the 11 who would be in the team at Middlesbrough. I then took the attacking players again to do more work with them, while Mervyn took charge of the back four and midfield three. We had a small-sided game and then we brought all the players together to do some shadow work, where we walked them through different set plays, both Middlesbrough's and ours, which might occur in the match and let them know what they should be doing.

Saturday: A short, sharp five-a-side and then the 11 stayed with Mervyn and I while Keith and Glynn Snodin took the rest of the squad that was going to travel. For 30 minutes Mervyn and me went over the Middlesbrough team slowly and individually. We set out what we thought would be their team and told our players what was required of them, highlighting the strengths and weaknesses of the opposition. Then we talked about our strengths, before rehearsing all the opposition set plays, making sure our team knew what they should be doing in situations such as corners and free-kicks. After lunch the team went up into the Pro-Zone room again to go over the major points we had been making throughout the week, and once that had been done the whole squad flew north for the next day's game.

That night was pretty typical of any away trip. The players had their meal while Keith, Merv and I ate ours separately. The three of us usually had a drink in the bar before eating, and then over a bottle of red wine we chatted about the team, the club and general football matters. By 10 pm we're tucked up in bed and then the three of us had a chat again over breakfast the next morning.

Sunday: In the morning I made my notes to use during the final team talk, just emphasizing key areas that I wanted to get across to the team. The players had their pre-match meal at the hotel and then the team bus arrived to take us to the Riverside Stadium. When we got on the coach I let everyone know who the subs were going to be, and after we got to the ground we had another little team meeting once we knew what their side was, going over any changes and what we could expect from their players, with Merv going over set-plays again. The players went out for their warm-up, came back in and then ran out for the match.

Once that happens all you can do is hope the hard work you've put in during the previous six days will pay off. On that particular occasion it did and we came away with a valuable 3–0 win, but it's difficult to really enjoy a victory after the game because there's always things like interviews and press conferences to be done. On the way back home Keith, Mervyn and I usually go over the game and talk about certain incidents, but in many ways the match is soon forgotten and the priority becomes making sure you prepare properly for the next game.

I may have been Charlton manager for 15 years but one thing that never changed during that time was the feeling of nerves I got on the morning of a match. It disappeared by the time a game started and I actually enjoyed it while the team played, although I can't say there were too many occasions during that time when I felt totally relaxed during the course of a match. I found that if you picked up the points there was a tremendous feeling of relief, because everybody in the Premiership knows how important it is and there's a big fear factor to contend with. There are perhaps as many as 14 teams in the division who know that if things start to go badly they could be in for a relegation battle, if it goes according to plan they should be alright, and if it goes a bit better than that they could be in Europe. Then there are the six clubs who don't really live with the fear of relegation and are looking to get in the Champions League or the UEFA Cup. Their pressure is in trying to achieve that.

There is pressure on every team in the Premiership and for a club like Charlton the main pressure was making sure we stayed in the division. The club is at a very precarious stage in its development as far as I am concerned. For the first few years after gaining promotion people predicted before the start of each season that we would be relegated. It didn't happen but if it had we could probably have coped with going down, and perhaps would have been strong enough to be in there with a shout of coming up again. But the longer you stay in the Premiership the more geared up you become to playing in it. Obviously that is a good thing in many ways and it means you can build your infrastructure as a club and begin to operate at a different level, but the flip side is the fact that relegation can then have a catastrophic effect. Look at what has happened to Leeds, Ipswich, Coventry, Derby, Sheffield Wednesday and Leicester in recent years, and it's not just about the football team, it's about the other people working at a club who, through no fault of their own, suddenly find themselves out of work because of relegation. I was very much aware that my responsibility didn't just stop with the team, because what we did on the pitch would ultimately impact on the staff throughout the club.

At Charlton the club always made sure thay didn't spend money they didn't have. For example, a couple of seasons ago everything the club had was already paid for. That included players, the training ground and The Valley, with the exception of a small and controllable mortgage on the North Stand. Making sure they didn't spend money they didn't have and making sure things were done in a sensible way has been at the heart of the success the club have had. Richard and the board have always tried to build Charlton brick by brick without taking the sort of huge financial risks other teams might have done. It's served them well and I always recognized that I wasn't going to be in a position to splash out the sort of cash on a transfer that some other managers do. It went with the job and in many ways it was no different from day one. A lot has changed in the game since I first took over with Gritty but the principle of good housekeeping is the same now as it was then, and it's been a major factor in enabling the club to grow and develop in the way it has done.

I operated in a very different environment during recent years and the biggest change was the amount of money that has come into the game, particularly at the top level. I've only ever seen the TV programme *Footballers' Wives* once and thought it was a bit over the top, but things like big houses, expensive cars and designer clothes have become part of the scene for Premiership players. I once heard a story about a player who suddenly panicked on his club's team bus as they were travelling home after a game. He insisted that they had to turn around and go back to the ground they'd just played at.

'Why?' asked the manager.

'Because I've left my earring there and it's worth £15,000!' said the player.

The influx of foreign players to our game has also had an effect at the top end of the scale. I'm certainly not saying it's been a bad thing, but the fact that in general they tend to come over and play in the Premiership has definitely had a knock-on effect. A foreign player can really map out his career these days, spending a few years here and then maybe moving off to play in another country. It's certainly made it more difficult for young English and British players to break through into the first team and stifled them to a certain extent but, at the same time, those that do make it are of such a standard that they are almost ready to start pushing for places in the international set-up. Stewart Downing at Middlesbrough is a good example of that. I have nothing against foreign players in the game – it's an inevitable consequence of progress and the way football has grown. It's a world-wide sport and the top players will want to play in the top Leagues for the top money.

They've introduced a lot of good things into our game and I think the lifestyle of our own players has improved because of them. One of the things so often levelled at foreign players is that they introduced diving into our game. Whether that is true or not, the fact is it's now part of football in this country and I would like to see some strong action taken to try and stamp it out. I firmly believe video technology should be used as part of the game in this day and age, and diving is one area where it could really come into its own. If a match is looked at by a third official and it is clear a player has dived in the penalty box, he should get a red card. If he does it elsewhere on the pitch, he should get a yellow. Once we get a few red cards for the offence I think it will put a stop to someone trying it in a match. The same is probably true when it comes to players being held at free-kicks and corners. I'm waiting for referees to start giving penalties when a player is held at a corner – if that happened the habit may disappear overnight.

A third official could also be used for possible penalty decisions. When an incident takes place in the box, I think they could wait for the ball to be played out of the penalty area and then call for the third official to have a look on the video so that a definite decision can be made. It wouldn't work if the game was continually stopped to look at incidents in other areas of the pitch, but for something as important as a penalty, I can't see why it shouldn't be used. And why not look at having some form of technology which clearly lets us know whether a ball has crossed the goal line? It may mean having an infra-red beam which runs from post to post, or it may mean having a micro-chip in the actual ball, but something has to be done to make sure there is definite proof, one way or another, as to whether the ball has crossed the line. Football is big business these days and crucial decisions can make such a huge difference to clubs.

Although a lot of money may be spent on transfers these days in order to get players who will improve your team, there is also a huge financial outlay on trying to produce home-grown talent. When I first took over with Gritty we didn't have a big squad and then had to sell players to balance the books, but at the same time we were lucky in having youngsters coming through who were able to make it into the first team. Over the years there was a steady stream of them, including players such as Robert Lee, Lee Bowyer and Scott Parker, to name just three. But the great irony for Charlton in recent years has been the fact that despite having their own academy, the club don't seem to be producing players in the way it has in the past. The training facilities, scouting system, coaching, money and structure are much better these days than they were in the past, but the youngsters still aren't coming through.

It's a common groan from a lot of clubs who have spent a lot of money on their academies. The home-grown talent just isn't developing in the way we'd hoped it would. Obviously the fact that players from all over the world are now playing in this country has made things harder, but I believe the problem is more wide ranging than that. I think youngsters have a lot more going on in their lives these days and the choice of leisure activities is a lot greater than it used to be, so maybe they just don't play enough football in general. They may watch it on TV and play football games on their computers, but they aren't physically playing as much.

Ten years ago one of the big selling points for Charlton as a club was to be able to say to the parents of promising youngsters that their son would have a much better chance of playing in the first team with us than he would at other bigger clubs. We could point to players in our team at the time who had come through the ranks and say they would always get their chance with us. That is much harder to do these days. Scott Parker, Kevin Lisbie, Jonathan Fortune and Paul Konchesky all came through the ranks and played for Charlton in the Premiership, but they made the breakthrough some time ago, and since then things have tended to dry up. Charlton are not the only club in that position and although there might not be as many boys coming through, if you look at the ones who have, such as Parker, John Terry at Chelsea, Ashley Cole at Arsenal, Ledley King at Tottenham, Stewart Downing at Middlesbrough and Frank Lampard, Joe Cole and Michael Carrick at West Ham, it's clear to see that the quality is there. We just need more of them.

After nine years away from the club Gritty returned as Charlton's new academy manager. He is the perfect man for the job, not just because of his abilities as a coach and administrator, but because he understands Charlton and knows better than anyone what the club is about, and I know he and the rest of his staff put a lot of work into making sure the kids start coming through again. The club have always given youngsters a chance and I think they will continue to do that if they are good enough, because it's vital for them in my view.

Charlton may be in the Premiership now, but one thing is for sure, there is a huge gap opening up between the top clubs and the rest of the teams. If you look at the finances of teams like Chelsea, Manchester United, Arsenal and Liverpool, they are in a different league to the other clubs, and because of that you'd have to say they are the big four of the division. They can afford to go out and spend the sort of money a club like Charlton can only dream of, and in terms of what the fans can expect I think the Premiership is in danger of becoming a little bit predictable as a consequence. The top four clubs are winning everything and getting bigger each season. They make more money from the gates they get, and also from things like being in Europe, TV money and their merit award. And although Newcastle have under-achieved in terms of winning trophies and where they finished in the League recently, they are still a huge club who fill their stadium and have the sort of buying power that allowed Graeme Souness to spend around £50 million on players like Parker and Michael Owen when he was manager.

When Charlton bounced back and got promotion to the Premiership in 2000, it was probably worth about £15 million to the club overall. Obviously there was the TV money and also things like sponsorship and commercial contracts that can be re-negotiated when you come up, but to reap greater financial rewards in the Premiership you need to stay in it year after year.

People talk a lot about the TV money that has flooded into the game and it often sounds as though all the clubs are getting the same amount, but it doesn't quite work out like that. It's true that there is an equal split between all the Premiership clubs, but that is only on 50% of the money. Another 25% is used as a merit award, giving a club different amounts depending on where they finish in the table, and the other 25% is for live TV matches. So the reality is that the big sides have bigger stadiums and take more gate money, finish higher in the League and therefore get more money from the merit award and they appear in more live TV games, taking more of the 25% set aside for that. The Champions League is another source of income, with Liverpool's winning involvement in 2005 said to be worth around £30 million to them.

I'm not grumbling about the big clubs earning so much, and I do realize that their wage bills are huge, but it does seem to be a fact that a handful of clubs are pulling away from the rest and I think the fans realize this as well. The Premiership is still exciting, but I think we all have to be aware of the fact that what supporters want most of all is competition. If that is taken away and the whole thing becomes too predictable, it could also become a bit of a turn-off.

As a club what Charlton have achieved on the pitch has been matched by what has been done off of it. Without the sort of initiatives that went on during my time at Charlton there is no way they could have grown and evolved in the way they have.

When we moved to Selhurst Park the club had a community scheme which became the only real point of contact with people from Greenwich, Bexley and north Kent, where we drew the bulk of our support from. It maintained an important link which was so crucial at the time. When we returned to The Valley the club had lost a generation of supporters, particularly amongst children, and they had to set about correcting that. A 'Target 10,000' scheme was launched in an effort to build support and one of the brightest things to happen was the 'Kids for a Quid' idea, where children got into the ground for just £1. The marketing of matches was another crucial aspect of the club's activities off the field, and through a series of advertising campaigns the sale of season tickets began to take off, growing from just under 4,000 to 12,000. After the play-off win the club made use of data from the 40,000 fans who attended the match in order to market the club to them. Charlton have always prided themselves on being a community club and players regularly attend events with fans, as well as joint activities with local councils. One of the most recent initiatives was the launch of The Valley Express service in Kent, which saw 1,600 new supporters using it for one of the club's games. For £5 return a supporter could come to The Valley from 70 pick-up points in the southeast, just another example of the way Charlton are constantly looking to improve and gain support. At one stage the club generated 2,000 new season-ticket sales by using advertising in local papers and radio emphasizing the fact that they were one of the cheapest prices in London, and by 2004 they had 21,500 season-ticket holders, with The Valley regularly sold out. The plan is to expand the ground to a 31,000 capacity, from its current 26,000, with a new East Stand and eventually have a stadium that will hold 40,000. Should that happen it will be another incredible milestone for the club – one that would have seemed impossible 15 years ago and a testament to all the people who have worked so hard for the club during the time I was associated with Charlton.

'Doing a Charlton' has not just been about the matches the

team played while I was there, it was about an attitude around the training ground from players and coaches, the commitment of the board and the support of the fans. In my opinion I think Charlton is one of the most successful clubs in the country even if they are not winning trophies every season. When I've sat in an empty stand at The Valley and looked around at the way the place has been developed since those portakabin days, I can't help feeling that what has been achieved is fantastic. I always believe Charlton Athletic has been built on a dream. I'm not talking about the dream of getting into the Champions League or winning the Premiership, I'm talking about the dream of turning Charlton into a football club.

As the 2005–06 campaign got under way, all of my thoughts had been on making sure that Charlton's remarkable story continued. It was my 15th season in charge as manager and almost 21 years since Lennie signed me as a player. What I didn't realize at the time was that it would prove to be the season in which I finally said goodbye to The Valley.

25 CAUGHT IN THE ACT

It was the beginning of February 2006 and The Valley was buzzing. We had just beaten Champions League winners Liverpool 2–0 in a midweek game and our fans were rightly in the mood for celebration.

The win took us to 33 points and after a terrible run following the great start to the season we had managed to steady the ship and were on course again to hit the all-important 40-point target. We were also still in the FA Cup and 10 days later were due to entertain Brentford in a fifth-round tie.

The victory over Liverpool, in a game that had originally been due to be played earlier in the season, was another indication of how far the club had come during my time in charge as manager, but there was something missing for me that night. For some reason I just didn't feel the way I knew I should after such a great win over one of the best sides in the country. The Liverpool manager, Rafael Benitez, had been in to see me and congratulate us on the way we played, which was nice of him. As the players got changed next door I felt I needed to have 10 minutes to myself and sat in my room next to the dressing room. I poured myself a drink and tried to take it all in. The atmosphere had been the best it had been for a very long time that night and the noise level was tremendous. It made a big difference and in many ways it felt like the old days at The Valley. I was really pleased with the result, but I didn't feel as elated as I should have done.

That feeling stayed with me the next morning as I drove to the training ground. I took the time during the course of the journey to think about myself and how I felt. I had often told people that I would know when it was time to leave Charlton. I said that either the fans would tell me, the chairman would tell me or I would tell myself because I wouldn't feel the same about making that familiar journey to work each morning.

Quite a few of the fans had voiced their feelings during the course of the season and towards the back end of the last campaign. It certainly wasn't the majority of them, but there had been some grizzles from a few. The phone-in shows on the radio after matches had taken calls from some fans being critical of me and saying that perhaps after such a long time at the club it might be better if I moved on.

One call upset my brother Billy so much that he actually pulled over in his car, rang the radio station and started to have a go back. He told them that not only was he a directors' box season ticket holder at the club but he also had shares in Charlton and so felt he was justified phoning to voice his own opinion. Needless to say he stuck up for me, but to be fair, so did the majority of the fans.

Richard had been his usual supportive self, despite some rocky form following a good start. But as I parked my car at the training ground following the Liverpool game I started, for the first time, to question the length of time I'd been at the club. It wasn't about the fans or Richard, it was about me and the way I felt. I'd mentioned to Carol the night before that I didn't have the same satisfaction from the result that I would have had in the past. She knows me better than anyone and said I hadn't been my normal self at home for some time. I had been a bit snappy and short tempered with her and the kids, but I knew I hadn't been like that at the club.

I realized that I had been putting a brave face on things and hadn't felt comfortable for some time. But despite the strange feelings I had at the time they weren't enough to distract me from the main task, which was to push on up the League and have a cup run.

After the win at Middlesbrough that I have already mentioned we got another away victory in our next match when we beat Birmingham 1–0. It meant we had started the season with four straight wins and had 12 points. Despite losing 2–0 to Chelsea and 3–2 to Tottenham in our next home games we still managed to win 2–1 at West Brom and Portsmouth to keep the points tally high, as well as getting a point in a 1–1 home draw with Fulham.

By the time we travelled to Stamford Bridge for a midweek third-round Carling Cup match towards the end of October, we had 19 points from nine Premiership games, and had played some terrific attacking football, particularly away from home. The confidence and form carried on in that Chelsea match because we came away from the home of the Premiership Champions and Carling Cup holders having knocked them out with a win on penalties after the match finished 1–1.

It was a fantastic result but a long night and just three days later we had to cope with the visit of Bolton in the League, a team who always ask certain questions of the opposition, just like Wimbledon used to some years ago. But Sam Allardyce and his team don't play in the same style Wimbledon did. Bolton have some very good players in their squad, although Sam makes sure they play in a way that makes it very uncomfortable for some sides, and you can't hope to compete with them if your side is not prepared for a physical battle from the first whistle to the last.

We simply weren't up to the task when we met them on the last Saturday in October and lost 1–0. As good as our away form had been, we certainly hadn't managed to reproduce it in front of our own fans and had recorded just one win in the five home League matches we had played at The Valley. Little did I know after we'd lost to Bolton that the match would be the first in a sequence of games that would see our form nose-dive. We managed just one win in our next six League games and also got knocked out of the Carling Cup at home by Blackburn 3–2 after leading the game and looking as though we were going to win.

By the time Christmas came around we had slipped down the table from being second early on in the season to 12th place and I knew I had to take some drastic action for the home match with Arsenal on Boxing Day. We had paid a price for having a team that wanted to attack and had done so well early on. The make-up of the side wasn't right and we didn't seem to have enough people who could defend and grind out a result when we needed to. Just as I had done the season before at Tottenham, I knew I had to change things around, only this time I think I caused a few eyebrows to be raised by dropping six players for the visit of the Gunners.

I got a performance from the team but it wasn't enough to get us a win. Arsenal scored the only goal of the game and took all the points, but I felt happier with the way the team had performed and after having our away game at Newcastle two days later postponed at the last minute because of snow, we ended the year with a massive win when we beat West Ham at The Valley 2–0. It was one of those games where I quite literally breathed a sigh of relief as the final whistle blew, because the result was so important to us and we'd managed to stop the rot.

During all the time in which we had been struggling to pick up points and had lost all those games, Richard never once put any pressure on me or demanded to have a meeting about the situation. It was something I couldn't really imagine happening at other clubs and at one point I actually said to him that I thought he should be having a go at me.

'What's the point?' he asked. 'I'm not going to do that; it's not the way we work. I know how hard you're working and I leave the football to you.'

Ironically, as the team struggled to get results during November and December, I became aware that another club weren't put off by our poor form and I was strongly linked as a successor to Glasgow Rangers manager Alex McLeish. They were having a fantastic season in Europe, but the domestic front wasn't so good and he was being put under increasing pressure. Eventually it was announced that Alex would be leaving the club at the end of the season. There was a lot of press speculation about a new manager and I knew for a fact that I was on chairman David Murray's list to replace him.

I didn't need Scottish reporters phoning me up to ask if I was interested. By the time that was happening I already knew it was a strong possibility for various reasons. But I wasn't about to jump ship and leave Charlton, and at the same time I'd made my mind up that I wasn't going to start talking about a new contract with Richard. I'd made a decision to wait until the end of the season and re-evaluate things.

After the West Ham win the team began to look like a more combative unit. We scrapped for things and managed to get some important results, including a 4–2 away win at Sheffield Wednesday in the FA Cup third round when a lot of people were predicting we could be one of the day's upsets against the Championship team. We also picked up a valuable win against Birmingham and then got a point at Chelsea.

Our scorer in the 1–1 draw was Marcus Bent who joined us from Everton during the January transfer window. As usual there was a lot of speculation during the month about possible movements and one of the names mentioned was Danny Murphy. Danny had played a big part in some of the early season games we'd played but I'd left him out of the side for some later matches, because I felt we needed a different sort of side on occasions. The speculation in January concerned a possible move to Newcastle with Charlton old boy Lee Bowyer heading in the opposite direction.

I think the speculation perhaps got to Danny a bit and although I was going to include him in the squad for the home game with West Brom on the last day of January, which was a Tuesday, I wasn't going to bring him back into the side until the window closed. By that time there would have been no chance of a move and I knew he could then just get on with playing for Charlton. I intended to try and go back to playing the way we had in the early part of the season once we had steadied the ship and picked up some points. That would have meant Danny having a key role for us in the final few months of the season. He had a lot of ability and I saw him as a valuable part of the squad.

On the Sunday night before the Albion game it became clear that Tottenham were interested in making a bid for Danny. I didn't want to lose him and I think that sometimes players and agents forget that a club has the right to say no to a bid, but in reality once something like that starts to happen it gathers pace quickly. It's virtually impossible to get a transfer done in a day but somehow Spurs managed it, and in the end Danny left us right at the death with the transfer going through at 11.30 pm on the last day of the month after we had drawn 0–0 against West Brom.

I don't think he ever really came to grips with what Charlton were about. He'd left a big club in Liverpool, and I don't think it was the same for him. Perhaps he became a little disenchanted with life at The Valley and maybe he expected a little more on the pitch and off it. We fitted a lot of our football around him and championed his cause when it came to him possibly getting back into the England set-up.

I made a few comments in the press about him when he left, but they were meant as being tongue in cheek, although perhaps I was a bit sarcastic when I said that his social diary might be a bit fuller after going to Tottenham, and Sven might go to White Hart Lane more than he went to The Valley. But I'd like to put on record my thanks to Danny for his efforts during the time he played for me at Charlton and wish him all the best with his career. Eight days after losing him to Spurs we recorded the win against Liverpool and by this time a new twist to the season had come along for me.

The biggest football story in England during January had nothing to do with transfers, instead it was all about Sven-Goran Eriksson and the fact that he was going to leave his job after the World Cup in Germany.

Eriksson was at the centre of a sting operation by the *News of the World* in what later became known as the 'fake sheikh' story, where the England manager talked to someone whom he believed to be a genuine oil-rich sheikh, but who was in fact an undercover reporter for the newspaper. Once he'd opened up and talked openly on several different issues, including his opinion on certain players and managers, the knives were out for Eriksson, and towards the end of the month the FA held a press conference at which it was announced that Sven would leave his post after the World Cup.

By that time there had already been calls for his head and once again the papers were full of possible candidates to replace him. My name was in the frame and on the day before Eriksson's announcement Sir Bobby Robson actually came out and said in his *Mail on Sunday* newspaper column that if Sven went he thought I should get the job.

'I would like to see the most experienced and effective current English manager, Alan Curbishley, given the chance,' he wrote.

Once the official announcement was made I found myself linked with the job along with other English managers like Sam Allardyce, Steve McClaren and Stuart Pearce. From that moment I not only had to deal with the business of running Charlton, but also with all the speculation surrounding the England vacancy, just as the others had to. Almost straight away the papers were full of things like 'Curbs watch, Sam watch and Pearce watch', in which we were all being analysed and scrutinized as we went about our jobs. I also found that my regular press conferences before games and even after them suddenly started to become hijacked by talk of the England job.

All of this began in late January but the truth was it was nothing more than speculation at the time. I hadn't been contacted by the FA at that point and all I knew about the job and the possibility of being considered for it was what I read in the papers. It was a bit of a sideshow but I just got on with things and all the talk certainly had no effect on the way I did my job.

The fact that the Liverpool game and the way I felt after it fell right in the middle of this period was pure coincidence. When I drove to the training ground that morning after the match I was thinking about Charlton and not England. I was thinking about my time with the club and trying to work out exactly why I was feeling the way I did. The season had been draining for me and in many ways and I think I developed a bit of a siege mentality to the job. I hadn't been happy the season before when the team had lost in that home game to Manchester United, but that was a different feeling. This time I felt down, but it was after beating the European Champions, and I felt uneasy about the whole thing.

After the great win over Liverpool we came down to earth with a bang in our next match, losing 3–2 at Manchester City, but overall the signs were better and after beating Brentford 3–1 in the FA Cup at The Valley a little less than a week later we found ourselves through to the quarter-finals and got a home draw against Middlesbrough. Most of the pre-match publicity for the game with Brentford centred on them, which suited me. There were also a few headlines about Charlton caused mainly by the fact that I'd let slip a story about taking Carol to watch one of their matches on Valentine's night. I'd asked her if she fancied going to the West End for a night out, and dropped in the fact that I needed to see Brentford play! She was fine about going to the game and actually likes football; it's just the matches that involve me which she hates because it makes her so nervous

Goalless draws at Newcastle and then with Aston Villa at The Valley meant we picked up a couple of valuable points before recording another 0–0 draw when we played Liverpool at Anfield. It was another very good result for us and showed that we had become a team that didn't give too much away after leaking goals during the bad patch we'd had towards the end of the year. Taking four points out of a possible six and remaining unbeaten against Liverpool wasn't bad at all.

The preparation for the game was as good as ever for the team, but for me there was a little added distraction in the form of a phone call from the FA.

Two days before playing Liverpool I'd been to an area league managers' meeting at Highbury and in the evening I was due to attend a dinner for Sir Bobby Robson at the RAC club in London's Pall Mall. When I turned my mobile phone on there was a message from Richard Murray asking me to call him. It was a bit unusual because I knew he wouldn't have left a message unless it was important. When I got back to him he told me that Simon Johnson, who was Director of Corporate Affairs at the FA, had been on to him asking permission for them to talk to me on a very preliminary basis. It wasn't going to be a formal interview and everyone was sworn to secrecy about the whole thing. It was up to me to decide if I wanted to meet with them and he gave me Johnson's number so that I could get back to them if I wanted to.

I thought about the whole situation for a while. I knew there would be certain things about it that I would love, and there would also be things about it that I wouldn't like, but I wanted to find out more about the job. There had been a lot of talk and speculation, but now the FA did want to have a chat, I felt delighted and honoured to be involved.

When I got to the dinner there was a lot of talk about the England job, but I couldn't say anything to anyone. I didn't even say anything to Carol when I got home that night. I simply didn't see the point. All I knew was that I was going to phone Simon Johnson the next day and see what he had to say.

We flew north the next day after training in preparation for our game with Liverpool. The build-up had been the same as it always was but at the hotel I have to admit that there was a lot going through my mind, including the call to the FA. That day I phoned Simon Johnson to try and fix a meeting. He gave me four or five possible dates to consider and said they would like to meet in a hotel.

I wasn't too keen on meeting in a public place, although I don't really know why that was. I hadn't done anything wrong, but somehow I felt more comfortable trying to keep the whole thing private.

My brother Billy was out of the country on business but he owned a house in central London and I thought it might be the perfect place to have the meeting. I talked to him and told him what had happened. He was more than happy to let us use his place and I arranged to meet Simon Johnson and Chief Executive Brian Barwick at the house just before five in the evening of Friday 10 March. It was two days before we were due to meet Middlesbrough in a League game at The Valley, and I had to do the usual training and press conference before leaving Sparrows Lane for the meeting.

As I arrived Simon Johnson parked next to me and after getting out of our cars we chatted and walked together to my brother's house. Brian Barwick arrived about five minutes later and was let in by Simon. The three of us sat down and began to have a very informal chat. I did joke with Brian at one stage that I bet he'd been followed and also that I didn't really know why we were all sneaking around. It was nice for me to put faces to names and they gave me an idea of what the job was about. They explained that they were just going through the preliminary stages of their search for a new manager and that there were other people they were going to be talking to.

It was clear they were going to take as long as they thought was necessary. In my view it all seemed very logical to take their time with the selection process, because it was such a big decision, bearing in mind this was Brian Barwick's first major appointment and he had to get it right. After about two hours the two of them left and I stayed to have a drink with Billy's friend Peter who was staying at the house. As I drove home I felt happy with the way things had gone and thought it had been a useful meeting.

I was up early the next morning because I knew I had a busy day. First of all there was the last training session before the next day's game with Middlesbrough, and then I had arranged to drive to France with Jeff Vetere to watch a game at Lens. I knew I wouldn't be back home until the early hours of the next morning.

'I'll be home at about one,' I shouted out before leaving and then got into my car.

That night as we drove back to Calais in my car with Jeff, I got a message from my son Michael asking where I was. I hadn't told them I was going to France for the game and my family obviously thought I had meant one o'clock in the afternoon and not the morning. His message was quickly followed by a text from my daughter saying that I needed to call her quickly.

When I spoke to Claire she explained that she'd had a call from her boss, Gary Farrow, who has a PR agency, telling her that he'd heard there were pictures of me meeting with Brian Barwick and Simon Johnson that were going to be splashed all over the front page of the *Sunday Mirror*.

I couldn't believe what she was saying. I'd been so careful not to let anyone know about the meeting and even Carol was unaware that it had taken place. I knew that on my side of the fence only me, my brother Bill and Peter, who was staying at the house, knew about the meeting and none of us had spoken to anyone. I'd even kept Richard in the dark about it and I knew I had to phone and warn him about what was going to happen.

Apparently when Claire had told Carol that I was going to be on the front page of the paper her immediate reaction was, 'What's he done?' I think she was relieved to find out I'd only been caught with Brian Barwick and Simon Johnson, and not walking out of Stringfellows with a couple of lap dancers! Mind you, perhaps my daughter's boss might have been happier with that because Peter Stringfellow is one of his clients.

The whole thing seemed crazy and, to top it all, as we passed through customs Jeff declared that he'd lost his passport. We managed to sort the situation out in the end, but it only seemed to add to the whole surreal atmosphere of what had gone on in the space of about an hour since getting Claire's text. I was even asked for my autograph by one of the customs officials.

'It's for my brother and his name is Llewellyn,' she said. 'Do you know how to spell it?'

She obviously didn't know that Llewellyn is actually my first name, but for some reason I've always been called Alan. Another weird moment in what had turned out to be a very weird day.

The next morning Claire went out and got a copy of the *Sunday Mirror*. Seeing myself on the front of a tabloid wasn't something I was used to. It looked as though I'd been caught in the act, and made the whole thing seem as though we were all up to no good. In fact, it was all very innocent and all we were doing was having a meeting. The fact that the story was on the front and back pages as well as a double-page spread inside seemed way over the top.

They said that I was 'set to be crowned England's new manager', but I realized how ridiculous that was because I knew the FA were only in the first stages of their search for the new man. It was a lot of fuss about very little really, but nobody on the outside reading the story that day would have known that.

26 DECISION TIME

After all that had happened I still had to deal with the most important issue of the day – trying to get three Premiership points from our home game with Middlesbrough.

I also knew that one of the first things I had to do when I got to the ground was speak to Merv and Keith to explain the situation and the fact that, despite the tone of the story, my meeting was nothing more than a preliminary discussion.

I'm sure a few people might have looked at the situation and compared it with the stance I took when Scott Parker and Danny Murphy wanted to leave. But the fact was I always had a clause in my contract dealing with the possibility of me talking to the FA if the England manager's job ever became available, and I had been given permission by Richard to speak to them.

I wanted to explain the situation to the players as well and clear the air before the Middlesbrough game, because I didn't want anything to interfere with the job they had to do that afternoon. I sat them down in the dressing room and briefly went over it all before turning to head back to my room. Just as I started walking Chrissy Powell broke the silence. 'Three lions on his chest' he sang, and they all had a good laugh at my expense!

We got just the sort of result we needed from the match thanks to a couple of goals from Darren Bent and finished the game 2–1 winners, but I did feel under a lot of pressure to get a result after what had happened. I had to deal with a battery of cameras as well as loads of questions from reporters and in the end I was relived to get home after the game. We were well beaten in our next outing, losing 3–0 at Arsenal, though it might easily have been worse. They played superbly and their passing was magnificent.

During the course of the game the Arsenal fans started having a dig at me. It had never happened before and it was all to do with the England business. 'England job, you're having a laugh,' they sang and perhaps it showed how I was being perceived since the Sunday paper story broke, but I was a bit surprised later in the match when some of the Charlton fans started singing it as well.

Just 11 days after beating them in the League, Middlesbrough were back at The Valley again for the FA Cup quarterfinal which was played on a Thursday night. I knew it was going to be tough for us and so it proved as we were held to a goalless draw and the prospect of a replay at the Riverside. I had always wanted to have a good cup run with Charlton and although a lot of people seemed to think our best chance of a semi-final place had gone after failing to beat them, I never believed that. We had a good record up there and always seemed to play well, we'd also put in one of our best performances of the season when we'd won in the League early in the season, so I was hoping we could produce a repeat and make it through to the last four.

The home League win against Steve McClaren's team had put us on the 39-point mark, and I knew that victory in the

Premiership three days after the Cup quarter-final against another side from the north-east would see us through the 40-point barrier and guarantee Premiership football for the next season.

When Newcastle arrived at The Valley for the Sunday afternoon match they had Lee Bowyer and Scott Parker in their side and both of the former Charlton players managed to get on the score-sheet. Scotty scored a brilliant goal but luckily for us Lee knocked one in his own net as we finished the game with a 3–1 score and all the points.

It was a really important victory for the club and, unlike the Liverpool game, I did feel the way I thought I should after such a good win. As I drove home that day I felt more relaxed knowing we had got through the 40-point mark by the end of March. Seeing Scott and Bowyer reminded me of the massive contribution both of them had made to the club, and the fact that Lee had always joked that he should have a stand named after him for the money Charlton got when he went to Leeds. It seemed incredible to think that his transfer had happened almost 10 years earlier.

The next day I attended a board meeting and Richard made a point of putting on record his thanks to me, my staff and players for getting to the 42-point mark. Like me he knew just how important it was to the club and on the way that was underlined to me when I picked up a newspaper after stopping for petrol. In the sports pages they had reprinted League tables from five, ten and fifteen years ago, and it brought home to me what had happened at Charlton during my time with the club.

How do people view what you've done? A lot of people were talking of Charlton and Middlesbrough being similar before we played them in the cup. But managing Charlton is not like managing Middlesbrough. They had players like Viduka, Yakubu and Hasselbaink in their squad, three players that even if I had wanted to sign them, I knew Charlton could never get anywhere near the wages they were on. Gauging one manager's success against another's in the Premiership is very difficult because they all do very different jobs in many ways. Having beaten Newcastle I knew Charlton could look forward to their eighth season in the Premiership during the last 10 years when the 2006–07 campaign started. In the other two seasons Charlton had been promoted.

The table from five years ago for that particular weekend showed us in tenth place in the Premiership with 42 points, the same number we'd just got with the win over Newcastle. In third place were Ipswich, Sunderland were fourth, Leeds fifth, Leicester seventh, Southampton eighth, Derby were fifteenth, Coventry at nineteen and Bradford were bottom of the table.

All of those eight teams who were with us in the Premiership five years earlier had gone from the top tier and some had suffered almighty financial problems in the process. But there we were jogging along with an average placing of tenth, and season on season the club had built and strengthened. Perhaps it seemed a bit boring to some people but I wondered what the boards and fans of those clubs who had been relegated would have given to have done what Charlton had during the past five years.

We went to Upton Park for our next League game knowing we could be meeting them again in the FA Cup semi-final if we beat Middlesbrough, because the draw had already been made. The game finished goalless, but we paid a price for the point because we lost Luke Young with an injury. It was also a game Jay Bothroyd will remember for non-footballing reasons.

During the last part of the game I wanted Jay to go on as a

substitute and told the bench to get him ready. What I didn't realize was that he'd needed to have a pee before coming on and instead of going back to the dressing room had instead decided to get down on all fours in the dug-out and wee in a plastic cup. Unfortunately once he'd started he couldn't stop and managed to fill up two of the things. After the game a couple of West Ham stewards came into our dressing room to find him. They'd seen the two cups and wanted him to take them away. Understandably there was no way they were going to attempt to do it themselves!

We had another 0–0 draw when we met Everton at home before travelling north for the Cup replay with Middlesbrough. The club had organized an extraordinary operation taking more than five thousand fans up to the Riverside by road, rail and plane. They created an amazing atmosphere but unfortunately we couldn't send our travelling support home happy as Middlesbrough knocked us out and ended our Cup hopes for another year with a 4–2 win.

We had five League games left after losing at the Riverside and I was determined that we wouldn't finish the season with a whimper as we had done so many times during recent years. With 15 points to play for I wanted the team to finish as high up the table as they could, but after losing at Fulham I started to wonder if a familiar pattern was emerging. I thought we could get a result at Craven Cottage, even though we hadn't won away in the League since October, but once again we let a soft early goal in and lost out 2–1.

Two days later we had a chance to redeem ourselves in front of our own fans when Harry Redknapp brought his Portsmouth side to The Valley on Easter Monday. The players knew that with four games left there was still a real chance of a top

10 finish, but they somehow managed to go out and produce one of the worst 45-minute periods of the season. Just to cap things off, D'Alessandro put Pompey in front just before the break and we got booed off.

When I got to the dressing room there were only about five players sitting down as the others were in the treatment room having knocks taken care of. I was short and to the point when it came to letting them know how I felt. I told them I felt cheated as the crowd were booing me and they should be booing them, and then I swore at them. I then went off to the treatment room and delivered the same verbal volley to the players who were in there, before going to sit in my room.

To their credit the players survived a rocky start to the second half and then managed to pull things around and grab the points with a 2–1 win. After the game I went straight into my room and then into the dressing room to thank the players for the way them had responded in the second half, but at the end of the game I couldn't help feeling that possibly the season had taken its toll on them, and it was going to be a bit of a struggle in the last three matches.

I decided to make some changes for the journey to Bolton, but it completely backfired. I picked a side that wasn't able to cope with the way the home team went about their work and after losing 4–1 I had to hold my hands up to the players and admit that the result was down to me and the team I'd picked.

Two days before the trip to Bolton I'd been on another journey that had a real cloak-and-dagger feel to it, when the FA had invited me for a formal interview.

After the initial 'getting-to-know-you' chat I'd had with Brian Barwick and Simon Johnson at my brother's house, I hadn't heard anything more from them for some time until Simon rang to say that, despite what I might hear, there hadn't been a short-list drawn up at that time and if they were going to take it further they would contact me.

Once again things went quiet until Richard called to say that the FA had been on to him and asked if they could see me at the beginning of the week leading up to our Cup replay at Middlesbrough. He told me the club had said no for the simple reason that he didn't want anything getting in the way of the preparation for the game and I agreed with him.

As soon as the Everton match had finished our focus was on the meeting at the Riverside, and I knew our preparation for such a big game had to be spot-on. We flew up on the Tuesday but on the morning of the match the next day I opened the newspapers to be greeted with details about how potential England candidates had been interviewed at a house in Oxford. The names of Steve McClaren, Martin O'Neill and Sam Allardyce were mentioned, and there were one or two comments in the papers about me not being there, and they were asking whether I was now out of the running.

All of a sudden on the morning of one of the biggest games for the club in recent years, I was getting phone calls from the press asking me what was going on. It was something I could have done without and it was a distraction, but I had to deal with it and get on with planning for that night's game. As I have already mentioned it turned out to be a disappointing time for us and a chance missed to get into the semi-finals and write another chapter in the club's history.

The next day I got a call from Simon telling me that there was only one date available for me to be seen for my interview and that was in one week's time on Thursday 20 April. It was scheduled for 6.30 pm and he told me that as part of the interview they wanted me to prepare an itinerary for a 10-day get-together for the England squad, which would incorporate two matches. Simon said that it would form a major part of the interview. He even asked if I would require any presentation equipment such as videos or flip charts, and I told him I would get back to him if I needed them. He also said that I was to keep quiet about the whole thing and should not keep talking about the England situation, which I found a little bit odd because I couldn't escape the press before and after games and they were the people asking the questions.

I would have liked nothing better than to have stopped talking about England, but the fact was that every time the press spoke to me all they ever seemed to talk about was England. Perhaps I should have cut them short and just said 'no comment', but there was certainly no way I had done anything to encourage the talk. Once again, just like the meeting at my brother's place, I never told a soul that I would be going for the interview, not even Richard, although when I had lunch with him on the day before the meeting he already knew because the FA had spoken to him.

I was contacted by Brian Barwick's PA and told that a car would pick me up and take me to the interview, but I wasn't told where the meeting would take place, and it all began to take on a bit of a strange feel. It was as though I was part of a plot in a thriller rather than a candidate for the England manager's job. I knew that on the day of the interview I wouldn't be able to get away from the training ground until at least 4 pm and I had to get to wherever the interview was going to take place by 6.30 pm.

I didn't want to raise any suspicion by leaving the training ground in a suit and so it was arranged that I would be picked up in Wapping. I knew that I could leave my car there and grab a cup of coffee from a nearby McDonald's if I had some spare time. So that afternoon I turned up, parked and used my car to change clothes into my suit. Barwick's PA phoned to check that I was there and ready to be picked up and told me the car would be with me in 20 minutes. Sure enough it turned up along with Dennis the driver and we set off for the meeting. He wouldn't tell me where we were going but at least he stopped short of blindfolding me!

It did seem a bit over the top and it soon became clear that we were going to be early for the meeting, so I knew wherever I was being taken couldn't be too far. Dennis suggested we kill some time by having a cup of tea and then we set off again. I wasn't really concentrating on where we were going and then suddenly we turned off into a side road and had to make our way through a group of about 50 people who were happily drinking outside a pub. The next thing I knew we were stopping outside some garage doors as they opened to let us in, and we were into the back of FA headquarters at Soho Square.

I was met by Brian Barwick's PA and shown to a glass-panelled conference room, but the coffee and tea had taken their toll, so I nipped to the toilet and made myself comfortable before what I had been told would be an interview lasting around 90 minutes. Arsenal vice-chairman David Dein was in the gents as I walked in and I congratulated him on their performance against Villarreal in the Champions League the night before, and then went into the interview room.

Once all the introductions were taken care of I sat down and the interview began. I sat directly opposite Brian Barwick, who was chairing the meeting; to his right were David Dein and Trevor Brooking and to his left were Geoff Thompson, Dave

Richards and Simon Johnson, who was taking notes. They asked me a series of questions and I noticed Simon Johnson's note taking got particularly furious when I was asked about handling big-name players, the press, what I saw as some of the pressures of the job and what I thought was expected of the England manager and team.

I hadn't looked at my watch but knew the meeting had probably gone on for an hour or more when Brian Barwick asked everyone if they had any more questions for me. Nobody had, but I wanted to mention a few things to them and I got some answers to questions I had. I could see that the interview was coming to an end but I realized that nobody had asked me about the itinerary I had been asked to prepare, and which Simon had told me should not take longer than 20 minutes to present.

I'd prepared folders for everyone going right through everything I would do on a day-by-day basis. From the time the players were called up until the time they left, and I gave a copy to everyone on the panel believing they would want to go through it with me. In addition I'd prepared a detailed breakdown of all the training that I thought I would elaborate on during the course of the presentation. I thought it might form a major part of the interview, but the whole thing was never discussed. Instead, they said they would take a look at the folders after I'd left and Trevor Brooking asked if he could have a copy of the training schedule.

I got up, shook hands with everyone and left the room. Simon Johnson saw me out and I thanked him for inviting me, then went back down to the garage where Dennis the driver was waiting to take me to the car. On the journey back I have to admit I felt a little flat. There were things I'd hoped they would ask me which didn't come up and there were answers, which on reflection, I might have done better with. I wasn't sure what the next move was going to be but I did reflect on the fact that as a manager I'd never signed a player after just two looks. The FA had decided on a certain type of selection process and although I'd felt exhilarated after the initial meeting at my brother's house, I didn't feel like that after the interview in Soho Square.

The presentation thing disappointed me and the overall feeling I came away with was that my interview had been a little bit rushed and perhaps not quite as relaxed as I thought it might have been. When I got the call for the interview I was pleased that the whole thing seemed to be kicking on, but on the day I didn't feel the meeting went as well as it could.

Having been unable to make the original interview date because of the Middlesbrough game, I realized it had probably been difficult getting everyone together at a time that would be convenient to all of them. But I couldn't help reflecting on the fact that a fairly cramped room at the FA was probably a bit different from a country house in Oxford. At one stage Trevor Brooking even had to lean back on his chair and call to a cleaner because he was making too much noise and we were inside trying to have a meeting.

I was disappointed with the fact that I hadn't been given the chance to talk about my itinerary, and I suppose the overall feeling I came away with was that perhaps my interview had been fitted in as a bit of a courtesy and that maybe they already had their man.

Four days after my interview the papers were full of stories linking Portugal's Brazilian coach Luiz Felipe Scolari with the job. When I met Richard two days later for lunch on the Wednesday before the last home game of the season against

Blackburn, and he had mentioned early termination of my contract, one of the other things he asked about was the England job.

'First of all I don't think I've got it,' I told him, 'and secondly it's not really on my agenda right now.'

I also told Richard about the interview and how disappointed I was about not talking through my prepared itinerary.

I hadn't heard anything from the FA following the interview six days earlier and it was clear Richard was becoming a bit fed up with the length of time the whole process seemed to be taking.

'I'm going to phone Brian Barwick,' he told me as we left the restaurant. 'I'm really disappointed with what's gone on. It's not right.'

I think he possibly felt the England thing being in the background for so long during the course of the last few months had affected things at the club, and a little more than a week later he went on record and said as much. After getting his number from me Richard went off to phone Brian. Because no decision had been made at that time I think Richard felt it put Charlton in limbo. He spoke to Brian Barwick's PA and she then got Brian to phone Richard back. I don't know exactly what was said between the two of them, but when Richard stopped beside my car as we were both pulling away he told me that he didn't really think I was in the running. What neither of us realized at the time was that Barwick and Simon Johnson were apparently in Portugal having talks with Scolari.

The England situation took a new twist in the couple of days that followed because at one stage it appeared Scolari had been offered the position and was about to take it, only for the whole thing to fall apart very quickly. In the end, it was no great surprise when Steve McClaren was given the job a couple of days before the end of the Premiership season.

On the same Friday I met with Richard and Peter to sort out details of my early termination, I switched my mobile phone on after meeting with them and heard a message from Brian Barwick. He said he wanted me to call him so that he could give me a progress report on where they were with 'the recruitment issue'. The message was recorded at 2.10 pm and at about that time in a hotel in Germany Scolari was apparently beginning to talk about withdrawing from the running for the England job. I didn't actually return the call. But I did speak to Brian again just before the official announcement of Steve McClaren as England manager, when he phoned to tell me the FA's decision.

I can honestly say that I always felt Steve was the favourite to get the job, if the FA were going to appoint an Englishman. He was already part of the set up as a coach with Sven, had managed a Premiership club for five years and been involved as a coach alongside Sir Alex Ferguson at Manchester United. He had started off at Oxford as a coach 15 years earlier, ironically at about the same time I first became a manager. He has learned his trade and I have to admit that I'm glad the job has gone to an Englishman.

I was surprised when Scolari's name came up and although nobody can argue with what he has achieved as an international manager, I think someone did make the point that being manager of Brazil with the players you have at your disposal might not make it the hardest job in the world when it comes to the World Cup, and as manager of Portugal when they lost in the final of Euro 2004 to Greece, I think the team had a distinct advantage because they were the host nation.

It was very difficult for the FA in many ways because they

always knew that no English manager they were likely to look at had experience of managing a team in the Champions League. At least Steve McClaren has been close to that as a coach with United, and I think he probably always had the upper hand. When you look at his CV I think he probably did tick most of the boxes. As for me I always felt I might just hit the post when it came to getting the job, and someone did say to me that perhaps it's the sort of thing a manager should take on towards the end of his career rather than at the beginning or in the middle of it, so who knows what will happen in the future.

After my lunch with Richard on that Wednesday and the subsequent meeting with him and Peter Varney at The Valley to sort out the details of my departure I drove home on the day before the Blackburn match to tell the family that I was about to take charge of my last home game as Charlton manager.

I told them that they mustn't tell anyone else and then let them know about the way Richard and Peter had outlined what they wanted to happen. The next day I arrived at the ground knowing that I had to tell Mervyn, Keith and then the players. Richard had said that he would pop down and have a word with Merv and Keith, but by the time he'd got to my room I had already broken the news.

I came straight to the point and said I would be leaving the club and the whole thing had been settled very amicably. As I was telling them I could hear Richard knocking at my door and when he finally came in he told Merv and Keith that he would be speaking to them with regard to their own positions at the club. Both of them had done great jobs for me and it's an unfortunate fact of football life that a manager's staff are usually tied to him. If the manager goes it can have a knock-on effect and shortly after the season ended Mervyn and Keith also left the club, but once again I believe the whole thing was settled properly, with Richard and the rest of the board knowing just what the two of them had done for the club.

After popping into my room Richard had the unenviable task of having to go upstairs to the boardroom and break the news to the other directors, while I got ready to tell the players. I said I wanted them all in the dressing room at 5 pm for a meeting 15 minutes before the game was due to kick-off. I still had a bit of an uneasy feeling about what the club was doing and the fact that it could detract from the business of getting three points, but when I spoke to Keith, he said they were doing the right thing.

I'd decided I wanted to give someone a bit of a lift because I knew we were safe and I made the decision to give 21-year-old Lloyd Sam a shot on the bench. I could see his eyes light up when I'd told him but he was a good kid and he deserved it.

When I went in to tell the players I was leaving I knew it would be difficult. I told them what had happened and the fact that I'd be going after the Manchester United game at Old Trafford the following week. I kept my head down a bit as I spoke to them and the dressing room was a bit quiet. I explained there was nothing sinister in it and if they could do anything for me perhaps they could go out and beat Blackburn.

By this time the fans in the stadium had been told as Richard and Peter's plan for my send-off started to take shape. I told Mervyn and Keith that I wanted them to walk out with me, not behind me. We had been a team and I wanted everyone to acknowledge them as well. Walking down the steps to make my way onto the pitch I felt OK, but as I walked onto the field and then saw all the fans, it hit me a bit. I kept my head down and just carried on walking to the dug-out.

It was very emotional and as I walked to the bench I saw

John Humphrey, Bob Bolder and John Bumstead standing at the side of the pitch. They were all part of the old school, people who had got us back to The Valley, people who did it without any great financial rewards, and people who did it because it was there to be done. I knew that if I got the chance later that day I was going to mention them.

There was no happy ending as far as the result was concerned and at times it seemed to take on more of a testimonial match feel. About five minutes from time I was standing at the side of the pitch and I could hear the fans suddenly starting to clap me. 'You should take a look at this,' said Keith, and I must admit I wasn't prepared for their reaction. They just seemed to carry on clapping and I will always remember it. When the final whistle blew we had lost the game 2–0 and I started walking around the ground with the players, the noise level from the fans seemed to grow and grow. I started choking up at the reception and once again I needed to keep my head down because of the emotion.

I was given a microphone and finally started speaking to the fans. I tried to thank as many people as I could, including the board, Roger Alwen and Richard, but I have to admit that because of the emotion of the occasion I found it difficult. Eventually I walked off the pitch and into my little room.

'That's it,' I thought, 'it's over,' and at the same time I made a note to take the three pictures I had on the wall with me. One was of me holding the play-off trophy, another was of me, Merv and Keith after we'd won the First Division title and the third was of the players celebrating the championship. Great memories and important moments in Charlton's history.

The week following the game with Blackburn was a bit weird. I called all the players in to the training ground on the Monday, but then gave them three days off. Carol had gone to

Spain for a short break and I was at home with the kids. Once Michael and Claire had gone off on Tuesday morning it felt strange. For the first time in a long while I was able to just think about myself, and after a few days I felt quite refreshed.

On the Thursday before the last game of the season at Old Trafford I attended a sponsors evening, which I really enjoyed, and the supporters there that night had some very nice things to say about me which I will always appreciate. It had been the same four days earlier at the club's Player of the Year awards, which turned into a very memorable night for me and the fans who attended were fantastic.

It was difficult coming to terms with the fact that I was still in charge for another game, because it already felt as though I'd left. But I suppose if you are going to have a last game then Old Trafford in front of a record Premiership crowd of 73,006 people isn't a bad way to end it.

The night before the game I sat with Keith and Mervyn in our hotel and shared the usual bottle of red wine that we had between the three of us. Chris Powell came into the room just as we were finishing, bought us another bottle and said thanks. It was a nice touch from a nice guy and a player who had done well for me. I also went out and had a few drinks with the staff in the hotel bar. The atmosphere was relaxed but not as it usually is the night before an away game.

I had promised Carol that for my last match in charge I would wear a suit instead of the training gear I usually opted for, but somehow I had forgotten to pack a pair of shoes and ended up borrowing a pair that were a couple of sizes too big from the football club secretary Chris Parkes. I had to stuff tissue into the toes and I felt very strange walking out onto the Old Trafford pitch before the game.

Charlton had bought two first-class tickets to New Zealand for Carol and me to use, so that I could visit my sister. She's been over to England several times but I'd never managed to get enough time to make the trip over there. It had been agreed that Alex Ferguson would present the tickets to me and after the game he also gave me a really nice bottle of red wine.

Once again our fans were brilliant to me and they were all holding up cards with the words 'Thanks Curbs' printed on them. I was just sorry that they made the long journey only to see us soundly beaten 4–0 by a very good United team. After a quick drink with Alex we pulled away from Old Trafford in the team coach and headed for the airport. When we landed at Stansted I shook the hands of all the players and then realized that was it, my last game in charge and the start of a new chapter in my life and in the life of Charlton Athletic.

I know the club probably sacrificed three points for me in that final home game against Blackburn. A win would have seen the team finish 11th in the Premiership instead of 13th and with it get another £969,922 in merit money.

What Richard decided to do that day was typical of what Charlton have been about, and after 15 years as the manager I was proud to be clapped out of the front door and not kicked out of the back.

Whatever happens in the future and whatever I do in my career I know Charlton, its fans and the people I worked with during my time at the club will always represent a very special and happy period of my life.

Career Summary

Llewellyn Charles ('Alan') Curbishley

Born: Forest Gate 8 November 1957.
Educated: Gainsborough Road School (West Ham), Trinity College
   School (Newham) and West Ham Technical School.
Role: Midfielder – 5' 10½'', 11st 4lb; coach; manager.

Playing career

Senrab Boys' Club (Poplar).

West Ham United – associated schoolboy; apprentice 22 July 1974;
professional July 1975.
(League debut in first division match against Chelsea at Upton Park
on 29 March 1975 (aged 17). Final match (sub) against Leicester City
at Upton Park on 26 March 1979. Total League and Cup record – 87
(+ 9) appearances, 5 goals).

Birmingham City (£225,000) June 1979.
(Debut in Anglo-Scottish Tournament against Bristol City at St Andrew's on 4 August 1979. Final match against Watford at Vicarage
Road on 22 March 1983. Total League and Cup record: 153 (+ 2)
appearances, 15 goals.)

Aston Villa (£100,000 + Robert Hopkins to Birmingham City) March
1983.

(League debut (sub) in First Division match against Birmingham City at Villa Park on 4 April 1983. Final match against Liverpool at Villa Park on 15 December 1984. Total League and Cup record – 39 (+ 2) appearances, 1 goal.)

Charlton Athletic (£38,000) 24 December 1984.
(League debut in Second Division match against Crystal Palace at Selhurst Park on 26 December 1984. Final match (first spell) against Oxford United at Selhurst Park on 24 March 1987. Total League and Cup record – 68 (+ 1) appearances, 6 goals.)

Brighton & Hove Albion (£30,000) 21 August 1987.
(League debut in Third Division match against Chesterfield at the Recreation Ground on 22 August 1987. Final match against Blackburn Rovers at Ewood Park on 5 May 1990. Total League and Cup record – 127 (+ 5) appearances, 15 goals.)

Charlton Athletic (free) as player-coach 3 July 1990.
(League debut (second spell) as a sub in Second Division match against Newcastle United at St James's Park on 24 October 1990. Final match (sub) against Portsmouth at Fratton Park on 17 August 1993. Total League and Cup record – 23 (+ 6) appearances, no goals.)

Honours and Representative matches
Forest Gate Boys; Newham Schools; Essex Schools (U15s); England Schoolboys (8 caps – scored on his debut against Northern Ireland); England Youth (10 caps); England U21 (2 caps); FA Youth Cup runners-up medal (West Ham United v Ipswich Town) 1975; Ron Greenwood's England XI v Ron Saunders Midlands XI (Nov. 1977) in testimonial match for former referee Jack Taylor – scoring England's goal in 2–1 defeat.

Career League and Cup record – 497 (+ 25) appearances, 42 goals.

Managerial and coaching career

Joined Charlton for second spell from Brighton as a player and reserve team coach, succeeding Peter Eustace, on 3 July 1990; promoted to first team coach-player 4 October 1990, following the departure of

Mike Flanagan; appointed join player-coach (title later changed to joint player-manager) with Steve Gritt on 24 July 1991, after the appointment of Lennie Lawrence as Middlesbrough manager; appointed team manager on 15 June 1995 after Charlton decided to dispense with the post of joint manager – Steve Gritt losing his job. Gritt was, however, reunited with Curbishley following his appointment as Charlton's Youth Academy Manager in June 2004.

In an emotional address to the crowd prior to Charlton's final home match of the 2005–06 season against Blackburn Rovers on 29 April 2006 chairman Richard Murray announced that Alan Curbishley would be leaving the club albeit with a year of his contract still remaining. Murray had wanted Curbishley to extend his contract to three years which the Charlton manager was not willing to do.

Honours and Representative matches
Manager of Charlton when they won promotion to the Premiership in seasons 1997–98, through play-offs, and 1999–2000, as First Division champions – Curbishley becoming the first manager in Charlton's history to steer the club to the top division on two occasions; Manager of the Year (the 92 clubs) 1999–2000; Nationwide Division One Manager of the Year 1997–98 and 1999–2000; eight Manager of the Month awards, including two in the Premiership – four of them as joint manager with Steve Gritt; Manager of the Nationwide Football League U21 team which faced the Italian League Serie B U21s at The Valley on 10 March, 1998 – the game finishing 0–0.

Players used by leading managers

From the 1921–22 season up to the end of the 2005–06 season, a total of 632 players had represented Charlton in the 78 seasons they have competed in the Football League/Premiership. The total figure (632) includes Arthur Turner who played in the 1945–46 FA Cup competition.

The breakdown of Charlton's 78 seasons reveals that Alan Curbishley has used more players than any other manager in the club's history.

By the end of the last campaign, Curbishley (along with Steve Gritt initially) had used a total of 138 different players of whom 114 made their Charlton debut under his reign.

Of the 632 players, a total of 380 (60.1%) were introduced by Charlton's four leading managers (i.e. in terms of matches played).

	New	*Total*	*Matches*
Alan Curbishley/Steve Gritt	114	138	729
Jimmy Seed	99	116	730
Alex Macfarlane	91	104	316
Lennie Lawrence	76	94	411

New = Charlton debut. Total = Includes players who made debut under a previous Charlton regime.

Top-flight football

Exactly one-third of Charlton's league history has been in the top-flight and during season 2005–06 the match at Newcastle on 22 February 2006 marked the Addicks 1,000th match in the First Division/ Premiership.

The 1,012 matches played up to the end of the 2005–06 seasons were split under the various managers as follows:-

	P	*W*	*D*	*L*	*F*	*A*
Jimmy Seed	551	216	120	215	866	886
Director (David Clark)	1	0	1	0	4	4
Jimmy Trotter	36	9	3	24	54	97
Lennie Lawrence	158	37	47	74	158	222
Alan Curbishley	266	85	72	109	308	382
Total	1,012	347	243	422	1,390	1,591

Seed record still intact – but only just!

Alan Curbishley broke many top-flight records during his managerial career at Charlton and fell just one short of equalling the legendary Jimmy Seed's record of 730 matches in charge.

It should be noted, however, that because of the war years, Seed lost seven seasons during which time Charlton played exactly 250 League and cup matches which are excluded from his total figure.

Late in the season, for Curbishley to equal Seed's fifty-year-old record, Charlton needed to reach the FA Cup semi-final but went out at the quarter-final stage in a replay at Middlesbrough – a club that ironically Charlton had performed the 'double' over in the Premiership.

The League and cup record of Charlton's top-three longest serving managers reads:

	P	*W*	*D*	*L*	*F*	*A*
Jimmy Seed	730	311	156	263	1,238	1,137
Alan Curbishley/Steve Gritt	729	280	183	266	937	950
Lennie Lawrence	411	128	109	174	496	579

Long-serving managers

While job security for managers of football clubs has always been precarious, three managers who managed to buck the trend in the Premiership, and brought relative success to their clubs, are Sir Alex Ferguson (Manchester United), Arsene Wenger (Arsenal) and Alan Curbishley (Charlton Athletic).

As of May 2006, these three team bosses – a Scotsman, a Frenchman and an Englishman, respectively – had aggregated a total of 44 years in charge. And while Ferguson and Wenger had won numerous trophies, Curbishley had just one big prize to show, that of steering the Addicks to First Division championship success in 2000; but in relative terms, when you compare the enormous wealth, and spending power, of Arsenal and Manchester United with that of Charlton's, his subsequent success in establishing the South-East London club in the Premiership was no less remarkable.

Before Curbishley's resignation in May 2006, the top four longest-serving current Premiership managers were:

	Club	*Appointed*
Sir Alex Ferugson	Manchester United	November 1986
Alan Curbishley	Charlton Athletic	July 1991
Arsene Wenger	Arsenal	September 1996
Sam Allardyce	Bolton Wanderers	October 1999

Success in the Premiership

Charlton were relegated at the end of the first season in the Premiership (1998–99) but went to the final match before suffering the drop.

The Addicks, however, returned to the Premier League after winning the new First Division championship the following season – the highest League honour the club has achieved in its history.

Charlton are one of only ten clubs who have been ever-present in the Premiership for each of the last six seasons, up to 2005–06.

In terms of wealth, status, and spending power, the other nine clubs in this select group are ahead of Charlton but while some of them struggled, the Addicks during this six-year period retained their much-treasured top-flight status with some ease.

During those six campaigns up to the end of the 2005–06 season, a total of thirty clubs played in the Premier League and of them fifteen were relegated, some of them on two occasions like Leicester City, Sunderland and West Bromwich Albion.

The following table details the overall average placing of each of the thirty clubs (2000–01 to 2005–06).

	00–01	01–02	02–03	03–04	04–05	05–06	Average placing
1. Arsenal	2	1	2	1	2	4	2.00
2. Man. Utd	1	3	1	3	3	2	2.17
3. Chelsea	6	6	4	2	1	1	3.33
4. Liverpool	3	2	5	4	5	3	3.67
5. Newcastle	11	4	3	5	14	7	7.33
6. Tottenham	12	9	10	14	9	5	9.83
7. Wigan	–	–	–	–	–	10	10.00
8. Blackburn	–	10	6	15	15	6	10.40
9. Aston Villa	8	8	16	6	10	16	10.67
10. Leeds	4	5	15	19	–	–	10.75
11. Bolton	–	16	17	8	6	8	11.00
11. CHARLTON	9	14	12	7	11	13	11.00
13. Ipswich	5	18	–	–	–	–	11.50
13. Middlesbrough	14	12	11	11	7	14	11.50
15. Everton	16	15	7	17	4	11	11.67
16. Fulham	–	13	14	9	13	12	12.20
16. Southampton	10	11	8	12	20	–	12.20
18. West Ham	15	7	18	–	–	9	12.25
19. Man. City	18	–	9	16	8	15	13.20
20. Birmingham	–	–	13	10	12	18	13.25

21. Portsmouth	–	–	–	13	16	17	15.33
22. Sunderland	7	17	20	–	–	20	16.00
23. Leicester	13	20	–	18	–	–	17.00
24. Crystal Palace	–	–	–	–	18	–	18.00
24. Derby County	17	19	–	–	–	–	18.00
26. WBA	–	–	19	–	17	19	18.33
27. Coventry	19	–	–	–	–	–	19.00
27. Norwich	–	–	–	–	19	–	19.00
29. Bradford	20	–	–	–	–	–	20.00
29. Wolves	–	–	–	20	–	–	20.00

Charlton all-time top transfers

In

Date	Player	From	Fee
July 2001	Jason Euell	Wimbledon	£4,750,000
July 2000	Claus Jensen	Bolton Wanderers	4,000,000
July 2001	Luke Young	Tottenham Hotspur	4,000,000
July 2000	Jonathan Johansson	Glasgow Rangers	3,750,000
June 2005	Darren Bent	Ipswich Town	*3,000,000
May 2002	Gary Rowett	Leicester City	2,700,000
Aug. 2004	Danny Murphy	Liverpool	2,500,000
Jan. 2006	Marcus Bent	Everton	*2,500,000

| July 2004 | Dennis Rommedahl | PSV Eindhoven | 2,000,000 |
| May 2001 | Shaun Bartlett | FC Zurich | 2,000,000 |

Out

Date	Player	To	Fee
Jan. 2004	Scott Parker	Chelsea	£10,000,000
June 1999	Danny Mills	Leeds United	4,375,000
July 1996	Lee Bowyer	Leeds United	2,812,500
July 2005	Paul Konchesky	West Ham United	*2,000,000
Jan. 2006	Danny Murphy	Tottenham Hotspur	*2,000,000
July 2004	Claus Jensen	Fulham	1,250,000
Aug. 2001	Shaun Newton	Wolves	1,150,000
Aug. 2002	Mark Kinsella	Aston Villa	1,000,000
May 2002	Andy Todd	Blackburn Rovers	1,000,000
May 1994	Scott Minto	Chelsea	862,500
Sept. 1992	Robert Lee	Newcastle United	750,000

Note: Six of the players in the above list of top sales – Parker, Bowyer, Konchesky, Newton, Minto and Lee – were all products of Charlton's successful youth policy.

*Reported maximum fee.

Other staff directly associated with the playing side at Charlton

First team coaches

Joint Charlton managers – Alan Curbishley and Steve Gritt also acted as first team coaches until Curbishley took sole control on 15 June 1995. Charlton then advertised for a first-team coach and 40 applicants, whom Charlton regarded as 'serious contenders', applied for the job.

Les Reed – from 25 August 1995 until May 1998.

Mervyn Day – from May 1998 to May 2006.

Assistant manager

Keith Peacock – from May 1998 to May 2006.

Reserve team coaches

Keith Peacock – from July 1991 to May 1998.

Gary Stevens – from July 1998 to June 2000.

Glynn Snodin – from June 2000 to March 2006.

Mark Robson – from March 2006 (initially to end of the 2005–06 season).

General manager – football

Andrew Mills – Appointment announced 9 May 2006 following resignation of Alan Curbishley.

Chief scout – Ted Davies

Head of medical department – Wayne Diesel

First-team physiotherapist – George Cooper

First-team doctor – Dr John Fraser

Youth Academy manager – Steve Gritt

Assistant Youth Academy manager – Mark Robson (17–21 age groups – also see above); Steve Avory (9–16 age groups); David Chatwin (7–11 age groups)

Academy education and welfare – Phil Gallagher

Academy recruitment – Dennis Coxall

Groundsman – Colin Powell. The former Charlton winger succeeded Bill Harrison in March 1989.

Full internationals

The remarkable growth of Charlton from the time Alan Curbishley took sole control as manager in June 1995 up to his departure could, in part, be measured by a comparison of the international honours gained during the seventy-four year period up to 1995 and the eleven years up to the end of the 2005–06 season.

	Players capped	Appearances	Goals
1921–1995	22	80(+ 10)	7
1995–2006	28	248(+ 68)	41
Total	50	328(+ 79)	48

Other facts about Alan Curbishley

- Played in the same Essex Schools representative side as Glenn Hoddle.
- When Alan made his league debut for his first club West Ham United, in goal for the Hammers was Mervyn Day who was to become first team coach at Charlton.
- Alan made his final first team appearance on 17 August 1993, 18 years 141 days after his debut for West Ham United. By the end of the 2005–06 season, as a player (515 matches) and manager (729) Alan had been directly involved in 1,244 first team competitive matches.
- Alan played under a total of eight different managers for his five clubs – i.e. Ron Greenwood and John Lyall (West Ham United), Jim Smith and Ron Saunders (Birmingham City), Tony Barton and Graham Turner (Aston Villa), Lennie Lawrence (Charlton Athletic) and Barry Lloyd (Brighton & Hove Albion).
- After his playing days ended in League football, Alan played for Havering Nalgo, managed by London *Evening Standard* football journalist Ken Dyer, in the Brentwood Sunday League (1998–99), Metrogas Vets and Charlton Vets.
- Alan's older brother, Bill, is famous in the music world, managing a number of bands including The Who and Led Zeppelin, and was joint producer, along with Rob Beard, of the hugely successful 1979 rock film classic *Quadrophenia*. When Bill brought The Who to their first concert at The Valley in 1974, Alan was only a youngster at

West Ham and along with a mate he showed his enterprise and ini-
tiative at this early age by making, and selling, badges with The
Who on them. They sold the lot and, relative to his wage as a West
Ham apprentice, 'made a fortune'. Alan is also the possessor of one
of The Who's gold discs as a result of a swap with Bill for one of
his England U21 caps.

- Alan's younger brother, Paul, became a West Ham United apprentice on 1 August 1976, scoring against the Charlton Colts in the
Hammers' 4–3 win at Chadwell Heath on 30 October 1976. After
a spell at Norwich City, Paul played for Charlton's Colts and midweek team in 1978–79, and later returned to Charlton to coach the
youngsters.

- Whenever a top managerial job vacancy became available, Alan's
name was, and still is, invariably in the frame. Probably the very first
approach came in December 1993 when Charlton officially rejec-
ted a request from Birmingham City to approach him. In 2006, he
was one of the leading candidates for the England job vacated by
Sven-Goran Eriksson.

- Awarded an honorary Masters degree by Greenwich University at
a ceremony held at the Barbican Centre in London on 3 November
1998. The University spokeswomen, Karen Jones, said: 'Every year
we award a small number of honorary degrees. They are awarded
to people who are particularly distinguished in their field or who
have made a major contribution to the region.'

- When Charlton won promotion to the Premiership in season
1999–2000, they did so by finishing champions of the Nationwide
League Division One. It represented the highest level Charlton had
ever finished champions and it was their first title since the 1934–35
season when they won the Division Three (South) championship.

In the boardroom

In July 1991, when Alan Curbishley and Steve Gritt were appointed
Joint Coaches (later renamed Joint Managers), the board of directors
of Charlton Athletic Football Club (CAFC) consisted of: Roger
Alwen (chairman), Michael Norris (vice-chairman), Richard Collins,
Richard Murray, Martin Simons and Derek Ufton.

In December 1993, Charlton Athletic plc (New Company) which had been incorporated in April 1993 entered into an agreement to purchase the entire share capital of CAFC and Charlton Athletic Holdings Ltd., the owners of The Valley ground.

Coinciding with the above offers, fans were invited to take up shares in the New Company and this proved very successful, producing 1,300 new shareholders.

Turnover in Charlton's first financial year as a public company (up to 31 May, 1994) was £2,916,000, which represented an increase of 31% on the previous year, over half of which was spent at Upton Park until the move back to The Valley in December 1992.

Since 1994, the turnover figures of the New Company have in the main been dramatic, and obviously necessary, for Charlton to retain their Premiership status.

Year to	Turnover (£'000)
31.5.95	2,720
31.5.96	3,691
30.6.97*	4,330
30.6.98	5,770
30.6.99	16,274
30.6.00	11,746
30.6.01	28,317
30.6.02	30,641
30.6.03	35,141
30.6.04	42,606
30.6.05	40,714

*13-month period.

As of May 2006, the board of directors of Charlton Athletic plc comprised:

Richard Murray (elected chairman during 1994), Robert Whitehand (deputy chairman), Gregory Bone, Derek Chappell, Gideon Franklin, Michael Grade, Michael Stevens, Martin Simons, David Sumners.

As of May 2006, the board of directors of Charlton Athletic Football Company Ltd was as follows:

Martin Simons (chairman), Richard Murray (deputy chairman), Roger Alwen, Gregory Bone, Nigel Capelin (deputy group chief executive), Derek Chappell, Richard Collins, Gideon Franklin, David Hughes, Michael Stevens, David Sumners, Sue Townsend (supporters' director) – succeeded by Ben Hayes on 1.7.06, Derek Ufton (former Charlton player and England international), Peter Varney (group chief executive), David White and Robert Whitehand.

Associate directors: Clifford Benford, John Humphreys, Diran Kazand-jian, Andrew Murray, Hannah Murray, James Murray, Paul Statham and Steven Ward.

Honorary Life President: Sir Maurice Hatter.

Picture credits

All photographs © Tom Morris, with the exception of the following:

Page 15 (top, centre and bottom) © Action Images
Page 16 (top) © Mirrorpix; (centre and bottom) © Empics

Index

Lightning Source UK Ltd.
Milton Keynes UK
UKHW01f1025050718
325270UK00002B/131/P